# THE WALK BACK TO EDEN

GOD'S WORD, YOUR STORY.
HIS PARADISE, YOUR PURSUIT.

Melody Westbrook
*and*
Emileigh Ziebka

WESTBOW PRESS®
A DIVISION OF THOMAS NELSON & ZONDERVAN

WestBow Press books may be ordered through booksellers or by contacting:

WestBow Press
A Division of Thomas Nelson & Zondervan
1663 Liberty Drive
Bloomington, IN 47403
www.westbowpress.com
844-714-3454



ISBN: 978-1-6642-9476-9 (sc)
ISBN: 978-1-6642-9477-6 (hc)
ISBN: 978-1-6642-9475-2 (e)

Library of Congress Control Number: 2023904558

Print information available on the last page.

WestBow Press rev. date: 03/28/2023

# *Contents*

# *Acknowledgments*

## MELODY

Being a first-time author, acknowledgment to those who have supported this endeavor could be endless. But to save you the long list, I will try to keep it short.

My first acknowledgment must go to my co-writer, Emileigh Ziebka. If I could wrap up all my thanks to her in a big box and embellish it with the most beautiful bow, it wouldn't begin to communicate my gratitude. The day we stood in a parking lot and I asked her to co-write with me, her look of confusion and disbelief will forever be etched in my memory. The fact that her first response was a hard no makes this adventure even more meaningful. Now that we have completed this book with unending conversations and relentless tears about God's story, we can see that our obedience to one crazy adventure has come full circle. After years of writing and Emileigh birthing two more children, what we have accomplished is in the hands of our Creator.

To my husband, Paul Westbrook, his overflowing support has meant the world to my heart. The days when I had no confidence in my writing, he was able to say exactly what I needed in order to spur me on. He knows me well in that when I feel inadequate, pushing me to want to quit, his compliments and praise keep me going. I am grateful for his kind heart when he took me out to celebrate the completion of the book (even though I still wrote for six more months because it didn't feel complete) to my favorite fondue restaurant and bragged to the waitress that his wife wrote a book.

To my wonderful sons and their precious wives, kids—I know

you are grown now—I want to say thanks for your support. Sarah Westbrook, thank you for the time you put in to help me title the book. Caleb Westbrook, my son who is a literature teacher, thank you for editing so many crazy beginnings of this book. Luke Westbrook, Joshua Westbrook, and Elena Westbrook Montoya, thanks for believing in me and supporting me in this endeavor.

To the many others who read a page here and there or a chapter here and there, thank you! Your words of wisdom helped mold this book.

## EMILEIGH

I am blessed with many who fill me to the brim with gratitude, but I'll spare you the novel and focus on the short list.

To Melody Westbrook, my co-author, mentor, and friend, the challenge you presented to me to write and then write better and then write more is something I will be forever grateful for. Your refusal to accept my initial decline to write with you on this project has propelled growth and strength in me that I will carry the rest of my life. You saw something in me I not only never thought possible but never knew I needed to accomplish. You teach, inspire, and encourage me. Our conversations are a breath of fresh air, and our friendship is an irreplaceable gift. Thank you for walking with me both on this endeavor and in life.

To my husband, Steve Ziebka, I can't imagine navigating the trenches of our life with any other person. You are my teammate and best friend. We are building a life together that is messy and altogether wonderful. Through writing this book, you gave me the time and space I needed amid the chaos of our home almost every time I needed it. Our gaggle has doubled in size from start to finish of this book, and it gets admittedly crazy at times. Along the way, your words of encouragement as writing material spurred me on, and the unending support you give helps keep my head above water.

To my children, Elizabeth, Lucas, Samuel, and Isaac, I have no idea why God chose me to be your mom, but there is no greater accomplishment I have or will ever attain that is better than the four of you. God uses each of you to challenge and inspire me. Thank you for unknowingly giving me writing material. One day when you read these words, I hope you are proud of the way God used you to apply His Word in my life. Thank you for loving me even when I don't feel I deserve it. Thank you for both the loving and frustratingly perfect words you spoke to me during this writing adventure that inspired many words written within these pages.

To my family and friends who read chapters, experienced some of the events recorded, and walked with me on the journey of life, thank you. Thank you for the encouragement, love, and wisdom each of you provides to keep me going. Thank you for being family and friends who point me to Jesus.

# *Introduction*

## THE WALK BACK TO EDEN, GOD'S WORD, YOUR STORY. HIS PARADISE, YOUR PURSUIT.

"Life is a journey!"

A phrase we commonly use to remind us that there are very few destinations in life. Printed on posters, kitchen décor, and t-shirts, this phrase embodies every walk of life, every generation, and every religion. No one can escape it! But how we walk this journey determines its outcomes, results, and even its destination.

Easy journeys bring delight; hard journeys stop us dead in our tracks. But even if we stop, we must start moving again, putting one foot in front of the other.

### OUR MYOPIC VIEW

On this path called life, our view is myopic. Imagine this with me: you are on a hike in one of the most beautiful settings in the world. Pick one. Whichever trail you choose, when you stop mid-trail, your view would limit you to whatever is in front or behind. The beauty captured would be the beauty limited within your range of vision.

What if we could widen our view, broadening our perspective? What if we could see the path we are currently standing on as only a small section of our journey? What if we stopped defining our lives by the current journey and defined it by eternity?

Defining our lives by eternity requires knowing the God of eternity. So, how do we get to know the God of eternity? We ask Him His story. His story written in His Word, the Bible!

So how well do you know His story? Our myopic view of life limits us to a myopic view of God's story. We pick and choose scripture that is meaningful and comforting. But when we see and understand God's word within the context it is written, it is like turning on the light in a dimly lit room. What were once shadows of truth become beacons of light guiding us on our walk of life.

God's word, His stories, surround us every day. We listen to podcasts, read books, and frequent our daily devotionals, highlighting amazing verses from scripture, but do we really know the characters played out in His Word? Are our lives touched by theirs? Do we walk alongside them, or are they characters in a book from long ago?

The Bible is the greatest story written, yet it sits on our shelf, gathering dust with no one to turn the page. We become frustrated in our attempts to read a book written centuries ago because it seems inapplicable and dry. But on the contrary, the Bible is filled with pages of stories about people just like you and me.

This book begs to be opened, to be read and studied. But until we open it up, it will forever be the story written outside of us. What if we could pick up the Bible and see His story written within us? What if we could see God's movement and hear God's voice? What if the story moved beyond the pages and became the story that lives within us?

## WHY DO I NEED EDEN?

Within God's story, the garden of Eden was altered because of the choices made by mankind. Since creation, God has desired for us to be in fellowship with Him. He designed the garden of Eden for us to dwell in His presence. But our sin destroyed that perfect union. From the point of destruction, we see in scripture how God desires to bring us back to Him, to Eden, a reclaimed paradise. For us to fully understand this, we must start in Eden in order to return to Eden.

This book will take you on a journey through the garden, into the wilderness, and locked inside a boat. You will feel the dirt between your toes walking the roads of Canaan, feel the heartfelt loss as Adam and Eve were kicked out of paradise, and sit in the quiet of an unformed universe. Practical lessons for today were taken from a book written centuries ago. You will not want to miss this journey!

## WHY THE OLD TESTAMENT?

Many years ago, as I made it my mission to begin studying the Old Testament with new and fresh eyes, I was amazed not just at the stories but at God's voice speaking through these stories. I was amazed at how practical the Old Testament was to my own life and how learning His story impacted my story. The Old Testament answers questions like, "Why is there sin? Why does heartache continue in our current world? Why did Jesus die?"

The Old Testament is the foundation for what we believe today. It is more than the Ten Commandments taken from the book of Exodus. It is more than disconnected morality tales taught to children in Sunday school. It is filled with stories of people, people with names, emotions, heartache, and laughter. As we sit beside them today with tear-filled eyes, our hearts would cry out to them as we told them our own stories.

Eve's heart would break in our story of feeling abandoned by God. Noah would resonate with us when we told him God's big ask for our lives. He would smile when we told him that we were scared and unsure. Sarah would weep when we told her that our womb was barren. As our hearts pour out to them, they would assure us that the journey toward God is worth every step.

Walk with me as we listen to their voices and learn their stories. Take my hand and let me guide you through a book rich with life lessons from those who have walked before us. Grab your boots and let's journey together.

## STARTING AT THE END

We will begin our journey at the end. We will first look at the Greats of Old at the end of their lives. As you put on your boots, the journey will begin in the book of Hebrews in the New Testament. We will pause and listen as the Greats of Old, who have long since passed, speak to us.

After we listen to the Greats, we will go back to the beginning, back to creation. Then we will continue walking until we step onto Abraham's front porch. With each account, we will begin to see how these stories can become a part of our story, our current twenty-first-century story.

## WHAT IS TESTAMENT?

Before we begin, let me ask you a question. Do you know the meaning of the word *testament*? Did you know that the word *testament* means "covenant"?

The Bible is divided into two sections: the Old Testament and the New Testament or the old covenant and the new covenant. There were four hundred years between the Old Testament and the New Testament called the Intertestamental Period, or the "400 Silent Years" where no new prophets were revealed.

So why the word *covenant*? Webster defines covenant as "a written agreement or promise usually under seal between two or more parties, especially for the performance of some action."

Throughout the Bible, God made binding agreements with His people. Why was this important? Why does He want to make an agreement with us? Why do we need a covenant?

His covenant is because of His love for us! God's greatest desire is to have fellowship with us, to be in a relationship with us. That is why He created us. His presence was known in the garden of Eden so He could fellowship with Adam and Eve. It was the perfect union between God and mankind. God made a covenant with them that if they would live their lives for Him, they would be blessed with paradise and blessed with a perfect union with Him. This is called the Edenic covenant, or Adamic covenant. But as we know, Adam and Eve broke this covenant with God by taking a bite from the fruit. At this bite, the covenant was broken. Within that broken covenant, salvation for God to save His people began.

At the bite, the fellowship with God continued to break time and again because of their sin. Then God destroyed the earth with a flood except for one family, Noah's. Once the water receded, God made another covenant. This covenant was called the Noahic covenant. God covenanted to never cause such destruction again by flood, a.k.a. the rainbow!

Man continued to break this covenant with God, so God made a covenant with Abraham called the Abrahamic covenant. Within this covenant, God promised Abraham that he would become the father of a chosen nation.

As time moved on, you guessed it. Man failed again and again, breaking the heart of God. So a covenant was formed between the Israelite people, God's chosen people and descendants of the promise given to Abraham, through a man named Moses, a.k.a. the Ten Commandments. This covenant was called the Mosaic covenant.

As man continued to break this covenant, God's desire to have fellowship with His creation never waned. So He made the ultimate covenant, the new covenant! Yes, the New Testament! This covenant was the final covenant given to us through the sacrifice of Jesus Christ.

Now, please do not take this lightly. When we look at the entire context of scripture, we will see the movement of God through these covenants. God's desire to fellowship with us burned so deeply that He offered up the most precious thing to Him, His only begotten Son. This was God's plan of salvation, the saving of His creation from the world of destruction.

We currently live within the new covenant given by Jesus. Everything in scripture points to Jesus, the ultimate sacrifice.

Our journey will be in the Old Testament. We will see how the Old Testament leads us to the New Testament, Jesus' sacrificial story!

## THIS BOOK

As we focus our journey in Genesis, we will walk until Abraham's death. This book will give you context to the familiar stories of the Old Testament, but it will also allow you to hear what God wants to say through His Word. You will depart with some new knowledge of scripture, but more importantly, you will part with life lessons God wants to speak through His Word.

At the end of every chapter, my dear friend, Emileigh, will lead you through probing questions pertaining to the lessons. Her uncanny way of unwrapping these lessons will speak to your heart and your life on a practical level. I thank God for bringing her into my life and for the opportunities she and I have to talk about God's story.

So let's go on a journey together walking back to Eden, the reclaimed paradise. Lace up your boots and grab your walking stick! I'll meet you on page one!

## A NOTE FROM EMILEIGH

Our faith journey is like a walk, and we all travel at a different pace. Some of us race through to accomplish our many to-dos. Others prefer to walk slowly and absorb completely the experiences and lessons around us. No matter what pace we approach our faith, God is leading, teaching, and prayerfully stretching our faith every step of the way. As we step into this study and these lessons, I pray each reader will learn at their own pace what God so desperately wants us all to see, His unending love, His all-consuming grace, and His overwhelming power. He wants to meet you exactly where you are.

My prayer is that you do the same with Him. Meet God where you are and surrender to what He is teaching you. Embrace His love through the power of His Word.

In the following lessons, we will walk together at a slower pace to absorb the key lessons God wants you to know. Through each lesson, I challenge you to find your walk-away, the key lesson or concept that resonated most with you. In each chapter and for everyone, the walk-away may look different, and that is beautiful. We each read scripture in different lights as well as walk different journeys; therefore, God will use these lessons to speak to you in unique ways. I will encourage you to share these walk-aways and your answers to the various discussion questions posed with a trusted friend or small group. God will use how He speaks to you to help lead others.

# 1

# A WALK TO REMEMBER

"Honey, grab your boots.

Do you have your jacket?

Oh, please lace your boots all the way to the top!"

These are the phrases I hear almost every time my husband and I set out on a hike. We love to explore new trails, but there is a checklist every time we head out the door.

While on the trail, I love observing nature, including a frog jumping into the water, a bird perching on a limb, and a worm moving as it slithers into the earth. It is easy for me to get distracted.

My husband, on the other hand, is enthralled with a destination. Don't get me wrong. He enjoys the path too. But place him at the beginning of the trail and point him in the direction of a waterfall, he is like a hound hunting its prey. Sometimes his desire for a destination and my desire for meandering through the woods doesn't make for a great mix. The temptation to throw his map off a cliff becomes more than I can bear. Ask him about Kauai!

My typical words are, "Just enjoy the journey, honey. By the way, would you like a snack?"

## JOURNEY TO HANGING LAKE

A few years ago, Paul and I went on a hike in the mountains of Colorado. To be honest, I really didn't want to go. I had gotten mad at him that morning and wanted to stay at the condominium to relax in the hot tub and eat donuts. (It was National Donut Day!) But if I were going to have any family time, I had better lace up my hiking boots all the way to the top! Our destination was Hanging Lake.

As we started this climb, I noticed the path was crowded, and I hate crowded hikes because I am keenly aware I have people behind me looking at my butt. Trust me: it's not pretty!

As we meandered up the mountain, I began looking for any excuse to get off the trail. An injured little girl and a beautiful waterfall were both great distractions, but neither worked. Waterfall to the left; Hanging Lake to the right! As I pointed my boots to the left, my husband informed me that the path to the lake was to the right. Ugh!

As I was pushing my way up the hill, exhaustion was setting in. I was about to quit when I saw signs of hope. My husband had said there would be a bridge that we would cross when we were close to the lake, and by golly, when I looked at my feet, I was standing on a bridge! Thank You, Jesus!

As we were crossing the bridge, other hikers were reassuring me that I was close. Seeing my look of desperation, they encouraged me. I appreciated their encouragement, but I did not want their attention. I was either going to punch my husband for taking me on this hike or throw up. Neither of those would be pleasant for them to witness. But either one would have given me great relief.

Huffing and puffing, I finally reached the edge of the bridge. Peering beyond the edge, I caught a glimpse of our destination. There it was, the most beautiful lake I had ever seen!

A hush came over the hikers as though we were entering a place of holiness. Meandering through the holy hush, I made my way to the other side of the lake. Finding a comfortable rock on which to rest, I sat and experienced God in all His glory. This beautiful, crystal-clear lake was hugged by beautiful pine trees and rock ledges as though they were the perfect frame to a beautiful masterpiece. The water provided the perfect window to the rocks and fish life below the surface of the lake. As I sat on a rock, I thanked God for the beauty in which I could worship Him.

In my serene moments, my husband's voice startled me. "Honey, Melody, are you ready to go? We need to get down the mountain before it turns dark."

I connected with God that day through His beauty! I heard His voice through His creation!

## HOPE FOR A DESTINATION REQUIRES FAITH

Before leaving for the hike, I had to have faith in my husband that there really was a hanging lake at the top of that mountain. The faith I had in him was rewarded by the sight of the lake hanging in the mountains. When we are given a promise that something exists, we want to have faith that we will receive what is promised. We want to be rewarded for our faith.

But what if our faith isn't rewarded here on earth? Most of us would quit. We would turn around on that mountain and head back down to sit in the hot tub and eat our donuts. But in the book of Hebrews, there is a long list of people who never saw their full reward yet remained faithful. The faith they held onto went beyond the rewards.

## PAUSE AND READ

Pause here and read Hebrews 11:3–12 and 17–21. I really do mean for you to pause here and read these scriptures on your own! (Smiley face!) Do you recognize these people?

- Abel
- Enoch

- Noah
- Abraham
- Sarah
- Isaac
- Jacob
- Joseph
- Moses

## LET THE JOURNEY BEGIN

As we begin our journey through the Old Testament, we are going to start in the New Testament. Let's imagine ourselves walking alongside these greats, conversing with them about life, absorbing their wisdom, and asking questions, such as:

- What was it like, Sarah, when you knew you couldn't give Abraham a child?
- Isaac, do you remember that day when your father walked you up the hill expecting to sacrifice you? Were you afraid?
- Jacob, was your deception toward your father solely influenced by your mom? Or was it something you wanted too?

The book of Hebrews gives us a peek into the lives of these people. It gives us an opportunity to see their faith and learn from the lives they lived.

## THE MYSTERY WRITER

The writer of Hebrews is a bit of a mystery. Within this mystery, we can gather characteristics of the writer without knowing who he was. One of the most important details to this mystery person is that they were of the Jewish faith and educated in both Hellenistic (relating to Greek history, culture, and language) and Jewish influences. This writer was learned in the Levitical law and the influences of it in lieu of the newfound faith of Christianity. He was kind of like a fish out of water!

Within the context of the Old Testament, the Jewish people, the Israelites, were God's chosen people. They had been given the Promised Land through the faith of Abraham and then regifted the promised land through the faith of Moses. This is foundational in understanding the emotions and fears of these people being referenced in the book of Hebrews. Throughout the Old Testament, we read chapter after chapter, book after book, of God pleading with His chosen people to return to the faith He called them to, the walk back to Eden!

In Hebrews 10, the author pleads with the people to remain strong in their faith in Christ. Because Christianity (following Christ, a man who was now dead) was such a far-fetched following, the writer knew he needed to convince these people it was worth it. Following meant sacrifice.

> Think back on those early days when you first learned about Christ. Remember how you remained faithful even though it meant terrible suffering. Sometimes you were exposed to public ridicule and were beaten, and sometimes you helped others who were suffering the same things. You suffered along with those who were thrown into jail, and when all you owned was taken from you, you accepted it with joy. You knew there were better things waiting for you that will last forever. So **do not throw away this confident trust in the Lord. Remember the great reward it brings you!** (Hebrews 10:32–35 NLT; emphasis mine)

These people had been ridiculed, beaten, thrown in jail, and robbed because of their faith. If they separated from Judaism into Christianity, they not only lost the protection of the Roman government but could possibly lose their lives for their faith.

Can you relate to that? Of course you can't! And neither can I! I have been ridiculed at times, but truthfully, I can't tell you any great ridiculed story. I have not been beaten, thrown in jail, or robbed because of my faith.

These people were risking everything for their faith in Jesus. They were tired, exhausted, and at the point of quitting. I would be too! Was this sacrifice worth the loss? How do you convince these people this was worth the sacrifices? How do you communicate that today to those you share your faith with?

So the writer moves to chapter 11 as a plea to these people to keep their faith. He wanted to speak to his audience in their own language, the language of the Old Testament. These people had studied these stories ad nauseum. Because they too were Jewish, they knew the stories of Abraham and Sarah, Jacob, Joseph and Moses. They could have taught an Old Testament survey class with their hands tied behind their backs.

The author wanted to connect their current faith in Jesus to the past faith of the Greats so he lays out the list of faithful people from the Old Testament in his plea for them not to give up.

For our faith to be renewed sometimes we have to walk alongside those who anchored our faith to begin with, the patriarchs of our faith! Think of those in your life who have anchored your faith. Why do you return to them when your faith wavers? Because they remind you the journey is worth it!

## FAITH IS THE EVIDENCE

"Faith shows the reality of what we hope for; it is the evidence of things we cannot see" (Hebrews 11:1 NLT). "Faith shows the reality of what we hope for." What do we hope for?

If I were to answer this today, I would answer I want hope in relationships, or hope for friends who are walking through hardships with their children. But there are days I cannot see the ending. In these days, faith must show me the reality of what I hope for!

Looking at the patriarchs of our faith from Hebrews 11, we see amazing people with amazing faith. But when you dig a little deeper, you will see brokenness and disbelief. Eden, the hope for peace and undisturbed relationship with the Creator, was disrupted with the disobedience of Adam and Eve, a broken paradise. Brotherhood was disrupted when Cain slaughtered his brother, Abel. Although Abel is long dead, he still speaks to us by his example of faith (Hebrews 11:4). Redemption was disrupted when Noah stepped out of the boat and found himself in a drunken disarray, lying naked in his tent. Promise was fractured when Abraham questioned God.

And the list goes on. We see these people in their belief, but they were filled with unbelief, just like you and me! But faith is the evidence of the things we cannot see.

- God does not ask us to heal; He simply asks us to believe that He can (faith becoming evidence).
- God does not ask us to provide; He simply asks us to believe that He can (faith becoming evidence).
- God does not ask us to be strong; He simply asks us to believe that He can (faith becoming evidence).

Is your faith evidence?

## FAITH IS ACTIVE OBEDIENCE

Faithfulness is active obedience. When I am obedient in my faith, the results of my faith are in the hands of God, not mine!

Think of it this way: faith is *in*tangible. We cannot see it. We cannot touch it. We cannot taste it. But obedience is tangible. Obedience can be seen. We can see it, touch it, and taste it. It is the tangible evidence to our faith. Therefore, it becomes active obedience.

Let's use Noah as an example. Noah's story is familiar to most. Big faith … big boat! Noah's sole responsibility was to have faith, and because of his faith (intangible), he built a rather large boat (tangible).

For what was Noah hoping? Why did he need faith? He needed faith for the hope of salvation for his family from this flood, something he had never seen before. He obeyed God, who warned him about things that had never happened before (Hebrews 11:7).

Noah couldn't see the future. He didn't know what would happen, "evidence of things we cannot see" (vs. 1). But his *in*tangible faith became tangible as he moved into active obedience stepping inside his boat. When that door locked, shutting him in, he trusted in his active obedience.

Have you ever gone on vacation and stayed at a place with a kitchen? It's breakfast time, and you want a piece of toast. You pop the bread into the toaster and walk away to get your cup of coffee. When you come back to check on your toast, it is still bread. Why? Well, the cord has been wrapped around the toaster by the housekeeper. It's not plugged in. Once you unwrap the cord and plug it in, you will have toast in a few minutes. If you don't, well, you will eat cold bread for breakfast.

The same is true for our faith. It does us no good if we don't use it. We must plug it in to the source, God, to get results. You can claim to have faith all you want, but until you really believe in something you cannot see, it is simply a great word to paint on a plaque and hang in your bedroom.

If Noah had never picked up a hammer, his faith would still be *in*tangible not showing the world his obedience! And his story would not be written in our Bible storybooks today. We wouldn't have the story of the rainbow!

Our intangible faith becomes tangible when we are obedient, obedient in our faith!

## FAITH IS FORWARD-THINKING, AND SOMETIMES THAT STINKS!

All these people died still believing what God had promised them. **They did not receive what was promised, but they saw it all**

**from a distance and welcomed it**. They agreed that they were foreigners and nomads here on earth. Obviously, people who say such things are **looking forward** to a country they can call their own. If they had longed for the country they came from, they could have gone back. But **they were looking for a better place**, a heavenly homeland. That is why God is not ashamed to be called their God, for he has prepared a city for them. Hebrews 11:13–16 (NLT)

Did you catch that? Read it again! They did not receive what was promised!

"I give up! If I never receive what is promised, then why should I even try?"

But these people made it into the Hall of Faith because they were "forward-thinkers." They were aware that this earth was their temporary home. " … they were foreigners and nomads here on earth." They had an eternal perspective knowing that their faithfulness would be rewarded in a "better place, a heavenly homeland."

Too often, we are current thinkers, looking only at the trials of the day, week, or year. We become overwhelmed juggling work, kids, and laundry. But life is a matter of perspective, "forward-thinking." We should be living with one foot in and one foot out, one foot here on this earth and one foot in eternity.

When you question where you are on this journey, look down at your feet! Where are they planted? One in and one out? Are you a "forward-thinker", or are you stuck in today?

## FAITH NEEDS PERSPECTIVE!

"These were all commended for their faith, yet none of them received what had been promised, since God had planned something better for us so that only together with us would they be made perfect" (Hebrews 11:39 NIV).

If our faith is based solely on what we see fulfilled here on earth, we miss the point. If our eyes are fixed on what surrounds us, what is in front and behind us, our myopic view, we will stumble with every step we take. But if we take our focus away from where we are currently standing and fix our eyes on eternity, every step will become purposeful.

The job you don't enjoy will become purposeful as you learn to depend on God for daily strength. That child who challenges every fiber of your being will be used to show you the eternal purpose of grace. The marriage that has brought you to your knees in pain will be the marriage that will bring you to your knees before Jesus.

Wherever your eyes are focused will become the journey you choose. It's all about perspective.

## FAITH BRINGS US TOGETHER!

Continue with me as we read the next part of this verse. It will blow your mind! Read this closely. "Since God had planned something better for us so that **only together with us** would **THEY** be made perfect."

Did you catch that? Read it again! Circle the phrase "only together with us."

… by combined action, jointly, in unison …

**ONLY TOGETHER …**

They need US …

Who are the us? Do you remember the context in which the author was writing? He was in a desperate plea to these people who had been beaten, imprisoned, and robbed for their faith. They were on the brink of giving up on their faith.

So the author throws out the net, hoping to catch their faith. In his cry of desperation, he says, "They need you!" The Greats of Old never saw the fulfillment of this promise, and they need you to finish this out to the wholeness the world was designed to be, the paradise God intended from the beginning.

Connecting this to us today, when we see our plight here on

earth with the perspective of eternity, we will see that the people in the book of Hebrews and the Greats of Old in the Old Testament need us here on this earth today to continue carrying this on to completion, the fulfillment of the promise, the reclaimed paradise.

If you think you have no purpose here on earth, think again! Look at your purpose through these lenses and remind yourself that you are needed to communicate the fulfillment of the promise through Christ Jesus.

## FAITH ALLOWS US TO SEE, BUT HOW DO WE DO THIS?

It's all in the eyes! What do you see? Where are you looking?

> Therefore, since we are surrounded by such a huge crowd of witnesses to the life of faith, let us strip off every weight that slows us down, especially the sin that so easily trips us up. And let us run with endurance the race God has set before us. We do this by **keeping our eyes on Jesus**, the champion who initiates and perfects our faith. Because of the joy awaiting him, he endured the cross, disregarding its shame. Now he is seated in the place of honor beside God's throne. (Hebrews 12:1–2 NLT)

This is it. This is the promise fulfilled: Jesus! When you keep your eyes fixed on Him:

- Every time your heart is hurting, look past the hurt and see Jesus.
- When you feel unloved, look past feeling unloved and fall into His arms of love.
- When you can no longer carry the load of this world, look to Him to carry it for you.

This is a conscience, purposeful pivot of the gaze!

## FAITH BRINGS US TO THE END OF THE STORY, THE LIGHTING OF THE TORCH

Over the years, the significance of the Olympic torch has evolved to our present-day enactment of this ancient tradition. The flame is the symbol representing the connection between the ancient and modern games.

Before the opening of the Olympic games, a torch is lit months prior in Olympia, Greece. That torch is then passed from person to person, town to town, and country to country until it reaches its destination to light the cauldron at the current Olympic stadium. When that torch was lit, there was no way only one runner could run the torch from Greece to the Olympic game destination. The torch must be passed to the next runner, swimmer, skier, and so forth. The first runner needs that final runner to complete the task or the purpose, or the promise! But interestingly, every runner in between is just as significant as the first and final runner.

Now, look at this in lieu of these verses in Hebrews. In the days of old, the days in the Old Testament, the torch was lit. Beginning with Adam and Eve, the torch was lit. It was then passed to Noah, Abraham, Moses, and so forth. With each runner, they knew they would never see the final lighting. But because of their faith, they continued to pass the torch, knowing the next person would carry it on to the next and to the next.

Today, you are standing on the path. As you are standing, you see the torch dimly lit in the distance. It is a faint light glowing from afar. But as it gets closer and closer, it gets brighter and brighter. As it approaches, you begin to feel the warmth from the fire. You see the runner before you looking weary as they carry the torch. But you also see their face is determined and delighted as they have been blessed to carry the torch.

As you reach out to grab the torch, there is an emotion of elation, yet an emotion of fear, wondering if you can complete this course. As you take your first step, confidence begins to well up inside you. With each subsequent step, you realize you are not doing this on your own strength. "Therefore, since we are surrounded by such a great cloud of witnesses … " (Hebrews 12:1 NIV).

Envision yourself as you run past those who have gone before you. As you run, they stand saying, "You can do this … Fix your gaze ahead of you … Don't give up … Your reward awaits you!"

As you run with the Greats of Old surrounding you, watching you and cheering you on, you need to continue to press on for the promise.

"Let us strip off every weight that slows us down, especially the sin that so easily trips us up" (Hebrews 12:1).

So throw everything else aside and
Press on,
March on,
Persevere on!

Your goal,
Your lighting of the cauldron,
Is the promise giver,
Jesus Himself!

In the final leg of the race, the torch will be handed off to Jesus.
You will stand and watch as He lights the cauldron,
Completing the promise!
Fix your eyes on Him!

Jesus was and is the completion of the promise.
He endured the cross,
Scorned its shame, and
Sat down at the right hand of God.
Promise fulfilled?
Check!
This is a walk to remember!

## TALKS WITH EMILEIGH

Let's start our journey together with Hebrews 11. Have you read it before? If you haven't, do so now. Read it slowly. If you are comfortable writing in your Bible, I encourage you to underline each time you read "by faith."

A wise friend once told me that when I'm reading scripture and find myself having to re-read it or pause, I am to take that as an opportunity to look for meaning from the Lord. Often when I read scripture, God pauses me at what seems to be the most random places. When I take the time to ask what He wants me to learn or simply reflect on that part, He reveals a deeper meaning than my original surface reading of it.

The Hall of Faith, as it is often termed, is full of great individuals who served and honored the Lord in their own unique way. We can learn so much from their lives. Though the book of Hebrews is found in the New Testament, the Hall of Faith references many Greats from the Old Testament.

*Do you have a favorite Old Testament story? If you aren't familiar with the Old Testament, did any of the Greats in Hebrews 11 cause you to pause or be curious about their life?*

Many of the greats listed cause me to pause. When I pause, I think about what God might want me to glean from their life. For example, we read of Enoch who pleased God. To please God, verse 6 tells us, we must have faith. To please Him, I need to trust the Lord wholeheartedly. Enoch did this with his life, and others learned from the way he lived. Do you live your life with wholehearted faith in the Lord?

Sarah is someone who catches my eye each time I read this chapter. Scripture outlines multiple layers of Sarah's walk with the Lord, but ultimately she lived a life of great faith. Further reading reveals that she didn't always trust God wholeheartedly, which is where her downfall began. Yet God used her life and story to exemplify great faith!

By reading the Old Testament account, we can better understand why the individuals included are considered great. I've included a listing of these individuals. Each one is included for a purpose, and it is by faith that we discover that purpose. Choose one of them, perhaps the Great who made you curious on your initial reading, and read the verses outlined.

## THE HALL OF FAITH

- Abel: Genesis 4:3–7
- Enoch: Genesis 5:21–24
- Noah: Genesis 6:9–22
- Abraham: Genesis 12:1–4
- Sarah: Genesis 17:15–16, 18:9–15, 21:1–7
- Isaac: Genesis 27:1–40
- Jacob: Genesis 48
- Joseph: Genesis 50:24–25
- Moses: Exodus 2:1–15, 12: 21–28, 14:26–28
- Israelites and the Walls of Jericho: Joshua 6:1–21
- Rahab: Joshua 2:1–21, 6:22–25
- Gideon: Judges 6:11–40, 7:7–20
- Barak: Judges 4:6–24
- Samson: Judges 13:24–25, 14:19, 15:20, 16:26–31
- Jephthah: Judges 11:9–11, 29–31
- David: 1 Samuel 16:12–13, 17:45–47; 2 Samuel 7:18–29, 23:1–7; 1 Kings 2:1–4
- Samuel: 1 Samuel 2:26, 3:19, 12:23–24

For many, the scripture reference is just a glimpse at the account of their life. For more extensive understanding of the way God worked in and through their life, read the corresponding verses. For example, the Hebrews reference of Sarah tells me she gave birth despite being beyond childbearing years. I needed to read the account in Genesis to fully understand her initial doubts and ultimate celebration that truly transformed her great faith! The accounts referenced for David, a man after God's own heart (1 Samuel 13:14), do not include his moments of poor judgment that God used to refine his character nor his valiant battle victories that truly made him a great king and representative of great faith. The accounts referenced of Moses do not mention his hesitation or fears, but corresponding scripture clearly shows how God used Moses' weaknesses for His glory. I challenge you to choose one from this list and seek what God may want you to learn through further reading.

***Which Great did you choose? What did you learn? Why do you believe they are considered great?***

Melody writes,

> Faithfulness is active obedience. When I am obedient in my faith, the results of my faith are in the hands of God, not mine!
>
> Think of it this way: faith is intangible. We cannot see it. We cannot touch it. We cannot taste it.
>
> But obedience is tangible. Obedience can be seen. We can see it, and others can see it. We can see it, touch it, and taste it. It is the tangible evidence to our faith. Therefore, it becomes active obedience.

***What is one way your faithfulness has become active obedience?***

As I write this study, I am being actively obedient to God's call. This was never part of the journey I thought God had lined out for me. I love the Lord. I lean heavily into my faith, but write a study? Surely that's not part of His plan for me. As I prayed and listened to God's call on my heart though, I knew to avoid the call to write for you now would not please God. I heard Him whisper through Melody's wisdom that I needed to act on my faith and be obedient. The moment I began writing, my faith took on a much greater tangibility. More so, I felt God telling me I needed to invite others in to pray for this journey. I needed their accountability and encouragement. As they pray for me, it becomes an opportunity for them to act on their own faith as well.

***When has your faith moved from intangible to tangible? Who in your sphere of influence might be looking at the tangibility of your faith?***

Have you ever read the story of Noah? Noah was a man of great faith. In short, the Lord told Noah He was going to flood the earth and he needed to build an ark for his family and many animals. Now I want you to picture your neighbor building an ark in their front yard. Unless your neighbor builds boats for his profession, this isn't a very common sight to see. Do you think you'd wonder what he was doing? Scripture tells us in Matthew 24:37–39 that his neighbors "didn't know until the flood came and took them away" but not specifically their response to Noah's act of obedience. What we know for certain is that Noah fulfilled God's calling on his life and made his faith tangible.

***When has the confidence of another affected your faith or your own confidence affected others? Did you (or the person who influenced you) stay on the path God called you? Did you attain the goal?***

Melody takes us a step deeper into Hebrews 11 as she reminds us that none of the Greats received what had been promised. Interestingly, this Hall of Faith is outlined in the New Testament after Jesus Christ sacrificed Himself and made tangible the promises of the Old Testament. The Greats didn't hear stories of the resurrected Lord nor bear witness to the perfection of His life. They simply believed what was to come and followed. They lived by faith. With their lives and faith, God had a purpose just as He has a purpose for you. God planned for their lives to be made perfect "with us." Our faith, our lives, and our stories are intertwined. The Greats of Old Testament times lived their lives with great faith. Though they were far from perfect, they have passed on the torch for us to carry. God intends for us to see their imperfections and successes and to learn from them so we can exercise great tangible faith ourselves. The even greater beauty in this purpose is that the journey doesn't end with us. We cannot attain the goal on our own. The glory of God will never be extinguished, but He invites us to take part in the race by carrying and passing on the torch. He calls us to keep the flame burning. We must continue the journey by taking steps of obedience, relying on His promises, and committing to passing on the torch.

***Who in your life are you investing in to pass your torch?***

Keeping your torch burning is not always an easy feat. It requires encouragement, accountability, and perseverance. As I take a step of obedience in writing this, I know my support system is praying for and cheering me on; that adds flame to my torch. I need those supporters on my sidelines to keep me moving forward. As I pour into my children and the women I attend Bible study with, I am making an investment.

Read Hebrews 12:1–2a. The author here calls us to lay down every hindrance. It is our responsibility to carry on the torch and keep moving forward in our pursuit of His righteousness. Imagine if Noah had perceived his inadequacies as an excuse not to build the ark. If I had let the lies of fear and inadequacy hold me back from writing, we wouldn't be walking through this study together. We each have a hindrance or obstacle that will threaten to stand in the way of our calling, threatening to dim our torch.

*What obstacle (or hindrance) is dimming your torch?*

Speaking the hindrances and obstacles aloud with trusted friends is the best way to begin combating them. Doing so can be scary but also freeing. It can take courage to fight against it. Those God has placed on your sidelines in the race of life will be there to encourage and cheer you on. You must look to them but also to your own perseverance to overcome the obstacles of life.

***What can you do to increase your confidence and faith to carry on your part of the story? Who in your life is cheering you on from the sidelines to keep running the race?***

We all will walk or run through life at a different pace, but despite our obstacles, considering His promises and with the Greats in mind, we must keep our eyes focused on the goal, not on those next to, in front of, or behind us. Our primary pace-setter in life should ultimately be Jesus. We, like the Greats, must rely on His promises and pace uniquely set before each of us to walk in faith more confidently. For it is by the Lord's strength that we take steps of faith (1 Samuel 2:9).

This week and each week, I invite you to challenge yourself in an area presented by Melody's words or brought forth by discussion with your small group or trusted friends. This week, I challenge you to identify one person you can encourage to keep running their race. Be a sideline supporter. Send this individual a message, email, or card letting them know they have your support. Write the individual's name somewhere as a reminder to invest in their race.

# 2

# THE QUIET WALK

Shhhhh! Quiet!

How many times did I tell my boys to be quiet?! One hundred times … a thousand times? When you raise three boys, the noise level can be intense!

We live in a world of constant noise. It surrounds us inside and outside of our heads, causing our sleep to become restless and our days to be chaotic.

But in the beginning, it was quiet! The earth was perfectly still, without motion or noise!

This is impossible for us to imagine because even in my quiet, I hear noise. Sitting outside, I hear the chirping of the birds or the singing of the cicadas as the males cry out. It is never totally and completely quiet.

But before the world was formed, it was quiet,…very quiet! …and there was a hover!

## THE HOVER

> In the beginning … the earth was formless and empty, darkness was over the surface of the deep, and the Spirit of God was **hovering** over the waters. (Genesis 1:1 NIV).

"The Spirit of God was hovering." Webster defines *hover* as "to hang fluttering in the air or on the wing; to remain suspended over a place or object."

As women, we are good at the hover. Whether you're a mom or not, hover is in our blood. Even as a young girl, I could hover with the best of them. I hovered over the playground, making sure everyone followed the rules. I hovered at church and the movie theater! Can you believe that she is with him? Hover extraordinaire!

Webster defines it as the "hang while fluttering in the air." Imagine this with me. The best example I can think of is the hummingbird. We are intrigued by their ability to hang while fluttering. But truthfully, I don't know why this so intrigues me. This is exactly what I did with my children.

> "Oh, you think I can't see you. Well, you are fooled, son. I have mom wings. You can't see them, but they allow me to hang while I flutter. This hanging and fluttering thing gives me all I need to watch you. And when I watch you, I see you do the things you think I can't see you do! I see it all!"

Webster also defines it as "suspended over an object." Can I just say, " You do not want me suspended over your object?"

I hovered until my flutter became more of a flailing, causing my wings to give out until I came crashing down with a loud thud. When I compare my hovering to God's hovering, there is a distinct difference. That difference has everything to do with noise. I hover with words.

- Don't do that!
- What were you thinking?
- Is that what Jesus would do?
- Just wait until your father gets home.

Lots and lots of words!

But God's hover was quiet! As God hovered over the waters, the earth was formless, empty, and dark. No creatures. Just dark and empty. Empty and quiet! Incredibly quiet!

## THE QUIET

So think of this:

- What has been the quietest moment in your life?
- What has been the darkest moment (not emotional darkness)?

Several years ago, I went to the Grand Cayman Island with a group of friends. While on the trip, I decided to do a little snorkeling. Since no one else wanted to go, I went alone while they waited on shore. Not a smart move on my part, I know.

Away from shore, I was able to see amazing beauty created by God. Every color of the rainbow swam peacefully below the surface of the water. Fish with stripes and polka dots danced around as though they did not have a care in the world. In this moment of intrigue, it was quiet, so quiet!

As I was swimming back to shore, my underwater world went dark. My face still in the water, it was as though someone had turned off the lights. When I brought my head out of the water, I was confused by this darkness. But my curiosity got the best of me, and back down I went. Below was a black abyss, an underwater cave. Holding my breath, I dove deeper below the surface. As I approached the edge of the cave (there was no way I was going to go in), an eerie feeling crept over me. I knew that if I dove any deeper, I would soon be engulfed in this darkness.

Looking back at this experience in my life, I realized I enjoyed the quiet but felt uncomfortable with the dark. But when I look at Genesis 1:1, I realize God hovered in both the quiet and the dark!

## THE QUIET DARK

Let us start at the beginning where it was quiet and dark. Finish this sentence, "In the beginning God … " (Genesis 1:1).

In that one statement, books have been written, articles

formulated, research cultivated, and controversy ignited. Our minds can quickly move to how the world was created and what we believe about creation.

As we look out in nature or walk alongside those we love, we look for an explanation of how all this started. When we see the intricacies and complexities within our world, we look for the how or the who. Holding a tiny baby, hiking up a mountain, and observing a simple sore healing on our arm are all examples of the detail built within our world. How? And who? Our focus will not be on the how, but on the who. Who created our world?

Looking to scripture, we discover in Genesis 1:1, "In the beginning God created the heavens and the earth." The God who has always been and always will be created!

It is quiet and dark. As we observed the quiet and contemplated the hover in the introduction to this chapter, we saw it was quiet! But once the lights turned on and creation began, the noise level began to rise. Sounds filled the air that had never been heard. Each creature brought a unique and distinct sound. Birds chirp; lions roar. Pigs oink; cats meow. Each sound brought distinction and noticeability! But with all this oinking, chirping, meowing, and roaring, noise soon filled the new world.

## HEY, TURN IT DOWN OUT THERE!

When God created the world, He also created a new sound every day. Discover the sounds of this world.

### Day One

> And God said, "Let there be light," and there was light. God saw that the light was good, and he separated the light from the darkness. God called the light "day," and the darkness he called "night." And

> there was evening, and there was morning—the first day. (Genesis 1:3–5 NIV)

What was created? What sounds were introduced?

**Day Two**

> And God said, "Let there be a vault between the waters to separate water from water." So God made the vault and separated the water under the vault from the water above it. And it was so. God called the vault "sky." And there was evening, and there was morning—the second day. (Genesis 1:6–8 NIV)

What was created? What sounds were introduced?

**Day Three**

> And God said, "Let the water under the sky be gathered to one place, and let dry ground appear." And it was so. God called the dry ground "land," and the gathered waters he called "seas." And God saw that it was good.
>
> Then God said, "Let the land produce vegetation: seed-bearing plants and trees on the land that bear fruit with seed in it, according to their various kinds." And it was so. The land produced vegetation: plants bearing seed according to their kinds and trees bearing fruit with seed in it according to their kinds. And God saw that it was good. And there was evening, and there was morning—the third day. (Genesis 1:9–13 NIV)

What was created? What sounds were introduced?

## Day Four

> And God said, "Let there be lights in the vault of the sky to separate the day from the night and let them serve as signs to mark sacred times, and days and years, and let them be lights in the vault of the sky to give light on the earth." And it was so. God made two great lights—the greater light to govern the day and the lesser light to govern the night. He also made the stars. God set them in the vault of the sky to give light on the earth, to govern the day and the night, and to separate light from darkness. And God saw that it was good. And there was evening, and there was morning—the fourth day. (Genesis 1:14–19 NIV)

What was created? What sounds were introduced?

## Day Five

> And God said, "Let the water teem with living creatures, and let birds fly above the earth across the vault of the sky." So God created the great creatures of the sea and every living thing with which the water teems and that moves about in it, according to their kinds, and every winged bird according to its kind. And God saw that it was good. God blessed them and said, "Be fruitful and increase in number and fill the water in the seas, and let the birds increase on the earth." And there was evening, and there was morning—the fifth day. (Genesis 1:20-23 NIV)

What was created? What sounds were introduced?

## Day Six

And God said, "Let the land produce living creatures according to their kinds: the livestock, the creatures that move along the ground, and the wild animals, each according to its kind." And it was so. God made the wild animals according to their kinds, the livestock according to their kinds, and all the creatures that move along the ground according to their kinds. And God saw that it was good.

Then God said, "Let us make mankind in our image, in our likeness, so that they may rule over the fish in the sea and the birds in the sky, over the livestock and all the wild animals, and over all the creatures that move along the ground."

So God created mankind in his own image, in the image of God he created them; male and female he created them.

God blessed them and said to them, "Be fruitful and increase in number; fill the earth and subdue it. Rule over the fish in the sea and the birds in the sky and over every living creature that moves on the ground."

Then God said, "I give you every seed-bearing plant on the face of the whole earth and every tree that has fruit with seed in it. They will be yours for food. And to all the beasts of the earth and all the birds in the sky and all the creatures that move along the ground—everything that has the breath of life in it—I give every green plant for food." And it was so.

> God saw all that he had made, and it was very good. And there was evening, and there was morning—the sixth day. (Genesis 1:24–31 NIV)

What was created? What sounds were introduced?

**Day Seven**

> By the seventh day God had finished the work he had been doing; so, on the seventh day he rested from all his work. The God blessed the seventh day and made it holy, because on it he rested from all the work of creating that he had done. (Genesis 2:2–3 NIV)

What was created? What sound was introduced? Sit back and think of all these sounds in your head. What do you hear?

For seven days, with the rising of the sun, a new sound became a part of the new world. Creation crescendoed, causing a gradual increase of sound reaching its climax on day six with the creation of animals and man.

## GOOD, GOOD … VERY GOOD

Within this creation, God completed each day with the phrase "and it was good." At the end of days three through six, God expressed how He felt about His creation. He was satisfied with His work. But in Genesis 1:31, He states it differently. It was not only good, but it was *very good.*

After the creation of mankind, God says, "And it was *very good*!" Creation went from good to "gooder." When He looked at man who had been made in His image, His heart delighted. He had created a being He could have fellowship with, conversations with, and laughter with! This was the desire of His heart!

This was as good as it gets … very good! But was it?

## HOLY MOLY … IT'S QUIET AGAIN

> By the seventh day God had finished the work he had been doing; so, on the seventh day he rested from all his work. Then God blessed the seventh day and made it holy, because on it he rested from all the work of creating that he had done. (Genesis 2:2–3 NIV)

## DAY SEVEN … GOD RESTED!

The word that God used to describe his creation of rest on day seven was not *good* or even *very good*. The word He used was *holy*! There was something about rest that caused God to go beyond good.

But why would the God of the Universe rest? Wasn't a world filled with sound His desire? Didn't He want fellowship with His creation every day of the week? Was He tired? Did He need a nap?

When I look back at this scripture, three things stand out for me: He finished what He began, He blessed His creation, and, He then rested.

## HE FINISHED, HE BLESSED AND HE RESTED

### he finished.

Let's think of a day in our own lives. For those who are list-makers, when the sun rises, the first thing you may do is to put pencil to paper or finger to phone, making a list of things you would like to accomplish for the day. When the day comes to an end, you look over your list to approve or disapprove of your accomplishments. Did you finish your work? The list you made this morning, did you cross everything off?

I am going to guess that you did not. Very seldom do us as listmakers cross out the entire list at the end of the day. On the rare occasion that we do, we are exhausted in our triumph but still not feeling elation from completed tasks. When we lay down to sleep, we toss and turn, agonizing over tomorrow's tasks, causing us not to rest.

The reason we don't rest is because we don't finish. We make it an impossible task for us to complete our list. Our to-do list could never be a done list because we try to cram too many things within a twenty-four-hour period. Sometimes it is as simple as a pair of scissors. We need to take those scissors and cut our list in half, making it a more likely possibility that we will complete our list for the day. Once we are finished, then we too can find rest.

When God reached the end of day six, He knew that with the creation of man and woman, His day was done and creation complete. He finished; therefore He rested.

**he blessed.**

God blessed rest and declared it holy. Each day of creation prior to day seven was declared as good. Okay, at the end of day six, it was very good. But nothing up to that point was labeled "holy." He saved the best until last. So on day seven, he declared it holy!

Good is good, but holy is, well, holy! Think of this. We live our lives in the good, the six days of creation, but we ignore the holy, the seventh day of rest. This day of rest is important, but we treat it with such triviality.

Why do you think it's a big deal? Why would God create it in the beginning within the seven days of creation and then have Moses chisel it on a stone tablet in the book of Exodus? I believe it is because God wanted us to go back to the "before the beginning" with regularity in our lives. Go back to the "before" where it was quiet, the quiet walk! God says,

> Every seven days, I want you to go back to "before the beginning" where it was quiet and you could hear my voice. Turn off the noise in your life for just a moment so we can have a conversation. If you do, you will hear what I want to say to you. Otherwise, you will continue in your chaotic noise called life, missing My voice. The words that I have to say will change your life!

Do you remember what it was like in the beginning? Do you remember the quiet? In the beginning, it was quiet, so quiet! In the beginning, it was dark, so dark! If we hover in the quiet, we hear God. We hear His voice, His heart, and His being!

But what was God's heart in the beginning? Why would God disrupt the heavens to create an earth? "For in him all things were created; things in heaven and on earth, visible and invisible… all things have been created through him and for him" (Colossians 1:16 NIV).

The disruption in God's being was because we were created for him! In context of scriptures, we can see God's intense desire to have fellowship with His creation. God longs to be in a relationship with us and to be joined in a beautiful and perfect union, Eden.

But as the beginning was no longer the beginning, the new world became loud. The more that was created, the more sounds filled the quiet expanse. But because He created us to have fellowship with Him, He created day seven. This was His blessing! God blesses in the quiet!

Day seven is powerfully beautiful but is greatly neglected. Day seven is holy! Yet we neglect holy!

**he rested.**

Rest …
We can't touch it.
We can't see it.
We can't taste it.
We can't smell it.
We can't hear it.
But it is BEAUTIFUL!

The most beautiful thing that God created was rest. Within our times of rest, we are able to see and appreciate the other aspects of creation. We see and experience the magnitude of the mountains when we rest. He hears the precious sounds of the birds when we rest. We taste the fruits of His creation. And we touch the coolness of the spring waters when we rest.

Yet we make rest optional. If the ocean were optional, we would find ourselves drowning in the deep. If livestock were optional, we would go hungry. We can't ignore the sky, the moon, or the sun because they are a part of our everyday world. But yet, we see the creation of rest as optional.

So why don't we rest?

That's easy...We don't have time because we never put a finish to our work! We have filled our lives with so much noise that the sound of rest gets muffled.

Unfortunately, not only does rest get muffled, but so does God's voice. We can't hear Him because it is so loud in our world. It's like walking into a crowded concert with your best friend. You have come to spend time together, but the crowd is so loud that you soon realize you won't be able to have any quality conversation with one another. It's just too loud. So after the concert, you go out for coffee so you can hear each other speak.

How do we expect God to speak amidst the chaos and noise? We say, "God, we need for You to speak," but we don't quiet ourselves to listen. If we don't pull away to hear God's voice, we will act or behave according to the chaos in our life.

It is in the pulling away, within the quiet and the rest, that we can hear God's voice. When our hearts are tuned to Him, the voices of others or our own quiets. We need rest to hear Him. We need to hear how much He loves us and cherishes us. We need to hear we matter to Him. We need to hear He is in control of our world.

If we don't rest, we don't get quiet.
If we don't get quiet, we don't hear His voice!

God wrote rest in His plan. Don't you want to follow His plan? Let's take a walk back to quiet!

## TALKS WITH EMILEIGH

Recently my daughter was working on her devotion. She was asked to use symbolism to draw a picture of what it must have been like when the Spirit of God hovered over our formless world. She began to draw a black circle, like the earth only without the picture-perfect blue waters and lush, green lands. Instead she began to draw spirals and lines this way and that in black crayon. In her photo above the blackness, she drew a picture of a dove. It was a simple but beautiful dove. It was a simple but beautiful picture of the Lord in His perfection hovering over what He would create to be a world of beauty. In the outer space around the blackness, she drew dots, which she told me were tiny stars all around our formless world. She knows that in the beginning, stars had not yet been created by God, but she told me she wanted to include them because they made her think of God's brightness and the pretty things He created. There was nothing more I could tell her than that her photo was perfect. In fact, her photo was quite thought-provoking for me, especially as I began to think of this lesson.

As God hovered over our world, I cannot begin to imagine the plans that circled through His mind. He must have envisioned it all from beginning to end, for we know that we serve an omniscient God. The incredible part to me is that He must have even foreseen our downfall and destruction of the world He was set to create, but He created it still, for us, His beloved children.

***Can you imagine the quiet as He hovered? Can you sense His peace when you think of His plan for us all along? What was your walk-away as you read this lesson?***

As I write this, I have two extroverted children, with a third child on the way, as well as a large dog who has separation anxiety and thus is constantly barking or howling if we happen to leave the room. What I'm saying is that my life is rarely quiet. I laughed when Melody asked to imagine my quietest moment because I don't have many of those! Recently though, my husband and I went on a weekend trip just the two of us (another rare occasion). We've been together for roughly fourteen years, so we have developed a comfort together that doesn't require us to have constant conversation.

On one afternoon as we hiked up the mountain, we paused to look out over the vast landscape before us. Now typically I am afraid of heights, but in this moment as we simply stood admiring God's creation, I couldn't help but be grateful for the beauty before me and the life the Lord has given me. It was a quick stop though because if I'm honest with you, my husband isn't exactly the slow pace through life kind of guy, so we had to get moving up that mountain. In step with him as we journeyed on, God's peace and the quiet love walked on with us.

As far as darkness, I avoid that at all costs, especially when darkness means the risk of stepping on a leftover Lego or Barbie shoe!

***What is one of the quietest moments you've had? What's one of the darkest moments you've experienced (physically, not emotionally)?***

When I try to imagine my life without the noise, I must imagine life without my family. I don't want to imagine that though because I love them! I'm certain this is what God thought as well. He knew our world would get noisy really quickly, and He couldn't imagine life any better way.

***What do you think it would be like to have complete silence and darkness all the time? Do you think maybe this is what God experienced prior to His creation? Do you think He enjoyed that peace? Why or why not? Can you remember what God created each day?***

My son is currently learning creation in preschool, and it has been a true joy to hear his sister help him remember each day's design and purpose. It may seem like small details in our minds as God's Word holds so much wisdom for us to retain and learn from, but as with all His Word, these days each held purpose and intentionality as well.

As our all-powerful Creator, He surely could have created the whole world in one day if He'd wanted, but instead He chose one day for each design within His plan.

He intentionally created each day with a purpose, and He intentionally created you with a purpose. God knew with each new day how much louder the world became, just as He knows how chaotically loud your life can get. For this purpose, He intentionally created quiet. There's a reason we often hear Him most clearly in a whisper. Have you ever noticed how much better others, especially children, listen when they know you're whispering to them? A shout can come across as aggressive, but a whisper makes you want to capture the words. A whisper makes you want to slow down, quiet down, and hear what is being said. God whispers to us with intentionality.

***Can you think of a time God whispered to you in your seeming chaos and you were able to quiet yourself to listen? What did He say?***

On the last day of the week, God created rest. It appears He saved the best for last. And sadly, so do we. As Melody phrased it, "It is powerfully beautiful but equally neglected." If you're like me, your to-do list is long, and opportunities for rest are short. It's easy to make a to-do list and spend every day of the week marking off each item. It's more challenging to take time off, to sit, and to slow down. It takes intentionality. It seems rest is the last item on our to-do list when it should be one of our first. When we operate from a place of rest, we are fueled to receive and offer the blessings of God. If we haven't heard His whispers, we can't adequately offer His wisdom to those around us. We must adjust our priorities and walk our journey from an intentional posture of rest.

***What brings you rest? Do you prioritize a day of rest in your week? Do you consider it easy or difficult to view a day of rest as a gift from God? Why or why not?***

In my life, rest is a fight. There is an expectation to be the perfect mom, wife, friend, and daughter of God, which entails many to-dos. (There's my list again.) But if I truly desire to obey the Lord, I will stop fighting all these expectations for perfection and simply trust and rest in the Lord's perfect love. When I stop fighting, the Lord is exalted. For me, this is a type of spiritual rest I need to find daily.

A way for me to do this is to operate from a posture of rest. To better operate from this posture, I need to be more intentional about rest. Examples in my life to do this can range from a walk or lunch with an encouraging friend, stillness on the couch with my husband, reading with my children, or waking early to meet the Lord in His Word. All the people and many of the activities in my life provide a beautiful noise around me. Sometimes, if I want to truly obey, I must give up a portion of that good noise to find the greater goodness of stillness, of quiet, of the gift of rest.

***What prevents you from honoring your day of rest? What is one way you can find rest this week—spiritually, physically, and emotionally?***

This week's challenge may be difficult for you, but it's incredibly important. Rest for at least one hour.

Don't let the gift from God be overlooked! Don't neglect the holy!

# 3

# WALKING WITHIN EDEN

Formless and Void
Brings about
Beauty and Solidarity!

As evidence of God's love toward His creation, He brought about a garden filled with treasures beyond our imagination: trees laden with fruit ripe for eating, rivers flowing throughout, delighting the eyes of mankind, and small rivers overflowing with gold, resin, and onyx.

Need was unknown because everything that was needed or wanted was granted within the boundaries of this garden. The garden was the backdrop of the union between God and mankind. This was a perfect union, a perfect paradise.

## OUR RELATIONSHIP WITH EDEN

Capturing a likeness of the garden of Eden is impossible for us because hatred and sin fills our world.. Every day is a battle wrestling with our sinful heart. We navigate through sickness and death, which was never intended for us. We struggle having our relationship with God at the forefront of our lives as we question our motives and priorities. We grapple with our marriages and our children. We watch families destroyed by selfishness and pain.

This is not God's original design. He designed us for Eden. He designed us to walk within paradise. He designed us to eat of the fruit from the trees, to float in the rivers of beauty, and to walk beside Him every moment of every day. Work within the garden was not tedious or taxing. It was pleasant. As man worked, he received the joy of reaping from his work. He did not toil or sweat. This was perfect living at its best, the perfect balance between God and mankind.

So what happened?

When God placed man into the garden, He said, "Eat this ... Don't eat that!" Simple and concise! But as we know, the "don't eat that" was the catalyst to our destruction.

## ALONG CAME WOMAN

Once the scene was set, God surprised man! Ta-da ... Woman!

"It is not good for the man to be alone. I will make a helper suitable for him" (Genesis 2:18 NIV). God took the man that had been created, and from his rib, He created the most beautiful creature of all... the beautiful, curvaceous WOMAN... full of life and glory!

When Adam looked at the woman, the garden paled in comparison to the beauty of what stood before him. At that moment, man chose to give his life for her, and he did! He gave everything he had to please this beautiful creature, even His relationship with God.

## THE BEGINNING OF THE END

As most of you know, this story did not end well! It didn't end well for man and woman, now named Adam and Eve, and it didn't end well for you and me. This was the beginning of the end, and soon Adam and Eve would lose their position in this beautiful garden and get kicked out to face a world of uncertainty.

We look at the fall of man through the lens of failure and

disobedience. We have temptation, deception, lies, disobedience, and punishment. But what we miss is grace!

Not only was this the beginning of sin, but it was also the beginning of grace. Up to this point, grace was not needed because perfection was present. But when perfection disappeared, grace appeared. Within the bite of the fruit, grace began to weave a thread into our lives.

## SIN CYCLE

Sin is a cycle. Sin never just happens. It's like when we ask our kids why they did what they did and a typical response is, "It just happened." We know that isn't true! A chain of events leads up to our moment of sin. As I see it, it happens in three strokes:

- Temptation is revealed.
- Tempter is released.
- Temptation is rewarded.

## TEMPTATION REVEALED

Temptation creeps up on us like a mistress to her lover. It is presented as a beautiful, mystical illusion. In this story, the allusion to beauty is a tree. This is not just any tree. It was a tree in the middle of the garden, a tree beautifully composed surrounded by other trees and plants that paled in comparison to the tree in the middle. Temptation is never hidden or ugly. There is something beautiful and alluring to be captured. Otherwise, we would not be tempted. God had given Adam the instruction to not eat from this tree even before Eve had been created. So I personally would rather blame Adam for my sin than Eve. He should have taken better care of the woman he loved and kept her from that tree.

## TEMPTER RELEASED

As temptation looms before us, often an outside source convinces us that this is good for us. My temptation to gossip often gets released by an enticing conversation that I am having with a coworker or neighbor. I might be tempted to share this nugget of questionable truth, but until I have someone (a tempter) to share it with, it is just a nugget of information tucked away in my brain. So in this story of Adam and Eve, the tempter is released in the form of a serpent. We often think of it as a snake crawling on his belly, but the serpent didn't crawl and slither on its belly quite yet. I envision the serpent approached Eve in a much more enticing way, maybe a puppy! There is no way I would listen to a snake, but I might listen to a puppy!

## TEMPTATION REWARDED

"Don't do it!"

"Don't do it!"

Like a slow-motion movie, the serpent creeps slowly and methodically. He is slick and handsome, using whatever tactics it can use to convince the tempted to bite!

> When the woman saw that the fruit of the tree was good for food and pleasing to the eye and also desirable for gaining wisdom, she took some and ate it. She also gave some to her husband, who was with her, and he ate it (Genesis 3:6).

The line has now been crossed. When temptation is rewarded, it is no longer temptation. It is sin … dark, ugly, unrelenting in! There is no turning back; what's done is done!

In this story of Adam and Eve, once they had given way to temptation and entered the unknown realm of sin, there was an immediate response. Their unclothed bodies were revealed, causing instantaneous concern. Personally, I'm okay with this reaction because you do not want to see this body walking around unclothed! Once their nakedness was revealed, they ran deep into the garden, hoping God wouldn't find them. Slowly read the verse below and try to imagine what this looked like!

> Then the man and his wife heard the sound of the LORD God as he was walking in the garden in the cool of the day, and they hid from the LORD God among the trees of the garden. (Genesis 3:8)

God was out for a walk in His garden. It was a beautiful day, as was every day, so it was a perfect time for a stroll. I can imagine that God went for a walk in the cool of every day, but this day was different. There was a heaviness in the air. Today did not seem as perfect as yesterday. Within God's home was peace and serenity. Today, that was disrupted. God's forever home with his forever family was now set off course.

God called out, "Where are you?"

Don't think for a moment that God was unaware where Adam and Eve were hidden. It's like a parent who asks their child what they have done when they know full well what the child has done. As parents, we want the guilty to step forward with the story already known.

"Where are you?" God asked.

Adam answered, "I heard you in the garden, and I was afraid."

"Afraid of what?"

"Afraid that you would see I was naked."

"Oh, child, what have you done? Did you take a bite of the forbidden fruit?"

"Yes, Lord, but it wasn't my fault. It is your fault for putting this beautiful woman here on this earth to entice me to eat the fruit. I would have been fine without her."

God was saddened because the sin of Adam and Eve not only disrupted their lives, but it disrupted His. No more walks in the garden enjoying the cool of the day. No more conversations sitting around the tree with His creation. No more peace and serenity. Adam and Eve had opened the box to destruction, and God was saddened.

We often think that our sin only saddens and disrupts our life. But think bigger than that, my friend! Our sin saddens and disrupts God. He longs for community with us. He created us to fellowship with Him. He created us to walk along the path of the garden with Him, to pick the fruit of the trees with Him, and to float on the rivers with Him. He is not sad because of our sin. He is sad because our fellowship with Him is broken. The reason God knows that our fellowship is broken is because every time we sin, we hide!

We hide by making excuses and justifying our sin. We hide by pushing the blame onto someone else. We hide by ignoring the truth.

## ROLL CALL

Because sin begs for consequence, God called the roll and asked each of the guilty to step forward for sentencing. Scripture starts with the serpent, but for the sake of the story, we will start with woman.

## EVE, STEP FORWARD, PLEASE!

Eve stands, trying to hide her body from God. Her head hangs in shame as she protects herself with a bush. The perfection of fellowship was now gone. Within this loss came consequences.

### Consequence #1

> I will make your pains in childbearing very severe;
> with painful labor you will give birth to children.

**Consequence #2**

> Your desire will be for your husband, and he will rule over you. (Genesis 3:16 NIV).

Well, girls, as we know, this is no joke! If you have birthed children, you know that it is one heck of a pain! And this ruling issue with the husband is never-ending! I battle almost daily with this concept that my husband is to rule over me. Pain with childbirth and husband ruling both equal pain! And other than taking medication for both reasons to ease the pain, I see no way out of this!

## ADAM, YOUR TURN, SIR!

Hi ho hi ho, it's off to work you go.

Your brow will sweat, or your stomach will be empty.

> Cursed is the ground because of you; through painful toil you will eat food from it all the days of your life. It will produce thorns and thistles for you, and you will eat the plants of the field.
>
> By the sweat of your brow you will eat your food until you return to the ground, since from it you were taken; for dust you are and to dust you will return. (Genesis 3:19 NIV)

This was Adam's curse. Day in and day out, he worked the fields, pulling the thorns and thistle.

## SERPENT, YOU HAVE NOT BEEN FORGOTTEN.

It is now the serpents turn to receive consequences.

> Cursed are you above all livestock and all wild animals! You will crawl on your belly, and you will eat dust all the days of your life. And I will put enmity between you and the woman, and between your offspring and hers. He will crush your head, and you will strike his heel. (Genesis 3:14–15)

Understanding the scripture…

Breaking this scripture into smaller pieces will give us a greater understanding of how we are offered a way back to Eden, a reclaimed paradise. When the gates of Eden were closed, it felt as though all was lost, but with God, there is always redemption. God stated His redemption story in the next few verses. Listen closely!

**Part One**

> Cursed are you above all livestock and all wild animals! You will crawl on your belly, and you will eat dust all the days of life. (Genesis 3:14 NIV).

As God looks upon the serpent, His first curse was to reduce Satan to one that crawls on his belly and eats dirt. This one is simple, double amputation or maybe quadruple! The serpent is cursed, his legs are severed, and his meals will now consist of dust. Pretty straightforward!

**Part Two**

> And I (God) will put enmity between you (Satan) and the woman, and between your offspring and hers. (Genesis 3:15 NIV).

This one is a little harder to break down. Let's first look at the players in this verse.

- God … here (of course!)
- Satan … check
- Woman … check
  And
- Offspring … double check!

All the players needed to play this out are written within this story. But some characters may leave us a bit baffled. We know who God is, and we certainly know who Satan is. But who is the woman, and who are the offspring?

- Who is the woman? The woman is Eve. Why do we think that? Well, she is the only woman alive at this point, and she played a very critical role in this saga.
- Who are the offspring?
  - Who are the offspring of Eve? This is a fairly easy conclusion. Just a few verses later in Genesis 3:20, Adam states that Eve is the mother of all the living. Her womb started all of mankind; therefore, she is the mother of all mankind including Jesus Jesus was her offspring.

Who are the offspring of Satan? That one is a little more difficult to answer. This could be the fallen angels or demons who follow him. It probably does not refer to actual biological offspring, even though we have all met people we would like to refer to as the "spawn of Satan." More than likely, it refers to those who choose to follow the ways of Satan. Quick pause: this does not have to be those who are Satan worshippers but simply people who choose not to follow the ways of God. When Jesus looked at the religious leaders in John 8:44, he said, "You belong to your father, the devil, and you want to carry out your father's desires. He was a murderer from the beginning, not holding to the truth, for there is no truth in him. When he lies, he speaks his native language, for he is a liar and the father of lies." I think that Jesus would have categorized these gentlemen as Satan's offspring.Placing God, Satan, Woman and Offspring in the ring, let the battle begin! Day in and day out, Satan will fight up against mankind. War will ensue for every walk of life, every race, every nation. There will never be a pause or break in this war. There will never be a cease-fire … until one day!

Let's continue reading.

**Part Three**

> he will **crush** your head, and you will **strike** his heel (Genesis 3:15 NIV).

This is the end written within the beginning; it is the final chapter written within the first; it is Revelation written within Genesis.

This statement is the foundation on which our hope for salvation lies referred to as *Protoevangelium*, the "first gospel." It is the Bible's first prediction of a Savior.

Truth, once bruised, will rise again!

**The Crush**

It's in the crushing.

"**he** will crush your head …" (Genesis 3:15 NIV).

Who is **he**?

This is explained in the earlier verse when it speaks of the offspring of the woman. If Eve is the mother of all humanity, then she also birthed the lineage of Jesus, Jesus being the ultimate member of her offspring. "Adam named his wife Eve because she would become the mother of all the living" (Genesis 3:20 NIV). Who is **your**?Whose head will Christ crush?

Continuing in this linear thinking, the offspring of Eve, Christ, will crush the head of Satan. Christ will crush Satan's head!

**The Strike**

Satan can only strike the heel of Jesus.

"and you will strike his heel" (Genesis 3:15 NIV).

As Jesus hangs on the cross, He is bruised. His body is torn and bruised in attempts to slay Him and bring Him down from Messiah, the Savior of our world.

Satan has attempted to put Jesus in a position of surrender making a way for Satan to destroy the story of Jesus.But don't be fooled. Satan's hands were tied, or, shall I say, his legs were short!

As Satan attempted to destroy Jesus, the only thing he could do was bruise or strike at His heel. Because Satan was a rather short fellow with no legs, the only part of Jesus he could reach was His heel. As he struck, he bruised. But the bruising was temporary!

In the beauty of this scripture, God is saying there will come a day when Jesus rises in this battle. And when He does, He will crush the head of Satan! Can I get an amen?! And maybe a hallelujah?

Let's break this down to make this picture as clear as possible. It is an image you need to carry with you every day. It needs to be in your pocket, on your phone, or taped to your mirror. It will get you through your worse days and make the good days brighter. It will give you the hope for triumph!

Jesus stands, Satan slithers!

Because Jesus stands over Satan as He hangs on the cross, Jesus has access to Satan's head. He could reach

> his long, slithering body too, but Jesus doesn't mess around! Let's go for the head and finish this once and for all.
>
> Therefore, because of the sacrifice that Jesus made on the cross for us, He struck the head of Satan. And this strike is fatal! The crushing of this head finalizes the battle.
>
> Now because Satan is a slithering creature, the only thing he can eat is Jesus' dust! No matter how hard he tries, he will never reach higher than Jesus' heel. He can try to jump on the back of his tail, he can try to slither up the wood of the cross, and he can even try to grow legs, but at the end of the day, he is just a serpent, a snake, Satan. He will never strike a fatal blow therefore only producing a bruise, a flesh wound. Can I get another amen?

So here it is:

> Satan can never give us a blow that will be fatal!

I know that it feels like it will. But he can't! Flesh wounds can be doggone painful, but remember they heal!

From the mouth of the Black Knight in the 1975 film, *Monty Python and the Holy Grail*, "Tis but a scratch … It's only a flesh wound." These flesh wounds leave scars, sometimes big scars, scars seen by others and not easily hidden. But scars that heal!

## HEAD-TO-FOOT PERSPECTIVE

So we need a head-to-foot perspective. In order to get that perspective, we must pause, stopping long enough to put things into perspective, a head-to-foot perspective. When that bite comes, and it will, just look to the head of Satan and remember that it is crushed. Lay it at the feet of Jesus and remember that even though Satan bit him, Jesus gave the final blow!

Remind yourself who wins this battle! So if I could do the honors and speak my truth to Satan, this is what I would like to say, "Nip, nip away!"

I don't know about you, but my heel is ugly. It is calloused and cracked, especially when I go too long without a pedicure. "Satan, if you want to take a strike at my calloused, cracked, and stinky heel, go for it! Because in the end, Jesus wins!"

Looking at the totality of this scripture, seeing things from beginning to end or, shall I say, "end to beginning," God gave us the exact, beautiful picture we needed from the very beginning. He gave us the end of the story, the end of our story!

Hang on, brothers and sisters, as we make our way back to Eden!
Jesus will reign from now and forever!
It was at this moment in scripture when grace began.
During the darkest moment for mankind,
God wove the thread of grace!

## TALKS WITH EMILEIGH

My daughter, Ellie, and I share a love for reading. It amazes me that she will read the same book repeatedly. Each time she reads it, she seems to have different questions that arise or a new favorite part. She reads with anticipation for the words, as if they might change from the previous three readings.

As I read the verses for this lesson, I realized this is how we should read the Bible each time we pick it up! We should read the Bible with anticipation because though the words are the same, we may learn something new. These verses in Genesis were full of insight I hadn't before considered as well as challenging moving forward. If this were the first time reading these verses or reading them from a new light, how did the words speak to you? What did Melody say that really spoke to your heart?

Have you ever thought about what Eden must have looked like? Our books and many children's Bibles give us a glimpse of what we assume it must have been, of what the Tree of Life and Tree of Knowledge of Good and Evil must have looked like perched in the middle of the garden. Was it surrounded by a deterrent moat to accentuate God's command, or was it budding with beautiful, aromatic flowers, enticing Adam and Eve to be near it? What about that cursed apple, pear, or plum, or was it some perfect fruit we've never imagined or tasted before? After all, God's Word says the trees "were pleasing in appearance and good for food" (Genesis 2:9). All His creation was good and likely very beautiful. I often imagine the garden of Eden as this blissful garden filled with exquisite colors and completely peaceful. The more I study these lessons with Melody, I realize how noisy it must have been with all those animals in a confined space and yet perfect. It's like a dream to imagine going for walks with God throughout this garden of perfection each day! But then again, aren't we going for a walk with God every time we open His Word and enter His presence?

Eden was a world of perfection before the fall. The animals and Adam and Eve all lived in harmony with one another. There wasn't chaos and heartache as we experience it these days. Can you imagine such a perfect world? What would it be like to live in a world free of sin?

God set up the story right from the start. He created this world for us, set Adam in charge of it, told him exactly what not to do, and even gave him a helper. God was very clear with His plan and command, "do not eat from the tree of knowledge of good and evil" (Genesis 2:17). He gave Adam all he needed and the freedom. He had made provisions, but He also had one important restriction.

Personally, I'm not a diet person, but I have been pregnant. With both dieting and pregnancy, there are restrictions. With each, there are limits to your freedoms, both for the good of your health and a goal of the best possible outcome. For me, I can avoid too much caffeine and alcohol when pregnant, but with our first child, I craved Jimmy John's sandwiches desperately. My husband tends to be stricter and more worrisome when I'm pregnant and really did not want me eating deli meat. (With that said, we are due to have our third child in a couple short months, and I admit I've eaten my share of safe deli meat! Shhh, don't tell my husband.) This deli meat restriction without a doubt is set for the best possible health of both my unborn child and me, advised to keep me safe. Wouldn't you know that having that restriction made me want a Jimmy John's sandwich even more! I tried to buy the bread and satisfy the craving. I tried the veggie club they serve. It just wasn't the same. I wanted what I was told I couldn't have. It makes me wonder: did Eve sample the other fruits in the garden, already tempted by what she couldn't have, in hopes that it would satisfy her desire? Was Satan preying on a temptation he already had been observing in her?

***When have you been distracted by something you were told not to do or eat? Have you ever dieted and felt more restricted? Did the restriction make it more tempting for you or easier with a set boundary in place?***

With my insatiable craving for Jimmy John's, I needed someone to encourage me. My husband had to be that person. He knew my restriction and helped me follow it. You better believe as soon as our daughter was born, I sent him out to buy me a Jimmy John's sandwich! With something as seemingly silly as a Jimmy John's sandwich craving and something larger like setting safe boundaries for our children, my husband is my partner in life. God did not intend for us to walk this life alone. He had great compassion for our need for companionship. For this, I am greatly thankful.

As I've walked through various seasons of grief, joy, struggle, and triumph, God has placed friends and family in my life to meet this need for companionship as well. My husband and these individuals intentionally placed by the Lord are the support I need to resist Jimmy John's and be faithful in my relationships. I keep these individuals close so my walk remains straight and steadfast.

***Who do you walk through life with? Do you have a best friend or a group you lean into? In what ways have these companions helped you on your walk? Can you think of a time one of them helped you overcome temptation?***

I enjoy reading books even if I can already predict the ending. For me, the real story is in the details, which bring beauty to the ending in such a profound way. Discussing those details or dissecting them helps to unpack the story in a tangible way. If my daughter, Ellie, is discussing a book with me that I haven't read, I feel lost and certainly unable to contribute much to the conversation. I wonder if that's how I'd feel if I missed the details our great Author has written for us, right from the beginning. Melody states, "During the darkest moment for mankind, God wove the thread of grace!" We serve a God who wove a thread of grace from the very beginning. The great story began long ago, and Satan has been trying since the garden of Eden to distort and confuse us with the details.

If I don't take the time to read the details and look for God's theme of grace written everywhere throughout my life, I'm vulnerable to the distortion when Satan rears his devious head. His tactics begin for me from the moment I wake up. Most days, waking up is a challenge for a night owl like me. It is a choice for me to choose kindness and joy when my family and the world expects me to hit the ground running. Satan wants me to be lazy and sleep in, so I miss reading God's details in His Word. Satan wants me to be impatient in my exhaustion. Satan wants me to wake up feeling inadequate for all I need to tackle in my day. Satan is daily, hourly, or sometimes by the minute tempting me to choose the easier path, to gloss over the threads of grace, to sin. When I begin my day in His Word and in connection with the Father, I feel better equipped to tackle those temptations. I need to be equipped to face those temptations and resist the sin.

***What is the difference between temptation and sin?***

Satan isn't the only one who tempts me to sin though. People around me also partake in that temptation. Even in those moments, I must choose the path of grace. I must pause in my weak moments and consider God's commands to love selflessly and to serve willingly.

*When has someone in your life been your tempter? What boundaries can you set in place to avoid moving from temptation to sin? Do you already have specific boundaries in place for this purpose?*

There have been more times than I care to admit when I have fallen prey to exhaustion or impatience. When this happens, I veer away from the storyline God has lined out for me. However, in His grace, I've woke again each morning since with an opportunity to try again. Part of my rewrite sometimes must include an apology for my harsh words. Sometimes it simply means allowing myself the grace to forgive my own imperfections. But always it should include meeting with the Author and asking for strength to move forward.

***Give an example of a time you rewarded the temptation and fell into sin. What was the resulting discipline? Or was there a discipline?***

For Eve's infamous sin, we read of her consequence in Genesis 3 (as well as Adam and the serpent). Upon first reading these verses years ago, I saw pain in it. I read and thought I understood the gravity of Eve's consequence, both for herself and her husband, who also fell into temptation and sinned against God's one restriction. I read these verses as the fall and kept reading in anticipation of some hope. Reading these verses now with greater reflection on verse fifteen brings greater light and brilliant hope to God's grace. A closer look into verse fifteen reveals God's glorious ending right at the beginning! Take a closer look at the words *strike* and *crush*. To strike is to have sudden, damaging effects, but to crush is to violently subdue or pulverize and even to bring about an overwhelming disappointment(dictionary.com).

Have you thought about the gravity of those actions considering this context? Satan will most certainly work tirelessly day after day to distort God's Word, to spring temptation in your way in seemingly surprising ways, and to study your desires and capitalize in exactly the right moments with temptation that will lead you away from God's great story. And yet, no matter how often, how suddenly, or how hard he works to strike your heel, it will be only that. He will be striking your heel. It will not be detrimental. In contrast, our Messiah pulverized Satan with a devastating blow on our behalf! Jesus Christ crushes the head of Satan each time we choose His light, His wisdom, and His path.

***What battle are you facing against Satan right now?***

Our neighbors recently got a new puppy that loves nipping at our nine-year-old dog's legs. She is constantly antagonizing our Bailey, partly to play but mostly just to get her riled up. Bailey will tolerate her for a time, visibly annoyed, and then ultimately walks away. The puppy is resilient and will proceed with this for some time. Bailey will entertain the puppy but always walks away unharmed. Satan is like that puppy, only not as sweet and snuggly. Satan will antagonize us, get us riled up, and persistently nip at our heels. He is unrelenting in his pursuit. Christ-followers can be that older, larger, more powerful dog though. We can walk away unharmed, confident in the hope we have in Jesus, assured by His greater dominance over the frustrating nips. There are times we feel stuck. There are times when we face battles with Satan, we're not confident we will escape, and there are certainly times it is difficult to see our freedom and God's grace through the seeming hopelessness. At those times, we must keep our eyes focused. We must pause and look for God's thread of grace.

***Can you see God's grace in the battle you are facing?***

We can keep our eyes focused on the One who gave that final blow, our Savior. He rewrote our story by offering grace and hope in the end. Contrary to many books I read, He doesn't finish our story with "The End." Just as in John 19:30 as He sacrificed His perfect life on our behalf, He uttered the words, "It is finished." In the garden, the story wasn't over; it wasn't the end. At the cross, He offered a new beginning to those who chose to follow Him. In Revelation 21:6, He promised us that "It is done." He offers us the gift of grace when we set our eyes on Him and allow Him to write each chapter.

***How can knowing the end of the story give you hope as Satan strikes your heel?***

God's grace is our hope amid our sinful, noisy world. In our home, grace sometimes means dessert even when you haven't finished your vegetables. It's playing outside with friends even when your room is still a mess. It's a hug from the child I lost my temper with earlier in the day. It's the breath of fresh air I take the morning after a rough day. It's living each day forgiven for all my failings yet redeemed for all His grace.

***What does grace mean to you? Where do you need to see God's grace in your life?***

Share a time you've seen God's grace in the midst of a battle.

Recently I told my son, Lucas, that if he didn't obey and get his teeth brushed, he wouldn't get a book before bed. As with most five-year-olds, he procrastinated until the book option was in fact removed. Less than five minutes later though, I was reading him a book. My husband walked into the room and reminded Lucas of what I'd initially said. Lucas responded simply, "Mommy's giving me grace, Daddy. Grace comes from God, and Mommy gives it too."

My son needed grace. He needed the assurance. He's learning what grace looks like by the grace I extend to him. I don't always give it, but I certainly don't deserve any of the grace God gives me. We all need to be reminded of God's grace in these tangible ways.

***Who do you know that needs to be reminded of His grace and the ending of the story?***

As you reflect on the story of your own life thus far and the chapter you're currently walking through, is there an area you need to surrender to the Author? Take the time now to re-read the details, to look for His threads of grace, and to view His Word from a new light. Cry out to the Author and thank Him for the grace He promises amid the battles you will face and the hope He wove into the details of your story so far.

# 4

## WALKING OUTSIDE EDEN

Adam …
    Eve …
        Chosen for communion with the Maker …

As the first man and first woman understood what they had done, they stood shaking in their fear and shame. They could never undo what they had done. The joy and peace they once knew was now replaced with confusion and chaos.

Still standing within the walls of the garden, they wrestled with their new life. These new emotions, unfamiliar ones, caused a chaotic fear crippling them in their movement, making it impossible to navigate in this new world, this new world tainted by sin.

Fear …
    Shame …
        Sin …

Words unfamiliar to the first couple, yet words we wear daily with extreme familiarity.

Peace …
    Quiet …
        Serenity …

Words familiar to the first couple, yet words we grapple to know their very existence.

As they sat by the tree in the middle, it took one bite, just one bite, and their world changed forever. Our world changed forever. As the flavor of the fruit was still ruminating within their mouths, their vision changed. When Eve looked at Adam and Adam looked at Eve, they began to see things they had never seen before. What was once delight in the perfection of their bodies became shame exposed. In the blink of an eye, in the bite of a fruit, all was lost.

They knew they had disobeyed God, but they didn't know at what cost. Sin had never been a part of their existence; therefore, the consequences of sin were also unfamiliar. God says,

> The man has now become like one of us, knowing good and evil. He must not be allowed to reach out his hand and take also from the tree of life and eat and live forever. (Genesis 3:22 NIV)

God's design for mankind was to never know evil. His design was for us to live forever within the garden. And that was gone.

> So, the Lord God banished him (them) from the Garden of Eden to work the ground from which he had been taken. After he drove the man out, he placed on the east side of the Garden of Eden cherubim and a flaming sword flashing back and forth … (Genesis 3:24 NIV)

Banished...

> The perfect union with God was now destroyed.
> Would they ever make their way back to Eden?
> Could paradise ever be reclaimed?

This act of disobedience set mankind on a trajectory of failure and sin. This path of destruction wove heartache and despair. Because of this destruction, paradise would become a thing of the past. As the gates were locked and the entrance guarded, they could only hope to glance beyond the gate in remembrance of this perfect union with God.

What had they done?

What had they done?

So often in our lives, we have felt the same! Just one bad decision and we set ourselves on the path of wondering, "What have I done? What have I done?" Misplaced and scattered, we wander aimlessly to find hope and healing.

From this point on, God set in motion the journey for all mankind to make their way back to Eden, the place of perfect union with Him.

Remember, it was never God's desire for us find our way back to Eden. His desire was for us to never leave Eden. His desire was for this perfect union and eternity to take place within Eden. But now that mankind was standing outside of Eden, God's plan of grace was set in motion.

Hearing the lock on the gate, Adam and Eve stood vulnerable to sin. Their bodies may have been covered with clothes, but their hearts were wide open to destruction, wide open to the unfamiliar wreckage of choices.

## STANDING OUTSIDE THE GATE

As they stood outside the gate, their minds began to wander, "What next?" Adam then looked at Eve in her little fig leaves covering the critical areas. Funny pause. Who decided what the critical areas are? Why not my arm, my foot, or my elbow?

Adam made a move. "How about some sex tonight, beautiful woman?"

I mean, think about it! They are standing outside Paradise, feeling lost and confused. Remembering Paradise, one of their favorite memories was sex. Would this wonderful, fulfilling, God-created activity work outside the garden? Well, why not try? It's always fun to try!

> Adam made love to his wife Eve, and she became pregnant and gave birth to Cain. She said, "With the help of the Lord I have brought forth a man." (Genesis 4:1 NIV)

Humor me here for a moment. First, Eve gets pregnant. She had never seen a pregnant woman because, well, she was the only woman. Over a period of months, she noticed her stomach getting bigger. Try to explain that one to her! After about nine months, she has these incredible, mind-blowing pains. No book tells her what to expect when she is expecting. She assumes this has something to do with this "pain in childbirth" thing. When God had told her that would happen, she probably smiled and nodded, having no idea what childbirth even was. Well, folks, she is about to find out.

Second, she said she had birthed a "man." How in the heck do you even birth a man? I had three of them, and I thank God they were of sizable proportion to get them out of my body. Maybe she looked at the baby's male parts and compared them to her husband's male parts, concluding they were of the same kind. Either that or Cain came out a full-grown man. God forbid! "Hey, honey, look. One of you just came out of me. Unbelievable!"

Over time, she birthed two more of these men, making a total of three. At least that is what is documented.

## JEALOUSY ON THE HOMESTEAD

After these brothers became men, jealousy struck. I know that jealousy between the menfolk can get rather dicey. Words don't fly as much as fists.

This jealousy stemmed from a customary sacrifice to honor God.

But in this story, one sacrifice was pleasing; the other was not. Cain was the target of this displeasure. Why? God only knows … No, really! God only knows! But we can assume!

> Now Abel kept flocks, and Cain worked the soil. In the course of time Cain brought some of the fruits of the soil as an offering to the Lord. And Abel also brought an offering—faith portions from some of the firstborn of his flock. The Lord looked with favor on Abel and his offering, but on Cain and his offering he did not look with favor. So Cain was very angry, and his face was downcast. (Genesis 4:2–5 NIV)

## REASONS FOR GOD'S REJECTION

### Good, Not Great

"Good job, son." This is a phrase I would often say to my children. I wanted them to know that I approved of what they had done. But oftentimes I knew that instead of good, they could have done great.

I am confident that God responds to us in the same way. He watches our obedience and knows we can take it from good to great if we just look to Him for guidance. And God desires great!

There was something missing in Cain's sacrifice. Maybe Cain missed the great.

### Handfelt, Not Heartfelt

Because Cain worked the field, his sacrifice came from the use of his hands. His hands provided food for the table and an offering for God.

In the mundane daily work, his hands worked the soil, producing his sacrifice. But his heart never produced a desire to give God everything. It was a completion of a task, not a worship from the heart. God wanted worship with heartfelt intentionality.

When we stand in worship to God, are we giving all that we have? Or is it customary worship or expected praise? God desires uncustomary … unexpected!

**Obedience, Not Trust**

God said, "Cain, I have laid out a simple formula for you. Do what is right! Obey! But you have to trust Me in your obedience!"

Can we obey without trust? This is a resounding yes. There have been times in all of our lives that we have obeyed out of fear and not trust.

Let me ask you a question, "Do you trust God?" The majority would say a resounding yes.

Now, let me ask you a second question, "Do you obey God?"

Well, I try! We would like to say, "Yes, absolutely!" but truthfully, our obedience wanes. Maybe our obedience wanes because our trust wanes.

If I trust God fully, obedience becomes the natural outflow of that trust. It no longer feels like obedience. It just feels right!

> Maybe for Cain, it was about trust and not about obedience. And that is why God didn't accept his sacrifice.

## ANGER KILLS

Anger is one of those life questions that confuse believers and unbelievers alike. The Bible hits the issue of anger directly, telling us to avoid it and rid ourselves of it. "But now you must also rid yourselves of all such things as these: anger, rage … " (Colossians 3:8 NIV).

Yet we encounter situations such as Jesus' reaction to the temple sales. We read about the anger of God yet are told to not let the sun go down on our anger. So which is it, anger or no anger?

I have learned in my life that anger can become a warning sign for me. If I dismiss my anger, I may also dismiss protection for my heart. Anger can become the spokesperson telling me that something is wrong. Yet if I fully embrace my anger and allow it to rule within me, it will destroy relationships. If we mishandle the anger in our lives, it will kill.

> If you do what is right, will you not be accepted? But if you do not do what is right, sin is crouching at your door; it desires to have you, but you must rule over it. (Genesis 4:7 NIV)

It desires to have you, but you must rule over it. With every temptation, there is a way of escape. God was aware of the danger of sin. He knew that if Cain did not rule over it, it would destroy relationships and, in this case, kill. To escape the collateral damage of anger, our hope lies within our relationship with God. It is our choice what will rule us.

But the anger Cain had toward his brother was all-consuming because he allowed it to be. It was as though something ignited within him and there was no way he could stop the burn. His answer lay solely in his relationship with God. But we have already learned that there was something displeasing in the relationship because he withheld a desirable sacrifice.

I think the lesson for us here is complex. It begins and ends with our relationship with God. Clearly, what we give to God needs to be pleasing to Him. We cannot halfheartedly offer ourselves and expect Him to bless or accept it. When our connection with God is loose, then He is not able to pour into us the fullness of His grace and wisdom. There will be leaks that will cause us to stray. But when we are fully tuned in to God, we can fight the destruction of anger that comes our way. It doesn't eliminate anger because anger is a God-given emotion, but we are able to recognize it and use that anger for protection and safety, therefore not allowing anger to kill.

## DEATH DOES NOT KILL

Heeding the warning of God and dealing with the anger where it truly lay would have produced a different outcome. But because Cain knew that anger toward God would not give him the satisfaction he craved, he directed his anger toward his brother, which resulted in a needless death. "Now Cain said to his brother Abel, 'Let's go out to the field.' While they were in the field, Cain attacked his brother Abel and killed him" (Genesis 4:8 NIV).

Abel was dead. His life here on earth was over. No more precious offerings to God. No more opportunities to be pure in his obedience. Just a life snuffed out in its youth.

Death gives us permanency of loss. When a loved one no longer walks into the room or calls us on the phone, there is a loss within that cuts to the core of our being. When the young die, we question even more as to why. They will never be able to make the impact on our world that they were designed to make. Or maybe they can?

In the brevity of Abel's life, he made such an impact on his world that he was able to stand in the Hall of Faith in the book of Hebrews.

> By faith Abel brought God a better offering than Cain did. By faith he was commended as righteous when God spoke well of his offerings. And by faith ABEL STILL SPEAKS, even though he is dead. (Hebrews 11:4 NIV)

Abel is still speaking.

When we lose loved ones, the life they lived on this earth is a life still lived within us. If they could speak, what would they say? What legacy is left in our hearts?

## LEGACIES LEFT; LEGACIES LOST

Abel is dead; Cain is alive! Despite the tragedy of losing his brother, Cain continued in his disobedience and denial. After Cain killed Abel, there was a moment when he could have regretted what he had done. This was his only brother, and now he was dead by his own hands. But there was no remorse, no regret. "Then the Lord said to Cain, 'Where is your brother Abel? 'I don't know,' he replied. 'Am I my brother's keeper?'" (Genesis 4:9 NIV).

Really, Cain! Your hole gets deeper and deeper! He wasn't going to take any responsibility for his own sin. He didn't want to confess it, and he didn't want to own it. Sound familiar? It sounds a bit like his parents. The apple doesn't fall far.

- God warns Cain of the sin crouching at his door. He ignores the warning and kills his brother in cold blood.
- God approaches Cain about the killing of Abel. Cain denies it and smarts off to God about some "brother's keeper" thing.

Then God says, "I know what happened. You can stop pretending. Just like your parents, you cannot hide from me. They may not have told you, but they tried to hide from me in the garden after they sinned. But I knew exactly where they were. I see, and I know all things. One of these days, I hope you will be able to learn that. So here is what we are going to do."

> Now you are under a curse and driven from the ground, which opened its mouth to receive your brother's blood from your hand. When you work the ground, it will no longer yield its crops for you. You will be a restless wanderer on the earth. (Genesis 4:11 NIV)

"A restless wanderer" … I've done that once or twice in my life, and it is not fun!

Looking to the New Testament for answers, we see the contrast of legacies.

- "By faith Abel brought God a better offering than Cain did. By faith he was commended as righteous when God spoke well of his offerings. And by faith Abel still speaks, even though he is dead." (Hebrews 11:4).
- "Do not be like Cain, who belonged to the evil one and murdered his brother. And why did he murder him? Because his own actions were evil, and his brothers were righteous" (1 John 3:12 NIV).

Two scriptures taken from the New Testament describe two brothers. These are legacies left and legacies lost.

Legacy left … Abel's faith. Legacy lost … Cain's evil. What will your legacy be? Make that choice today! Time is running out!

## EVIL WINS

Every time I watch a suspenseful movie, the big surprise at the end is not a big surprise. The bad guy or gal will be captured or killed. Everyone knows that. The suspense in the middle determines how good the movie is. But in the story of Cain and Abel, it seems as though evil wins. Simply cursing Cain to be a restless wanderer seems to pale in comparison to what Cain had done to Abel.

> Cain said to the Lord, "My punishment is more than I can bear. Today you are driving me from the land, and I will be hidden from your presence; I will be a restless wanderer on the earth, (then Cain adds a little extra to his punishment) and whoever finds me will kill me." (Genesis 4:13–14 NIV)

"Oh, woe is me! I can't bear this punishment, so just let me die!"

On the surface, it seems as though Cain was sorrowful for his actions. But when you take it all within the context of the story and scripture, Cain was unrepentant. He was simply feeling sorry for himself and did not want to die the same death he had invoked on his own brother. "But the Lord said to him, 'NOT SO … " (Genesis 4:15 NIV).

Not only did God say "NOT SO," He went on to make sure it wouldn't be so. " … 'anyone who kills Cain will suffer vengeance seven times over.' Then the Lord put a mark on Cain so that no one who found him would kill him" (Genesis 4:15).

It seems as if God goes to drastic measures to save the life of Cain. Why? Why would God allow evil to live and good to die? This is a hard one to answer, a question we still ask today.

It is clear from the New Testament passage (1 John 3:12) that Cain was evil. God could have taken out this evil. He clearly has the power to do that. But God chose to keep Cain alive after murdering his brother. Why?

- Could it be that God needed Cain to remain on this earth to procreate the earth? Think about it. There were not a lot of people around in those days.

- Was this God's grace? Possibly. Many times in our lives, we do not get what we deserve.
- Was this God's way of punishing Cain? Possibly! Obviously, Cain would not live a great life post-murder.

At times, things happen in life that simply give us no answer. We search hard and fast to make some sense of a horrible situation, but sometimes we never get that answer. It just remains a perplexity in life. Maybe that is where we leave this one, a perplexity!

But as I looked a little deeper into the scriptures and continued reading this story, there is one verse at the end of this chapter that brings all of this together for us. Well, at least it did for me.

Before we land on that verse, let's look at what happened with Cain. "So Cain went out from the Lord's presence and lived in the land of Nod, east of EDEN. Cain made love to his wife and she became pregnant and gave birth to Enoch" (Genesis 4:16–17 NIV).

Life continued …

To Enoch was born Irad.

To Irad was born … and the list goes on.

Throughout this time, the world was developing in many ways. We have the first city built by Cain, the first ranchers living in tents raising livestock, the first musicians who developed music playing stringed instruments and pipes, and the first craftsman making tools from bronze and iron. This was the new earth, a developing world.

> Adam made love to his wife again, and she gave birth to a son and named him Seth, saying, "God has granted me another child in place of Abel, since Cain killed him." Seth also had a son, and he named him Enosh. **At that time people began to call on the name of the Lord.** (Genesis 4:25–27 NIV)

Life continued, children were born, and the earth was replenished. But read that last verse again**, "At that time people began to**

**call on the name of the Lord."** This is the bow on top of the package, the whipped cream on an iced latte, or the cherry on an ice cream sundae. It seems like needless extra to the ending of a story of destruction.

But within this one statement, we are given hope amongst an evil world. It answers the question why God left evil to restlessly wander.

## HOPE IN EVIL

After the destruction caused by Cain's rage, life continued. God chose not to destroy Cain but allowed him to live. Through his life, new lives were formed. Children and children of children replenished the earth. But there was more than procreating that was taking place. God was working in the lives of these people. He was teaching them about His love and His grace for them. As He taught, they listened. There must have been moments when they enjoyed fellowship with their Maker once again. Moments when they walked with Him along the road. Moments when they bowed down to His sovereignty.

Amongst His teaching, **they called on His name!**

In our lives when evil seems as though it is winning. We have a choice. Will we let evil win or will we "call on His name"?

Looking at this through the lens of God, we must go back to Eden, the place where God desired peace and fellowship with His creation, the place where Adam and Eve called on His name.

When sin destroyed this fellowship, it was a temporary destruction. At every twist and turn, God is using situations in life, even the evil circumstances, for His creation to learn to call on His name!

When I look at this story, my lack of understanding that God allowed Cain to live gives way to God's sovereignty. What if God allowed the evil to live in order for His creation to learn to call on His name?

There are stories in our lives filled with complexities that we long to find a deeper understanding of. In these complex life stories, the question of why attacks us every moment of every day. No matter how we shake it, it simply does not make sense. We have seen good people die young. We have experienced evil people that prosper. And none of it makes sense to us. But when God uses these horrible situations in life to teach us to call on His name, this is God's sovereignty at work. This is the way He is leading us back to Eden to fellowship with Him. God uses evil for good!

## EVIL IN MY LIFE

The dream of having my father love me unconditionally never escaped my desire. I longed to have a father who would keep me safe and protected from this evil world. But instead, my father was the evil from which I needed to be protected. He was the evil in my world.

My father was not a drunk, or "wayward." In fact, he was a pastor of growing, thriving churches, but he used the "goodness of God" as evil in my life. He positioned himself as a man of God when in reality he used his religious position to manipulate and groom me. My young life was tainted as I battled his sexual advances and abusive behaviors.

In my journey of healing, I questioned countless times why God did not remove him from this world. Why didn't He stop it? Why didn't He end this abuse? Why did God leave the evil? I don't think that question will ever be answered.

But I can answer this: because of this evil in my life, I called on His name! Calling on God was my choice, but it is a path worth choosing. Statistically following God in my life should not have been my path. But it is! I have determined that my trust is going to be in God and God only. Separating from the evil of my father has allowed me to find the goodness of God.

In the midst of my healing journey, one of my journal entries is titled "I Looked Evil in the Eye and Survived." It was a stark reality that evil had raised me. But it was an even greater truth that I had survived.

I will never be able to tell you that this was okay. The damage and destruction in my life is beyond explanation. But what I can tell you is that through the midst of evil, I called on His name! The name of God is the only constant I had in my life. God was my survival and my hope. He still is.

When we don't understand the why, we simply need
to look to the who and call on His name!
Whose name are you calling on today?

## TALKS WITH EMILEIGH

Grace, goodness, and God are the three Gs.

Over the weekend, Lucas, our five-year-old, needed some Grace, with a capital G. We had been out earlier in the day and had talked about getting a car wash, but it had been closed. Hours later, he was helping my husband wash his own truck. When my husband needed to go inside briefly, Lucas decided it was a great time to wash Mommy's car as well. His intentions were spot-on. He's such a sweet and thoughtful boy, right? Well, not only was my car in the garage during said car wash, but my window was also open, neither being a deterrent Lucas noticed nor was concerned about. As a result, the interior received a thorough washing. It truly is amazing what can happen in a few short, unsupervised minutes.

In this moment, we had two options: Lucas could be punished for his poor choice or receive some Grace. We chose Grace. We knew Lucas's intentions were good. We knew where his heart was when he did this. He didn't have mal intent. He truly wanted to do something kind for his mom. We easily could have missed this opportunity though! Sometimes we do miss the opportunity to extend Grace, and far too often, we miss when God extends us Grace.

God knew Cain and Abel's hearts just like He knows each of ours. He knows our motives. He knows what I refer to as our why—why we act the way we do, say the words we say, or why we set on the course chosen. Jealousy filled Cain's heart. God saw that. That jealousy led Cain to temptation and ultimately to a sin he could never take back.

***Has jealousy ever led you to sin? What happened, and what were the resulting consequences?***

The root of Cain's jealousy was a direct result of his own choices. Abel brought to the Lord the best of what he had to offer. He brought God his firstfruits, his best. Cain, on the other hand, brought God what he had available and maybe just what was convenient.

***Do you believe you're currently giving Him your best?***

Cain and Abel were taught to bring their firstfruits, their best, but it seems possible the emphasis on bringing their best to Him was missed. We don't know if this were the fault of their parents, Adam and Eve, or simply their difference in why, the reason for the offering.

Cain strikes me as the child who needed an extra push. He either missed his parents' directives to sacrifice his best to the Lord that Abel clearly picked up or simply had a half-hearted personality. God does not find favor in half-heartedness though. In fact, in Jeremiah 29:13, He calls us to seek Him wholeheartedly.

In the dictionary, *wholehearted* is defined by a complete sincerity, enthusiastic, and earnestness. We ought to pursue the Lord and His purpose sincerely and earnestly. Living this way every day, especially during challenging seasons, can be quite difficult. It is much easier on my tired days to check my time with God off my to-do list, to sign up for a ministry because it should be done, to tithe the bare minimum, or to squander my talent because I feel inadequate. This is not a wholehearted approach to my relationship with God and certainly not pleasing to Him.

***Do you ever struggle to give to God half-hearted or out of obligation instead of wholeheartedly?***

When I'm truly listening to God's voice and His direction, wholeheartedness seems more attainable. I admit that too often I silence Him with my busyness, my fears, my worries, and my need for control. When I do this, I silence His convictions as well, just like Cain. "If you refuse to do what is right, then watch out! Sin is crouching at the door, eager to control you. But you must subdue it and be its master" (Genesis 4:7).

Years ago, I was in a relationship with someone who it seemed everyone told me I shouldn't be in. I have always been determined and headstrong and, thus, didn't listen. I thought I could change him. I thought I could bring him to Jesus. Little did I realize that in fact, he was pulling me away from Jesus. I ignored my friends. I ignored the Lord's shouts. (Whispering wouldn't work for me then.) I chose my own path. One day, I hit a breaking point when I finally saw what everyone had been warning me of, what God had been trying to redirect me from. The issue became much less about who or what I was entangled with but about why I wasn't following God's will.

***When have you heard God or even a trusted friend warn you of your inclination toward sin? Sometimes this is referred to as a blind spot. Did you heed the warning?***

As a result of this relationship, I learned what God didn't want for me in my future spouse. I needed to take more seriously the boundaries and standards God wanted for me. I needed to refocus on my relationship with Jesus. Praise God, those boundaries and willingness to listen to God's guidance in dating have led to my husband. Now he is an additional voice of wisdom in my ear, encouraging healthy boundaries and a deeper walk with Jesus.

***What kind of boundaries can you put in place to help you refocus and heed warnings rather than fall into sin?***

Read Genesis 3:8 and Genesis 4:9. Do you notice the commonality? Adam and Eve hid physically, and Cain tried to hide verbally. With so few humans on the earth in both cases and surely knowing God on an intimate level, I would assume they realized God knows all. There's no hiding anything from Him! This commonality makes me wonder if it were a learned behavior or simply our sinful human nature.

As a parent, I recognize many habits and traits both my husband and I have inherited from our own parents, both good and bad. There are some habits we've determined don't work best for our family, some we hope to pass onto our own children and still other habits we don't realize we picked up until one spouse points them out to the other. In the account of Cain, hiding was not a good habit to repeat! Not only did Cain try to dance around the sin after being caught, but he then proceeded to place himself in a pit of despair, complaining and whining about how rough the consequence was. In my opinion, Cain killed his brother. Anything that included staying alive is pretty gracious. Cain missed it though. He was so caught up in his own agenda, his own misguided why, that he missed God's thread of grace. How often am I too caught up with my own plans and desires that I completely miss the opportunities and second chances God is handing me?! I don't want the good or bad habits I carried on from my own parents to deter me from the habits God wants me to live by. Though I recognize the need to surrender, it is often difficult to step out of my comfort and simply seek His forgiveness and embrace the grace.

Forgiveness is a good habit I was taught as a child. Perhaps this made it easier to recognize the grace Lucas needed when he drenched my car interior. I was offered forgiveness often as a child. I needed it often for honest mistakes but didn't deserve it. Because of Jesus, I never get the consequences I rightly deserve. What turned out to be two days without a vehicle for interior water damage repairs, our family experienced an expensive learning opportunity. The honest mistake led to healthy conversations and a little boy with good intentions who felt loved instead of condemned. Instead of a need to lie or dig a hole of despair, Lucas sought forgiveness and received it wholeheartedly. I can only pray this will further his foundation of honesty, forgiveness, and grace.

***What is your typical response when you sin? Do you hide it? Ignore it? Repent immediately? Or do you let it consume you?***

Grace, Goodness, and God are "words with a capital G" in my home. What about when this broken world hands us an unexpected loss, a devastating circumstance, or a true act of evil? When life deals these cards, does it negate God's goodness and Grace? How must Eve have felt when she discovered her eldest had murdered her son?! Did that act of evil push her from God, or did it draw her nearer?

Even after our vehicle was fixed, there are spontaneous moments when lingering damage causes the screen to black out or the radio to freeze. They are lingering effects to a temporary misguided act. They are lingering reminders. True evil is rarely a singular moment. It is rarely short term but has lingering, wounding effects on our lives. Our response to these moments can determine our course and whether we simmer in the temporary or rest in the eternal. Does God want evil to linger in our lives? Absolutely not. Does God allow evil to exist? Unfortunately, yes. Does God want us one choice and one day at a time, to choose goodness and to choose to call on His name? Every single time.

In my life, I have been handed some moments that have left me asking why—whether it be the tragic and unexpected loss of a far-too-young family friend, watching too many friends and family suffer through infertility, or even the seeming silence from God when I desperately want an answer. These moments can keep my mind trapped in a fury of "Why, God?!" When I simmer in the temporary evil of this world, it can be suffocating. When I choose to step back and call on His name (see Genesis 4:26), I can rest in the eternal. I must call on the One who has the power to take this evil and use it for His glory. I don't always see it, but that part also isn't for me to understand. I am certain Eve did not understand why she lost her son, but I would bet she called on God to help her forgive her surviving son. We must make the choice to focus on who our grace comes from, no matter how many why questions this broken world hands us.

***How does the grace Jesus offers propel you to extend grace more willingly to others?***

When I reflect on the grace Jesus offers me, it can be quite overwhelming. I never deserve it and often don't realize I'm even receiving it until I take the time to slow my soul and seek Him. The more my kids need grace, the more I realize how much I've already been given. Everyone around me needs grace at some point as well, and that's sometimes where we can get caught. Abel wasn't extended grace by his own brother, and yet Cain received it from God. The driver that cuts me off in traffic doesn't deserve grace from me, but that driver is just as loved by God. The disgruntled waitress that brings me the wrong order doesn't deserve grace and gratitude from me, but God may still call me to tip extra. I certainly don't deserve grace when I lose my patience and use unkind words to my kids or husband, but they love me anyway. I don't deserve grace when I'm too busy to meet with God in the quiet, but He's still waiting for me. I certainly don't deserve grace when I'm too weary to pray, but God still whispers His promises and love, simply waiting for me to quiet myself long enough to hear. He whispers hope and grace. I don't want to miss that grace, that freedom, or that fulfilling life.

Reflect on God's unmerited favor in your life. Take some time to thank Him for it, for Jesus' sacrifice and areas in your life where you can see His thread of grace. If you can't see the thread, ask Him to open your eyes and heart to start noticing the areas He's pouring out His abundant grace on you.

# 5

# WALKING INTO THE DARK

Abel is dead.
Cain is restlessly wandering.
And the earth continues to procreate.

Seth begat (procreated) Enosh … and so on and so forth until Noah came forth from his daddy, Lamech.

Generation after generation produced more and more chaos. Sin became the prevalent form of entertainment to the point that God simply became fed up. When God created, He created peace, beauty, and paradise, Eden! But He also created will within man. The will of man superseded and dominated the earth.

In God's frustration, he shortened the life span of man. Man will no longer live nine hundred years. Listen to what God said about His own creation, "My Spirit will not contend with humans forever, for they are mortal; their days will be a hundred and twenty years" (Genesis 6:3 NIV).

God says, "That's it! I have had it with you. I have given you opportunity after opportunity to pull your lives together. My heart has longed for you to walk back to Eden so we can have fellowship once more. But I will no longer put up with you living such long lives. You will live 120 years, and that's it."

From then on, the life span of man began to decrease.

As destruction continued, "The Lord saw how great the wickedness of the human race had become on the earth, and that every inclination of the thoughts of the human heart was ONLY EVIL ALL THE TIME" (Genesis 6:5 NIV).

We went from one act of evil of Cain to "the human heart was only evil all the time." This was bad. This was really bad!

Living in our current world of destruction, I am not sure that God would describe this world as only evil all the time. To imagine only evil all the time makes me cringe. There was no escape from the evil—no Bible study group to escape to, no weekend church service to find respite, and no prayer group to lean into. It was evil all the time, every moment of every day.

## GOD REGRETS

Have you ever thought that God would regret anything? He is perfect, and perfection has no regrets! But listen to this.

> So the Lord said, "I will wipe from the face of the earth the human race I have created—and with them the animals, the birds and the creatures that move along the ground—**for I regret that I have made them.** (Genesis 6:7 NIV)

That is a solemn thought to think that God regrets what He had created.

Do you remember God's statements that what He had created was good? The sky was good, the land was good, the waters were good, and humankind was very good. What happened to the very good in which God had created?

He created man in His image for fellowship. But that fellowship had been destroyed because mankind (Adam and Eve) allowed sin to rule over them.

## GOD REGRETS, AND GOD IS SAD

"The Lord regretted that he had made human beings on the earth, and his heart was deeply troubled" (Genesis 6:6 NIV).

Our sin troubles God. He longs for us to have a peaceful fellowship with Him, but when our sin breaks that fellowship, it saddens Him. I can feel God's sadness when He banished Adam and Eve from Eden. He was sad because He wanted to be perfectly connected with His creation, but sin, our drug of choice, separates us from Him. Repeatedly, God gives us His grace to bridge that gap of separation. But as we continue to choose sin over grace, the divide widens. So God is deeply troubled! Remember that the next time you choose sin over grace.

## GOD'S DESIRE TO DESTROY

> So, the Lord said, "I will wipe from the face of the earth the human race I have created—and with them the animals, the birds and the creatures that move along the ground—for I regret that I have made them. (Genesis 6:7 NIV)

This could have been the end of the earth. You wouldn't have been born; nor would your children have been born. In this moment, God said this was it, the end! His heart was so broken over the loss of fellowship with His creation that He was wanting to end it all.

**But …**

"Buts" can be good or bad. This "but" is good! "But Noah found favor in the eyes of the Lord" (Genesis 6:8 NIV). One simple statement and the world was saved … kind of!

God used one man to redeem this earth, one man to carry His longing to have fellowship with His creation, one man to carve out the path back to Eden.

There was something different about Noah. Of all mankind now living on earth, he was the only one who was righteous. "Noah was a righteous man, blameless among the people of his time, HE WALKED FAITHFULLY WITH GOD" (Genesis 6:9).

Amid only evil all the time, Noah walked faithfully with God. I can envision that every time Noah stepped out of his tent, he stepped into wickedness, a wickedness that my mind cannot even begin to imagine.

What made Noah choose faithfulness? If there was wickedness all around him, what made him look up instead of around? What did Noah do differently to find "favor in the eyes of the Lord?"

Do you remember Cain? " … but on Cain and his offering he did not look with favor" (Genesis 4:5 NIV).

Cain—no favor
Abel—favor
Noah—favor

Is favor with God random? Does God have two jars: one marked "favor" and the other marked "no favor"? Does He randomly put our names in whichever jar He chooses?

## FAVOR … FAITHFUL'S COUSIN

We all want God's favor! Let His favor pour down on me! Give me all the blessings—healthy children, a great husband, a good job, a nice house, and a car that runs! We don't want much, just some good things in life.

But we struggle with faithfulness, favor's cousin. When our child gets sick, I mean, really sick, we ask God why. When our husband isn't so great, again we ask why. When we lose our job or the hot water heater goes out, why?

Our faith begins to disappear because our favor hid itself from us. We feel sorry for ourselves and struggle with the hard work it takes to make a marriage good. Where is my favor? My child is sick. Where is favor? What happened to our faith when favor took a pause?

We could go on and on about this, but you get my point. We want the favor, but we are not so keen as to what it takes to remain faithful. Ask yourself this, "Could you remain faithful without the favor?" Hmmm, thought-provoking!

## NOAH HAD IT ALL

So apparently Noah had it all. Because of his faithfulness, he had God's favor. His faithfulness and God's favor saved his life. It also saved the life of his wife and children. It also saved our life! Just one family left on earth made way for the whole earth to be replenished. If my life depended on your faithfulness, would I exist?

Let's walk with Noah.

> Now the earth was corrupt in God's sight and was full of violence. God saw how corrupt the earth had become, for all the people on earth had corrupted their ways. So God said to Noah, "I am going to put an end to all people, for the earth is filled with violence because of them. I am surely going to destroy both them and the earth … " (Genesis 6:11–13 NIV)

So build a boat, a really big boat!

> I am going to bring floodwaters on the earth to destroy all life under the heavens, every creature that has the breath of life in it. Everything on earth will perish. But I will establish my covenant with you, and you will enter the ark—you and your sons and your wife and your sons' wives with you. (Genesis 6:17–18 NIV)

## GOD'S COVENANT WITH NOAH: THE NOAHIC COVENANT

God makes a covenant with Noah. *Covenant*, according to Webster Dictionary, means "a written agreement or promise usually under seal between two or more parties especially for the performance of some action."

When God said, "But I will establish my covenant with you," what was He saying? What agreement was God making with Noah?

We have all seen a rainbow. Most of us know that a rainbow represents God's promise, a covenant to us that He will never destroy the earth again by way of a flood. Other than the fact we don't have to worry about a worldwide flood, what does this mean to us?

When God created the earth and mankind, He longed and desired His creation to be in perfect union with Him. Man failed, and that covenant between man and God was lost because of man's failure. The beautiful hope of Eden was lost, and destruction set in.

Over time, the destruction was more than God could bear. His heart was broken. He was going to destroy His entire creation, but one righteous man warranted a do-over. This tiny bit of hope wrapped up in one man allowed God to make a covenant not only with Noah but again with mankind. This was God's desire to bring us back to Eden, a reclaimed paradise. His desire to live life with us takes precedence.

So the earth was destroyed of all living things, allowing the earth to start over. The trees started over; the flowers started over; the oceans shifted, and the animals were reborn. We go back to God's original desire for Adam and Eve in the garden of Eden. But there is one thing God couldn't take back, man's will to sin. Sin had entered, and sin would not leave.

God did not create robots, but humans created in His image were now aware of the good and the evil, the bite from the fruit on the tree.

How many times has God given us a do-over? An opportunity

to get it right? Because of His grace, opportunities for forgiveness abound!

I am confident that God's heart has been broken many times by the choices I have made. But because of my relationship with His Son, Jesus Christ, this covenant of grace is what saves my soul. The covenant of Noah gave way to the covenant of Jesus!

## NOAH DID EVERYTHING

"Noah did everything just as God commanded him" (Genesis 6:22 NIV).

"And Noah did all that the Lord commanded him" (Genesis 7:5 NIV).

## THE DOOR ON THE BOAT WENT "CLICK"

After Noah and crew had done all they needed to do to prepare themselves for something they knew absolutely nothing about, God shut the door, and the door on the boat went "click." "Then the Lord shut him in. For forty days the flood kept coming … " (Genesis 7:16–17 NIV).

Let's think about this a bit. Noah and his family had worked for approximately fifty-five to seventy-five years building this monstrosity of a boat. There is a possibility that they had never seen rain.

Once the structure was finished, Noah yelled, "Load it up, everyone. Let's get this show on the road … or on the water."

After a quick shower to get the goat smell off their bodies, they stepped onto the boat. As they stepped in, the Lord said, "Seven days from now I will send rain on the earth for forty days and forty nights and I will wipe from the face of the earth every living creature I have made" (Genesis 7:4 NIV).

So for seven days, they spent time together in the boat before it started raining. I imagine they stayed on the top deck as much as possible, anticipating a long, hot, stinky ride for the next forty days! As they were sitting on the deck lounging in the sunshine, something wet dropped on their face. That was peculiar. After wiping the damp spot off their faces, another drop of wetness hit their legs and then their arms. There were water drops now coming at quite a rapid pace. Noah looked at his family with a puzzled look. Then he concluded it was time to go inside.

"Then the Lord shut him in" (Genesis 7:16 NIV).

The loud creak from the door was startling to Noah and his family. Once they heard a thud from the closing, they heard the bolt latched from the outside. This was the point of no return.

There are times in our lives when we feel as though the Lord has said "shut THEM in." Maybe it 's that moment when God has said no to a request that we really believed to be right. Maybe it's the sickness of one of our children or our own sickness. Maybe we have had a dream in life that hasn't come true. Maybe God is telling us to wait, and we don't want to.

As we are shut in and the door is closed, many things go on inside of us. Many times during the "closed door" moments …

We feel angst, anxiety, and turmoil as to what is next.
We cry out to God to let us out.
We want to be free.
We want to see the light of day.

But so many times we remain in the dark, closed behind the door, wondering what is next. We waste those moments that God wants to work inside of our own hearts because we are so anxious to get out from behind the door.

Don't you think Noah and his family had many moments of that angst and anxiety just waiting for God to open the door?

But as they waited …
day after day,

raindrop after raindrop,
the door stayed closed.

Yes, they had their everyday chores they needed to do, but don't you wonder what went on inside their own hearts? How many times per day did they ask themselves, "When do we get to get out from behind this closed door? When is God going to open the door so we can see the light of day?" But God waited until the time was perfect before He opened that door.

## OUR SHUT DOOR

As we stand on the inside of our "shut door," we hear the lock turn and the bolt latch.

It's dark in here!
I don't like this!
I want to get out!

But the moments tick by …

Seconds turn to minutes.
minutes turn to hours.
hours turn into days.
and days turn into weeks.

We often frequent the locked door, hoping that someone on the outside has unlatched it. But it remains locked!

We begin to fret and worry about what's going on outside. Then we begin to pace behind the locked door, hoping that the faster we pace, the sooner the door will be unlocked. But our pacing does no good.

After our pacing wears us out, we choose to sit down. Our position of sitting becomes a position of reclining.

As we recline, we get quiet.

As we get quiet, we begin to rest.
As we rest, we feel peace.
In the quiet, we seek God.

Over the course of time as that door remains locked, we have conversations with God that we never thought we would have. We talk about our hopes and dreams for ourselves and our children. We talk about our heartaches in life. We start to put some of the pieces to the puzzle together. We laugh with God. We cry with God. We get to know God in a way we never thought possible. We settle into this moment, not wanting this moment to end. We become grateful for the locked door. We are grateful to be shut in!

As we recline, enjoying our position of surrender, we hear a knock on the door. Someone says, "Come out!"

Approaching the door, we notice the bolt is unlatched and the door is cracked open with the light of the sun shining through. We have a sense of release and regret running simultaneously within us, knowing the moments between being "shut in" and "let out" are our moments. These are moments never to be recaptured, but also moments we will never forget! In those moments, we saw God!

Throughout our lives, we have had these moments, these moments of feeling trapped, trapped within a job, a marriage, or ourselves. We fight to get out and be freed. But with each swing of the fist, it is as though we sink deeper and deeper into our trapped state.

When God shut the door for Noah and his family, they had a choice. They could either accept the reality of their situation or battle their way through the next forty days. The truth of the matter is that they probably did both.

Acceptance of our reality is a part of the journey. We are placed on a path that wasn't the path that we thought we chose. But we have traveled so far in that we can't turn back. The door has been shut, and we have become lost inside. We run to the door and try to open it, but it's locked with no key to turn. We pound on the door for someone to let us out, but we hear only silence on the other side. What we do now is up to us! We can pace and fret until we wear ourselves out, or we can surrender to the moment. In the quiet of that surrender, we can seek the face of God. We can learn to lean on Him for all we need. We can seek His wisdom and His grace. We can find His peace.

Jesus gives us one of the most important gifts as we feel trapped inside. Jesus said, "Peace I leave with you; my peace I give you" (John 14:27 NIV).

There is a beautifully wrapped box sitting in the corner of our silence, but we ignore the box. Inside this box, we could have everything we need. It is the solution to our locked door. It isn't the key to open the door, but it is the key to open our heart.

Struggle after struggle, pace after pace, we ignore the box until one day we realize it is our last resort to get us out of the place of restlessness. Reaching down, we unlatch the box. As we slowly open the lid, we have an immediate release in our soul of angst. There is a "peace that passes all of our understanding," a peace of release within the very room we are trapped in. Inside the box is Jesus' gift of peace. It is ours for the taking.

What if that door never opens? What if we never get released from our marriage we feel trapped inside? What if the job we hate is the job God says to remain in? What if the hopelessness of a wayward child traps us?

We can thrash around until we wear ourselves out. We can pace the floor, looking for the way out. We can climb the walls, hoping we can crawl out. Or we can walk over to that box and receive the gift of peace that Jesus left for us. Our circumstances may never change, but we can! The peace of Jesus coats the hopelessness. It soothes the despair! "Then God said to Noah, 'COME OUT of the ark, you and your wife and your sons and their wives'" (Genesis 8:15–16 NIV).

## COME OUT

It's time to step out into the light of the peace of God!

## TALKS WITH EMILEIGH

One of my favorite songs is "Only Jesus" by Casting Crowns. I cannot count the number of times I have heard this and never allowed it to sink in until recently. "I don't want to leave a legacy. I don't care if they remember me. Only Jesus."

It's not about what I do in this life but to whom my life points others. I will never forget my grandfather's funeral when my dad shared, "My dad didn't tell me how to live. He showed me."

My grandfather modeled a life of devotion and love. He didn't have to tell my dad how to do that. He lived it. Years later, his love, devotion, and legacy live on, and I am certain that my own father's will also. When you live your life not concerned about doing but about only Jesus, your legacy speaks for itself.

Enoch was a man with such a legacy. He "lived faithfully then God took him away" (Genesis 5:24). The details of Enoch's life didn't matter. His faith mattered. His legacy still matters. In fact, in what is referred to as the "hall of faith" in Hebrews 11, we read of Enoch again. Neither his story nor his life was long (compared to others at his time), and it didn't award him his legacy; his faith did.

***Who do you know that has left a legacy? What do you think people will say about you after you pass? Are you leaving a legacy?***

At a time when the Lord regretted His creation of man (Genesis 6:6), He chose Noah. God recognized Noah's righteousness, and Noah was shown favor. His legacy is a representation of God's thread of grace. When God wanted to flood the whole earth, He spared Noah and his family. He offered them the grace to carry on.

***Would God choose you? Why or why not?***

Noah lived by faith and therefore not only heard but listened to God's voice. "By faith Noah, when warned about things not yet seen, in holy fear built an ark to save his family" (Hebrews 11:7).

There is such a definitive difference between hearing and listening. I can hear of God's commands and His guidance all through a decision-making process or during worry, but until I pause and actively listen to what He is speaking to me, I will not fully embrace what He wants me to hear. This is true of scripture as well. We can listen to the words written on the pages, but until we study the words and discover their hidden treasures, we will not fully embrace the gift His Word truly is.

"Noah did everything just as God commanded him" (Genesis 6:22).

Did you catch that? Noah did everything God commanded him. He didn't pick and choose the parts that were convenient for him and that he had time for in his busy day. He listened to the Lord's directives, and he followed them. We don't know what, if any, backlash Noah received for building a giant ark in a time that had never yet seen rain or even if he questioned the task, but we know he followed through, obeyed, and did everything to which he was called.

If you haven't been to the Ark Encounter in Kentucky, you should. They've constructed a life-sized replication of the ark Noah built. It is truly remarkable. From the impeccable construction down to the sanitation and living conditions, I marveled at the intricacies and beauty. This magnificent design was planned by the Lord Himself and constructed in every way by the man who found favor and listened to the Lord's commands. It must have been a huge undertaking and one fueled by ark-sized faith. There is no doubt that Noah must have quieted his mind and heart to clearly hear the specifics of this task.

***Have you ever felt God speak to you this specifically? Do you think you'd listen if given such a large task?***

God not only gave specific details of the ark itself, but He made all the provisions as well. God must have known how overwhelming this undertaking would be for Noah and therefore made sure to also account for and provide for all their needs. Not only would the ark need to home the animals needed to repopulate the earth, He made sure to provide enough for sacrifice as well. The importance of giving back to God and honoring His mercy was and still is very important. God wants us to be taken care of but, more importantly, wants us to remember where all of it originated from. Better yet, from whom it all originated.

I often forget this truth and take for granted the blessings He has bestowed on my family and me: health, security, and safety. I am grateful for all God gives my family, but am I doing more than thanking Him verbally for His blessings? Am I giving back to Him a portion of that which He has allotted me? Am I using the spiritual gifts He's given me for His glory?

***Do you live your life to sustain you and your family only? What type of provisions are you making to give to God?***

Remember how we talked about the parts of scripture we read past and don't immediately notice its significance? The raven and the dove were another of those moments for me. In the past, I read it and thought about the frustration Noah might have felt after the raven returned, knowing he was still stuck in the ark, and then the beauty of the pure-white dove. I missed the intentional significance though. The raven, the blackbird with nowhere to land, now symbolizes to me the darkness God saw in our world in His own creation. There was no room for it anymore, no place for it to land in the world He had designed. That darkness needed cleansing. The dove, however, returned with an olive branch. The pure white, cleansed of darkness, offered hope of a fruitful land and life ahead. This dove offered the pureness of His blessing, a representation of the grace He would one day offer us with His pure, hope-filled Son.

There are areas in my own life I need to replace the raven with the dove. I need to replace the darkness of comparison with the pureness of being fearfully made. I need to replace the darkness of insecurity and seek fulfillment in His unique calling for me. I need to cleanse the darkness of deceit and embrace the hope of eternity.

***Where in your life do you see a darkness that you need to cleanse your heart of? What olive branch could you replace that darkness with?***

Noah and his family didn't miss that hope. They seized it and left the ark, ready to embrace the new life the Lord had planned for them. I can imagine after being in the ark for so long, there was a mixture of excitement and anticipation, and as they exited the ark, they remembered who had delivered them, the One who had rescued and provided for them. They built an altar in gratitude to the Lord (Genesis 8:20). There was cause for celebration, and the first place they looked was up.

***When something celebratory happens, who is the first person you tell? When do you receive a blessing, what's the first thing you do?***

God's thread of grace continues to be unraveled after the flood but, this time, in a tangible way we still see today. Though God regretted what He had created, He found favor in Noah's faithfulness, cleansed the earth, and promised never again to do so. He placed a rainbow in the sky, signifying the covenant with man to never again flood the earth. He not only gave Noah a promise that could be passed along from generation to generation but offered a promise we are able to see each time it rains. We can see the reminder of His grace for ourselves and be reminded of the hope He has available for us.

My children are a reminder of this love and grace for me. There are days that feel like I'm being poured on by tumultuous rain and even days of a light drizzle that are simply irritating. Yet their lives, their health, and their unconditional love for me are constant reminders of His grace. Of all the mothers in the world, the Lord has entrusted them to my care. That's grace.

***What examples has God placed in your life to remind you of His promises?***

I assume Noah and his family didn't realize just how long they'd be in the ark or just how long this new form of precipitation bursting from the earth would last. I doubt they anticipated being in for over a year!

That uncertain waiting period is likely one of my biggest faith struggles. I will never know how long a challenging season will last, how deep the despair of a loss will be, or how long I must endure before seeing His rainbow. I do know I trust the One in control though. He knows the pits and mountaintops I will hike through, and He knew exactly how long Noah and his family would be in the ark, from entrance to exit. I truly believe in these uncertain times. He has us, exactly where He wants us, for exactly as long as we need to be, to hopefully learn exactly what we need to learn.

In lighthearted terms, this waiting period for me currently is pregnancy. I do not know when this baby will be born. I do not know what this baby will look like. I do not even know what the gender of this baby is. I do know I'm uncomfortable. I do know I'm not able to do the things with my body I'm used to during non-pregnant days. I do know that I'm weary and feeling uncertain about the other side of this wait. I do know that God knows all these things. I do know this baby is a blessing. I do know this wait is worth every minute. My baby is growing for exactly the amount of time God deems necessary, and I'm using that time to be with my other children and in His Word before I'm likely too tired to do so. I'm trying to maximize this waiting period.

As I write this, our world is walking through the coronavirus pandemic. At the beginning of it, they essentially shut us in, advising and then ordering us not to leave our homes. We didn't know how long this would last nor what it would look like on the other side. It still doesn't feel like we're on the other side of it in many ways. Yet again, God knows. Just as he shut Noah into the ark with an ending in sight, He knows the ending of this pandemic. What many of us don't know is the toll being shut in will have on us. While Satan is taking every opportunity to use this pandemic to induce fear, anxiety, and hatred, God intends this time for growth, love, and opportunity. He's calling us to use this time to settle our hearts and minds and rest in Him. Our family has embraced this time together, finding more time to simply be with one another, slow our typically busy pace, and enjoy the gifts of life without the hustle. I've taken time to study different scripture and even make talking about God with my children a greater priority, mainly because we have more time to do so. During what many call this time a trial, I am calling it a blessing.

***Describe a trial you endured much longer than originally anticipated or a time you felt "shut in." What is your inclination during times of trial? Do you seek rest and peace, or do you complain and pound on the door to get out?***

Consider these trials you've faced and those you will inevitably face. After all, we will experience suffering in this life, but He who is in control has overcome (John 16:33). I challenge you in those times of trial, uncertainty, or being "shut in" to get to know God in a way you never have. Rest in His peace and connect with Him intimately.

# 6

## IT'S A LONG WALK HOME

"My plane is right above you!" This was a text I received on Christmas Eve as my son was coming home for the holiday.

As a retired mom, I love to hear my children say they are coming home. My trip to the store is filled with joy and hope as I anticipate their arrival. The pot on the stove emits a sweet aroma, and the Christmas decorations are brought from the basement.

The lights are hung …
The candles are lit …
The table is set …

And now I wait …

I wait to hear the sound of their car in the driveway.
I wait to hear their laughter as they approach the door.
I wait for the doorbell to ring.

Running to the door, I shout, "Honey, they're here! They're home! The kids are home!"

The word *Home* is like a warm blanket on a snowy day. It has an unsung calm, a restful peace. Why does one word take on such deep meaning?

Why does it allow us to breathe air deep into our lungs? Because it represents a place where we can be ourselves, a place where we can let down our guard and be authentic, a place where we are loved and accepted for who we are.

Home can be our place of origin or a temporary residence. It can be a suitcase or a car. It can be something we touch or just something we feel. It can be filled with laughter or tears. No matter how it is defined, it is still home!

Do you remember the stories from your grandparents or great-grandparents about how long they had to walk home from school? Five miles … uphill … barefoot in the snow! It didn't matter how hard and how far it was, they always seemed to make it home.

From the book of Genesis, the story of Abraham talks about Abraham going home to a place he had never seen. This is an interesting perspective because typically home is a place you return to. In Abraham's story, home is a place he journeyed to find. One day in the life of Abraham God told him to go, to leave his familiar surroundings and find his home.

But before we sit on Abraham's front porch and sip lemonade, let's go on this journey with him.

## WHERE'S HOME?

I would love to ask Abraham the question, "So where's home?"

When someone asks you where home is, how do you respond? Do you respond with your place of birth or your current place of residence?

Looking at my own life, I can count seven different places I have lived since birth. But if you were to ask me where home is, I would say Edwardsville, Illinois, my current place of residence. The old adage is true, "Home Is where the heart is."

Throughout Abraham's wanderings, he hung his hat in many places. His original place of birth was Ur of the Chaldeans. We conclude that because Abraham's brother, Haran, died at a young age in his birthplace, which would be the same birthplace of his brother, Abraham, which was Ur of the Chaldeans (Genesis 11:28).

Ur was a city. It was in the southern part of Mesopotamia. Since it was centrally located, it was a great city for trade and commerce. This city was of great wealth and a bureaucratic state. The people of Ur were of the tribe of the Chaldeans, whose main god of worship was not the God of Creation. In the ancient times, there were thousands of gods that were worshipped. Often these gods would represent something needed in the lives of these people. The purpose behind this tedious detail is to allow us to know the surroundings in which Abraham was raised. He was not raised in a God-fearing society who knew and understood the Creator of the Universe. He was surrounded by pagan worship as people embraced the beauty of the palaces and temples built for worship of the gods. The foundation for Abraham's faith is up for debate. We assume that he surrounded his life worshipping the God of Creation simply because of the depth of his faith. But that is simply an assumption.

While living in Ur, Abraham had two brothers, Nahor and Haran. Haran died while living in Ur, leaving behind his son, Lot. After Abraham married Sarah and Nahor married Milkah, Abraham's father, Terah, decided it was time to move the family. So they set out for the land of Canaan, which was due west of Ur, but because of the topography of the land, they headed north toward Harran, six hundred miles away. Once in Harran, they would be able to cross over into a more palatable terrain. But while camped in Harran, they chose to settle for a while. Terah was growing old, and travels became more and more difficult for him. At the age of 205, Terah died.

We are not sure how long Abraham and his family remained in the land of Harran, but using the context of scriptures, it would seem as though they had stayed there long enough for it to become home. In later scriptures, Abraham sends his servant back to Harran to retrieve a wife for his son, Isaac. Then even later, Jacob, a descendant of Abraham, flees from Canaan to the land of Harran to find refuge from his brother Esau. Abraham's brother, Nahor, established roots in Harran, therefore making Harran home to Abraham's relatives.

After Abraham's father died, God had other plans for Abraham than staying in Harran. God had a promise, a covenant He wanted to make with Abraham. He had a new place for Abraham to call home.

## GOD SPEAKS!

It is so interesting how we often say we wished that God would speak to us like He spoke to the people of the Old Testament, you know, an audible voice from God so we know exactly which direction to go.

But maybe we need to pay attention to what we are asking for. Think about this. You are going about your daily duties, for instance, driving to work. Suddenly you hear a voice, a deep, demanding voice. You begin to panic. Making your way to the side of the road, you pull over so you can focus on this voice. Once you hear what God says, you realize that you really didn't want to hear it after all. I wonder if Abraham felt the same.

Listen to this conversation between God and Abraham. Maybe it went kind of like this.

*God says, "Hey, Abraham!"*
*Abraham stumbles out of his tent to see what all the commotion is. Never hearing the voice of God before, he does not recognize the voice, so he climbs back into his tent.*

*God says, "Abraham, it's me, God. I have something I want for you to do."*

*Abraham stumbles out again, this time a little more attentive to this voice. "God, is that you? I mean, God, the Creator of heaven and earth, is that you?" Standing outside of his tent, speaking to what seemed the air, Abraham begins to listen.*

*God states, "Abraham, I want you to pack up everything you own and leave this place. I have your new home waiting for you."*

Many of us have struggled trying to decide on whether to move or not. Having this clear guidance would be great! But what if God wanted to take us to a place we didn't want to go? Would we climb back into our tent until God gives us what we want? "The Lord had said to Abram, 'GO from your country, your people and your father's household to the land I will show you'" (Genesis 12:1 NIV)

*Abraham says, "You have my attention, God."*

God responds, "'I will make you a great nation, and I will bless you. I will make your name great, and you will be a blessing. I will bless those who bless you, and whoever curses you I will curse; and all people on earth will be blessed through you.' So, Abram went, as the Lord had told him" (Genesis 12:2–4 NIV).

Just like that, Abraham packed his bags, his family, and his livestock and left for an unknown land.

When God calls us to something in life, we often ask for details, lots and lots of details. When do I leave? How am I going to get there? What do I do once I get there? Why do I need to go?

But have you ever thought that God gives us what we need when we need it? His plan rolled out for us is never too early and never too late. It is perfectly orchestrated long before it reaches us.

Stepping out into this world of faith, Abraham was called to follow God. His steps were undoubtedly filled with questions: where, why, and what.

filled with fear … what if.
filled with anticipation for the future … what is ahead.

But God had already answered these questions. The path had been constructed for this journey. Abraham simply had to walk.

We live in such fear of the what-ifs that it paralyzes us within what is secure and what is known. When we choose not to walk in God's calling, we choose disobedience because we fear the whole journey. Sometimes obedience is just that first step, not the whole journey. Abraham needed to take that first step,...

> and they set out for the land of Canaan, and they arrived there (Genesis 12:6 NIV).

Simple fulfillment of God's request ...

> they set out ...
> and they arrived.

God asks us to do two things, set out and arrive! But we will never arrive until we set out.

What has God called you to do that you have yet to take the first step?

## THEY ARRIVED THERE!

Those three words were the basis of going home. As Abraham stood on new soil, he was home, home in the place of the unknown.

> *God says, "Child, you are home. You are in the place I have chosen for you. You are in the place I have chosen for my nation ... for my people. Just keep walking and I will continue to show you how all of this will unfold. Welcome home!"*

## GOD CONTINUES SPEAKING

The Lord then appeared to Abraham, and as they stood at the edge of the land, with Abraham's feet dirty and blistered from the journey, God spoke, "The Lord appeared to Abram and said, 'To your offspring I will give this land.' So, he built an altar ... " (Genesis 12:7 NIV).

Abraham bent down collecting rocks that scattered the soil. With his hands resting in the dirt, he knew this was home. Collecting rock after rock, he built an altar to God one stone at a time. When he finished building this alter he fell on his knees worshiping the God who led him from the known to the unknown.

From the known to the unknown, that is not what we want. We want to be led to the known. When I get to the known, then I will worship God. "Praise Jesus for all the wonderful things that He has done," not "Praise Jesus because He has led me to the unknown!"

When I head out on a journey, a move, or a change, I want to know where I am heading. I want to know the street I am going to live on, have my curtains selected, and meet the neighbors. But this was not the case for Abraham. He had no place to live, no curtains to hang, and no neighbors to call friends. So, his worship seems counterintuitive. How could he worship a God who had led him to the land of nothing?

Standing in the land of the unknown, he was only at the beginning of his journey. Looking to the future was a blind attempt. So, His faith had to be anchored in the unknown.

Think about it, anchoring our faith in the unknown! Could you do it?

## THE JOURNEY CONTINUES

As the journey continued, Abraham and Sarah moved deeper into the land of Canaan, settling in the desert of Negev. Deserts are dry and dusty, and the desert of Negev did not disappoint. After settling in this land, famine struck the land, causing Abraham and his family to travel to Egypt to survive.

This is such an interesting pause in this story. Abraham had traveled to the land that God was giving him. This land was a promise from God not only to Abraham but for a nation that would come from this land, yet a famine struck. So often we think that when we follow God even to the unknown, we would never be struck by famine. We think our obedience deserves a reward. We think we are deserving of good. But rewards don't always come in the package of obedience. It's kind of like opening a box of Cracker Jacks and not finding your prize inside. It kind of stinks!

Can we be happy with our obedience without the reward?

## BACK TO CANAAN

As the story continues, Abraham and his nephew Lot, who had also traveled to Canaan with Abraham, grew too large for the land they were both residing in. Canaan is a large piece of land, but Abraham and Lot tried to squeeze everything they both owned plus their families into too small of a parcel. So they parted ways. Given the first choice, Lot chose the lush and beautiful land in the east.

> Lot looked around and saw that the whole plain of the Jordan toward Zoar was well watered, like the garden of the Lord, like the land of Egypt … So Lot chose for himself the whole plain of the Jordan and set out toward the east. The two men parted company … (Genesis 13:10–11 NIV)

Even Lot wanted something similar to the garden of Eden. We all want the garden of Eden, but we are not all willing to do what it will take to return there.

I love what God says next.

## GOD SPEAKS AGAIN

As Lot began his travels toward the east, Abraham looked to the west. As he gazed toward his new home, God took Abraham to the corner. My friends, a lot of things can happen in our lives when we stand on the corner with God.

Imagine this with me. God takes the hand of Abraham and says, "Look!"

Abraham stands with his feet in the hot, dry sand, and God says, "Look! As far as your eye can see … look!"

I'm not sure if you have ever been to a desert, but there isn't a whole lot out there. Since it is barren, eyes can see pretty doggone far!

As they stand together looking out over this land, God speaks to Abraham.

> The Lord said to Abram after Lot had parted from him, "Look around from where you are, to the north and south, to the east and west. All the land that you see I WILL GIVE TO YOU and to your offspring forever. I will make your offspring like the dust of the earth, so that if anyone could count the dust, then your offspring could be counted. GO, WALK THROUGH THE LENGTH AND BREADTH OF THE LAND, FOR I AM GIVING IT TO YOU." (Genesis 13:14–17 NIV)

It is like standing in the middle of a candy store and the owner says, "As far as you can see, it's yours! Every lollipop, every licorice stick, every gumball … it is all yours!"

God says, "Look around, Abraham. Everything you see is yours! I want to give it to you. This is your new home, your forever home here on earth! I have a plan far greater than the newness and adventure a new land will give you. It is here that I will build my kingdom. It is through you that I will build my kingdom. Don't look any further than home."

"Don't look any further than home." Can you imagine what that would have been like for Abraham? He had traveled far from his birthplace. Leaving the land of Ur, he had settled with his family in a land that was not his home. Hearing an unknown voice, he moved to an unknown land and placed his feet onto unknown soil.

God promises He will use Abraham in a mighty way if he just stays home. Don't look any further than home!

So many times in life, we look beyond home, hoping that there is something bigger for us. But what if God wants us to stay home? What if He doesn't want us to look any further than where we currently are? What if standing on the edge of our streets, porches, and towns was like Abraham standing on the edge of the desert? What if God is saying for us to look as far as we can, to the north and to the south, and capture everything we can see as His promise for us right where we are? Would your vision be corrected? Would your perspective change?

## HOME: PURPOSE OR PLEASURE?

God did not choose this home for Abraham's pleasure. God chose this home for His purpose! So often we choose where we want our home to be out of comfort, pleasure, or adventure. But what if we chose for God's purpose?

What if God put us exactly where we are because He has a bigger purpose than just our pleasure? The street you live on, the neighborhood where you reside, is it your pleasure or God's purpose? The neighbor you like or don't like, is it your pleasure or God's purpose? The story of Jesus that you hold on to, is it your pleasure or God's purpose? You choose!

## THE STORY ISN'T OVER

> As the sun was setting, Abram fell into deep sleep, and a thick and dreadful darkness came over him. Then the Lord said to him, "Know for certain that for four hundred years your descendants will be strangers in a country not their own and that they will be enslaved and mistreated there. But I will punish the nation they serve as slaves, and afterward they will come out with great possessions. You, however, will go to your ancestors in peace and be buried at a good old age. In the fourth generation your descendants will

> come back here, for the sin of the Amorites has not yet reached its full measure." (Genesis 15:12–16 NIV)

"In the fourth generation your descendants will come back here ..." Where are they coming back? They are coming back home! Here is home!

Laying his head on the soil called home, Abraham was laying his head on a story that wasn't over. There would come a day he would no longer walk the roads of Canaan, the land of promise. His feet would become weary, and his body would rest in eternity. But the land that God promised to Abraham would also become the land He promised to the nation of the Israelites. The nation would begin in the womb of his wife, Sarah. It was this land that God's people would call home! They will come back home, to Canaan, to the Promised Land, a land flowing with milk and honey, home sweet home! In about five hundred years after heartache, death, and disobedience, they would come home to the land of promise, the land of purpose.

## WHAT'S YOUR ADDRESS?

What is your address? What do you call home? Is it your current place of residence, or do you long for something more? When you hang your hat at the door, are you looking for another door? Are you wasting the moments on your front porch longing for a different porch?

God brings us to a place to call home for a purpose, a reason. Even if we spend our lives moving from one place to another, each new place is our home. Home is the place where God wants to plant His purpose, His plan. If we live our lives longing for a new home, we miss that chance for God to work His purpose through us. We waste those opportunities for God's divine moments. Remember, home is where God's heart is!

Drawing from the scripture in chapter one of this book, I believe the Greats of Old said it best as they were looking for their permanent home.

> They agreed that they were foreigners and nomads here on earth. Obviously, people who say such things are looking forward to a country they can call their own. If they had longed for the country they came from, they could have gone back. But they were looking for a better place, a heavenly homeland that is why God is not ashamed to be called their God, for he has prepared a city for them. (Hebrews 11:13–16 NLT)

As wanderers here on earth, they were looking for a place to call home. They could have returned to the place from where they came, but they were looking for something better, something beyond what they had seen here on earth. Instead of looking at what was around them, they looked at what was above them. Their eyes were fixed on their Creator, longing for their final home, their heavenly home.

As we wander here on earth, whether that is in the same place of residence for life or scattering around to different parts of the world, there is only one place that is our permanent residence, and that residence is placed in eternity. When we set our eyes on Jesus, troubles of this world fade within the light of eternity. Jesus says,

> Do not let your hearts be troubled. You believe in God; believe also in me. My Father's house has many rooms; if that were not so, would I have told you that I am going there to prepare a place for you? And if I go and prepare a place for you, I will come back and take you to be with me that you also may be where I am. You know the way to the place where I am going. (John 14:1–4 NIV)

It is in this place that we will be always home!

## TALKS WITH EMILEIGH

Can you imagine how difficult it must have been for Abraham to leave his homeland, not knowing where he'd end up? He just said goodbye and left. He trusted the path laid before him. He put faith in the goodbye. He did this because he trusted in the promises of the God he followed.

A part of my heart resides in El Salvador. It's a love that began the day my husband and I chose to sponsor a child through Compassion International. Our home church visits this community typically a couple times a year, and something about this little boy's face tugged at our hearts. The first time my husband and I met him, our lives were changed. I've since traveled with our church to their community three more times, but the last trip I took was by far the most difficult. I hadn't intended to go on their trip last September because with two young kids at home and a husband with an extremely busy fall work schedule, it seemed unfeasible. There was a familiar voice whispering to me though. I knew the voice well, but I simply didn't understand. It wasn't the right time. It wasn't the right trip. "Go" is what I heard. After prayer and conversations with my incredibly supportive husband, I signed up. Telling my kids goodbye for eight days when I typically stay home with them every day was incredibly difficult. I can still remember their tears and the tough phone calls during the trip. When I returned, we talked about all the ways God worked on this trip, both on me and through me. We talked about obedience. My children heard their mom, whom they did miss, tell of her decision to follow God's path even when it was difficult. That made the goodbye worth every tear. That was faith in action, active obedience.

***Have you ever been called away or even to move away from family due to work, school, and so forth? Was it easy? Difficult?***

Thankfully on my trip to El Salvador, we are all so thrilled to be together there's no quarreling (or at least none that I get involved in). On Abraham's journey, however, he and Lot's herdsmen began to quarrel. Abraham and Lot had accumulated many things after all, and with many things come more things to quarrel over. I wonder if Abraham and Lot saw or heard of this happening and tried to ignore it for a time. I wonder if they even tried to use subtle ways to intervene and dissolve the issues before they got out of hand. I've certainly ignored plenty of bickering from my own children, hoping they'll just figure it out and play nicely together. Sometimes, it's just not worth involving ourselves. Sometimes getting involved in the argument makes things worse, and often, in my home, it's a fight that shouldn't have happened in the first place. Unfortunately, the quarreling got to be too much on their long journey, and uncle and nephew were forced to choose separate ways.

***Have you ever been pulled into an argument/quarrel/debate that really shouldn't involve you? How did you respond? Did the situation or outcome of the argument affect you in a meaningful way?***

As we learn, Abram and Lot getting involved in the argument and parting ways was simply part of the plan. Abraham, in either his graciousness or trust in God's provision, allowed Lot to choose his direction first. Knowing that Abram trusted God enough to leave his homeland and travel for an unknown amount of time to an unknown land, Abraham also trusted God enough to bless him in any direction he went. Just like nine times out of ten I would choose a bowl of ice cream over a bowl of Brussels sprouts, Lot chose the option that looked more appealing. He chose where the grass looked greener. As we find out, unfortunately for Lot, the grass isn't always greener. The land that looked better was filled with wickedness (Genesis 13:13). On the other side of the greener valley, God blessed Abraham and, in a sense, rewarded his gracious heart. I do not intend to imply that Lot was not gracious or faithful, but I do recognize generous when I see (or read) it. Abraham was generous with his love for Lot, his offer of first choice and his contentment with whatever decision was made. I don't believe Abram did so for recognition either. It was a heartfelt offer of love.

My dad is one of the most generous people I know. It surely is one of his spiritual gifts. I've learned over the years that he never gives for recognition. In fact, I've watched him be intentional about disclosure often when giving. The amount of joy it brings him to help those God leads him to is undeniable. He has a generous heart toward those he shows generosity to because he leads a life of generous love toward God. This is likely one of my most treasured gifts I've learned from him over the years. As a result, I have seen the Lord bless him and our family in both obvious and subtle ways. Of his many blessings, he is both a successful business owner and soon-to-be grandfather of five. There is no doubt he lives his life trusting the path God has, offering time and love to those God directs him to and showing gratitude to the One who bestows the blessings.

***Who is the most generous person you know? Do you see God's blessing in their lives? Is their gratitude directed to the One who blessed them? How can their generosity inspire you to use your own blessings?***

By no coincidence but rather divine intervention, Abraham's act of generosity led exactly where God wanted him to go. While Lot chose the land that may have physically looked better, Abraham's land was full of purpose. Lot seemed to be blinded by the looks of the land and what it might offer him while Abraham kept his focus upward. Again, Abraham trusted in the path set for him and not only listened for but responded to the whispers directing him. He remained focused on the One who was blessing him. Abraham's focus allowed him to live out God's purpose rather than be derailed by distractions like greener pastures. With quarreling herdsmen in tow, I am certain there was also some rebuttal from them as well. Their focus and maybe the focus of many in his caravan may have been for a land of ease and pleasure. After all, they left their homeland in search of something better. The paramount lesson we learn is that God didn't choose Abraham's path or land for Abraham's pleasure but for God's purpose. As He always does, God had a great plan and chose to use Abraham to be part of it. It was Abraham's pleasure to choose in response to obey.

In my own life, I have allowed myself too often to be distracted by my worries or frustrations to see what God's purpose is. This year has held a myriad of challenges and opportunities for my family. It would be easy for me to feel overwhelmed and distracted. I work remotely from home. I have two young children, one of which we have decided to homeschool this year, the other with more energy than the Energizer bunny. I am nearly thirty-nine weeks pregnant, and I have felt called to write these lessons. Nothing about the timing of that combination seems reasonable to me on the surface. That's the funny thing about God's timing though, isn't it? It's always right on time. Whether it be a mission trip to visit my El Salvadoran family or plunging into homeschooling, I trust God has a great purpose. I trust His timing because it is far wiser than my own eyes can ever see. There are certainly days I get caught in my exhaustion or a routine of productivity rather than investing in and enjoying the laughter of my children. It's a difficult balance to understate the challenge. I realize there are too many opportunities I'm missing with the gifts running around my feet because I'm distracted by all I need to do or expecting more from what I've been bestowed. Yet as I read this lesson on Abraham, I was reminded of Jeremiah 29:11 and God's promise of hope and a prosperous life. He knows those plans. I must trust the purpose and avoid the uncomfortable or inconvenient distractions along the way.

***When have you missed God's purpose because you were distracted by your own comfort or convenience? Where in your life can you switch from a mindset of enjoyment and begin looking for His purpose?***

Read Genesis 15:12–21. Abraham followed where God led. He trusted in His purpose. He's made it … or at least Abraham has. There's a legacy for Abraham to carry on and a long walk ahead still. Though Abraham now stands in the Promised Land, God tells

Abraham the walk for their people will be difficult. They will be oppressed and will suffer. They will be separated from this land the Lord has now made their home. Yet the Lord has a purpose, a redemptive plan to save His people and return them one day back to the land Abraham now stands in. The Lord prophesizes and promises deliverance and hope. He tells Abraham that he is exactly where he needs to be. He tells Abraham that this Promised Land is now his home and he is to stay right where he is. Abraham is just at the beginning of all God has in store.

In second-grade math, in the uncertainty of what impending day this baby will be born, in the pure exhaustion of just one more game of hockey, one more dinner to cook, and one more report to process, I am exactly where I am intended to be. I am in my Promised Land. Though there are days it may not feel like pleasure, I am reminded of His greater purpose and much more joy to come. I'm just at the beginning of a great plan.

***What area of your life do you find yourself at the beginning, looking ahead to what God has in store? What area of your life do you feel you have reached His promise or feel accomplished and could help lead others on their own journey ahead?***

Read John 16:33. Years later, Jesus tells us the same: in this life, we will experience trouble. We will experience trials and distractions, but there is hope. He has overcome the world, and with Him at our side, we can overcome. For many, they may not grasp that hope. Some may be suffering or feeling oppressed by the many trials of this world. Maybe you are just at the beginning, discovering what God has in store, or perhaps you are in your Promised Land, enjoying the richness of His goodness and blessings. Wherever you may be, share that with a trusted friend or mentor. Sharing where we are on our walk can take courage but also provides an avenue for growth in a wilderness of distractions.

***Where are you on your walk? Are you at the beginning, discovering who God is and what He has in store? During oppression, feeling lost and looking for God in a seeming darkness? On the journey, growing, seeking, and allowing God to refine you as you seek His promises? In the Promised Land, celebrating His promises and embracing His grace?***

The walk I'm currently on always leads me back home to those I love most, to those the Lord has given me, to those the Lord has entrusted to my care. Home is where I spend the majority of my time. For some, that has proven challenging. For me, I'm simply home, and that's exactly where I'm meant to be. I am amid God's journey plotted out for me, and I do not take that responsibility lightly. I am purposed with a goal, a goal to lead my children on a legacy of faith toward the One who has planned it all.

***Where is home for you? Where your family lives? Where you grew up? At your church? What makes it home for you? The people? The feeling it gives you? What purpose do you believe you have in your home?***

Each day is a new step on your walk. Yours may look different from your neighbor's, your sister's, or your best friend's. Abraham's walk certainly looked different than Lot's. Each day is an opportunity to move forward or stay stuck in the distraction, to look toward greener pastures or to rest exactly where God has placed you. No matter which direction your journey leads, our lives can look drastically different if we begin living with purpose. Begin living with the expectation of what each new day can hold. Look for the opportunities right where you are and ask God to reveal His redemptive plan in your life and the lives of those in your home. No matter the address, no matter the people you share it with, home is exactly where God wants you to be.

***How might your life look different if you began each day looking for His purpose in your actions, words, and relationships?***

No matter where you plot yourself on your walk, there is purpose. God is moving. He is beside you and ahead of you, leading the way and whispering His promises. It is your choice to be stuck or move forward. It is your choice to live with purpose or waste the time you are given. To truly live out and even discover your purpose, you must start by living with expectations. Start now.

Read Psalm 5:3. Are you living with expectations for what God can do?

# 7

## TAKE A WALK IN SARAH'S SHOES

Have you ever wanted something so bad you think you'd die if you don't have it? That the mere thought of it keeps you up at night. You can't sleep, you can't eat, you can't drink. You are so consumed by that desire nothing else matters, and you're not sure life is worth living if you can't have it.

—Katie Ashley, *The Proposition*

Webster Dictionary defines obsession as a persistent disturbing preoccupation with an often unreasonable idea or feeling.

I define obsession in this way…

> You are sitting in your "comfy" chair. The evening settles in like a soft blanket. Your tummy is full of the delicious dinner you fixed (or purchased). The television is set to your favorite series. Then it happens, you know, "it" happens. Your mind locks onto that one piece of chocolate still sitting in that box on the shelf in your pantry. You try to push that thought out of your mind, but the harder you try to push it out, the harder that thought shoves itself back into your brain. Picking up the remote, you pause your show, go through the discomfort of crawling out of your chair, make your way to the pantry, and snatch up that final piece of chocolate. You would

> think that because of the internal battle you endured to resist the chocolate, when you finally gave into it, you would have savored every little morsel, chewing it slowly and methodically. But nope … you snatched it from the box and devoured it in one fell swoop. As you make your way back to your chair, the thought barely lingers as to why you rose from your chair in the first place.

Sound familiar?

Obsessive thoughts control every fiber of our being, causing us to move robotically through life, longing for the gratification of our obsession. Our thoughts are irrational, and our behavior is equally irrational. We are blinded to those around us, not caring about the damage our obsession may cause. We become caught within a whirlwind, turning us around like a lost sock in the dryer. When someone tries to pull us out of the whirlwind, we stick ourselves to the side, hiding from anyone who offers help. We are completely and totally consumed.

In the book of Genesis, there is a story that paints obsession with colors of green for envy and black for destruction, an obsession that caused one woman to take a walk on the wild side that I am confident she never fathomed she would walk.

In chapter six, we looked at Abraham's long walk home. But as we read the scriptures, he didn't take this walk alone. He had his beautiful bride, Sarah, at his side. Sarah and Abraham had married many years prior in their hometown of Ur, south of the land of Canaan. They had traveled together to the land of Harran and then on to Canaan.

Abraham was approximately seventy years old when God called him out of the land of Harran. Since Sarah was his half-sister (yep, a bit disturbing, but this was acceptable during Old Testament times), she was close to his age. The Bible says they were about ten years apart making Sarah around sixty years old when they started to make their way to Canaan.

## SARAH'S OBSESSION

Sarah had an obsession, one that ran deep within her veins, much deeper than craving the last piece of chocolate. Her obsession? To conceive a child. "Now Sarai was childless because she was not able to conceive" (Genesis 11:30 NIV).

Contrary to that in Genesis 12:7, the Bible says, "The Lord appeared to Abram and said, 'To your offspring I will give this land.'" What? I don't get this. How could Abraham have offspring if his wife was barren?

Remember in chapter six when Lot chose his land, the lush land? And Abraham was given his homeland, the land of Canaan, by default?

> The Lord said to Abram after Lot parted from him, "Look around from where you are, to the north and south, to the east and west. All the land that you see I will give to you and your offspring forever." (Genesis 13:14–17 NIV)

This word *offspring* was becoming common in these conversations between God and Abraham. Does God not know that Sarah can't have babies? In Genesis 15:2, Abraham, out of frustration, finally speaks up to God and says, "what can you give me since I remain childless … " In other words, he states, "God, you keep talking about my offspring, but I ain't got no kids!"

God then says, "Hey, Abraham, let's go outside for j a bit." Folks, when God takes us outside, it's time to listen!

> He took him outside and said, "Look up at the sky and count the stars -if indeed you can count them."

> Then he said to him, "So shall your offspring be." (Genesis 15:5 NIV)

At this point, Abraham's faith moved from intangible to tangible. As in chapter one in this book, "obedience is the tangible evidence to our faith." "Abraham believed the Lord, and he credited it to him as righteousness" (Genesis 15:6 NIV).

Sarah can't have babies.

God promises offspring.

How can offspring come from a barren womb?

Let's see what happens next.

## THE PLAN

Sarah devises a plan, a "if you want something done, you gotta do it yourself" kind of plan. "Now Sarai, Abram's wife" (Genesis 16:1) took a walk on the wild side!

Throughout this story of Abraham, God has alluded to offspring over and over. In a previous chapter, God said, "To your descendants … " Little baby descendants were coming. They were cranking up in the descendant factory as Sarah speaks. But she couldn't wait for God; therefore, she took the matters into her own hands. Or, I guess, we could say she pushed the matters into her husband's arms.

Even in the Old Testament, God forbade extramarital sex. But the world was tainted by sin, causing even men of faith to have more than one wife or concubines they could pleasure themselves with. Because this was culturally accepted, Sarah succumbed to the acceptable, therefore bypassing God's desires and design.

Sarah's obsession became irrational thinking, resulting in irrational behavior. When we allow our obsession to become our mania, we will act accordingly, resulting in destruction.

Taking a walk on the wild side, Sarah orchestrated a sexual skirmish between her Egyptian slave, Hagar, and her husband, Abraham. Her irrational behavior brought on by her irrational thinking caused by her obsession to have a child resulted in pain, hurt, and destruction in the form of a precious baby boy.

## THE STORY

> Now Sarai, Abram's wife, had borne him no children. But she had an Egyptian slave name Hagar; so she said to Abram, "The Lord has kept me from having children. Go, sleep with my slave; perhaps I can build a family through her." (Genesis 16:1–4 NIV)

Stop! Here's the slo-mo of the story. "Sarah, please stop! You are obsessing, and your obsession will soon result in destruction if you don't stop your irrational thinking."

But because of Sarah's selfish desires and her lack of pause, she put sin in motion. She created a story that affected and destroyed the lives of those she loved the most and some she didn't love so much. One unwise choice not only affected her own life, but affected the lives of her husband, her slave, her slave's son, and ultimately a whole nation.

Look again at Genesis 16:2 (NIV). "Go, sleep with my slave; perhaps I can build a family through her."

Did you catch that pronoun? "perhaps I can …" Not we or us, but I. What happened to God? What happened to the us? When our obsessions become irrational thinking, we lose any connection to others that would allow truth to be spoken into us. The word *I* is the flashing red light, screaming danger.

> Abram agreed to what Sarai said. So, after Abram had been living in Canaan ten years, Sarai his wife took her Egyptian slave Hagar and gave her to her husband to be his wife (polygamy, which is against God's design). He slept with Hagar, and she conceived. (Genesis 16:2–4 NIV)

In the beginning of creation, it was quiet … oh, so quiet! With each twist and turn of the stories since creation, the level of noise grew greater and greater. As Abraham and Hagar's son was born, he let out a cry that would change the course of a nation.

Two women … one man

One pregnancy!

One baby!

Two moms! Yikes!!!!

Heaven help us! There is no way that this arrangement between Sarah, Hagar, and Abraham was going to work.

## BATTER UP

As the batter steps to the plate, the pitcher steps to the mound. He looks toward home plate, targeting the batter for a strike. First to bat is … Sarah!

The announcer grabs the mic as Sarah steps to the batter's box.

> Folks, stepping to the plate is Sarah. Sarah, the wife of Abraham, walks daily in her shame of being labeled childless. Sarah wants to have a child more than anything in life. So going against God's plan, Sarah devises her own.

The pitch is thrown. Strike one!

> Next to the plate is Abraham. He too wants a son. He too was told by God that he would have descendants. He too wondered if God would complete His plan. So taking matters into his own hands or, should we say, arms, he conceded to Sarah's plan of sleeping with his wife's slave.

The pitch is thrown. Strike two!

> Our third batter is stepping out of the dugout. Yes, our third batter … wait, where is our third batter? Who is our third batter? Will it be another strike, a base hit, or a home run?

Batter number three is not quite ready to appear, but she will! Hold on … it's coming! Strike three needs its own chapter … So wait for it! Wait for it!

## THERE IS GRUMBLING IN THE TENT

Once it was learned that Sarah's slave, Hagar, is pregnant, an argument ensues between Abraham and Sarah. There is grumbling in the tent, folks.

> Then Sarai said to Abram, "You are responsible for the wrong I am suffering. I put my slave in your arms, and now that she knows she is pregnant, she despises me … (now, here is the kicker) … MAY THE LORD JUDGE BETWEEN YOU AND ME. (I have a feeling she didn't mean this in a deep spiritual way!)" (Genesis 16:5 NIV)

**Note:** Sarah had taken God out of the equation throughout this entire process. When she needs God for leverage, she yanks Him back in. This was not an attempt to allow God to work. It was simply for convenience to emphasize her own point and make this argument sway to her side. When we throw in the God card, it stops people dead in their tracks, not allowing them to continue with their voice. Who can argue with the God card?

Setting herself up as the hero in this story, she says, "I PUT MY SLAVE IN YOUR ARMS … I am such an unselfish and giving wife. I cared even more than God. In my unselfishness, I sacrificed my own husband by allowing him to take Hagar as his wife and have sex with her. What is wrong with everyone else?"

The grumbling in the tent is now an all-out fight between Abraham and Sarah. I can hear the anger in their voices and imagine the people within the camp walking closely to the tent to hear the scuffle. The king and the queen of the campground were in all-out marital conflict.

Then Abraham responds, "'YOUR SLAVE IS IN YOUR HANDS,' Abram said. 'Do with her whatever you think best.' Then Sarah mistreated Hagar" (Genesis 16:6 NIV).

Abraham states, "YOUR SLAVE IS IN YOUR HANDS ... this isn't my responsibility. She's your slave, not mine. This was your idea, not mine. I just followed what my wife said to do. I was just trying to keep the peace, and now I get blamed! I'm not going to suffer for your wrongdoing, so do with her what you want."

Sarah says, "I PUT MY SLAVE IN YOUR ARMS."

Abraham replies, "YOUR SLAVE IS IN YOUR HANDS."

I feel as though I'm at a tennis match and the ball is Hagar. From the sidelines, I want to yell, "Stop right here. Everyone take a time-out and think about what is happening."

But Sarah walks away with no change of heart. The anger she was still feeling toward Abraham continued to spill over onto Hagar. It says here, "then Sarah mistreated Hagar." We don't know what that mistreatment looked like, but we know it wasn't good.

## RECAP

Sarah was not getting what she wanted, so she took matters into her own hands. When she does that, she destroys the lives of the people around her. This affected her marriage. It affected Hagar, putting her in a position that compromised her as a woman. It affected the people they were surrounded by who looked up to Sarah and Abraham but were witnesses to the destruction.

We often think that when we choose for ourselves and not for

God, it only affects our lives. But our choices cause a ripple effect of destruction.

## REMEMBERING CAIN AND ABEL GIVES INSIGHT TO SARAH

Do you remember the statement God made to Cain? In Cain's anger and bitterness toward God, he was warned that if he didn't get his act together, things were going to get bad.

Genesis 4:7b reads, "But if you do not do what is right, sin is crouching at your door; it desires to have you, but you must rule over it." And yet, Cain ignored God and killed his own brother.

Sarah needed to heed the same warning. Sin was crouching around her door, her living room, her kitchen, every room of her tent. But because her obsession to have a child blinded her, she allowed sin to creep in and control her at every turn. Her heart was not humbled before God or the people around her. She wanted what she wanted, and it came with a price, a huge price!

## BUT WHO WAS SARAH REALLY?

Let's pause for just a minute and get inside the head and heart of Sarah. Who was she? When I look at this story, I see Sarah as someone who is arrogant and self-centered. My judgmental side, which raises its ugly head often, says, "I would have never acted like that." How could a supposed woman of faith behave like this (nose lifted high in the air)?

We should never judge a book by its cover, yet that is what we do. We look at others and judge them by their actions or behaviors. What we don't see is what led them to this point of a bad decision.

Maybe instead of us turning up our nose at Sarah, we should ask, "Why did Sarah step off the path of faith and step onto a path of uncertainty and confusion, the path of disobedience?"

We know that Sarah was a woman of faith. It states that in

Hebrews 11:11 (NIV). "And by faith even Sarah, who was past childbearing age, was enabled to bear children because she considered him faithful who had made the promise."

How could a woman with faith of this magnitude make such a horrible decision, one that affected so many lives around her? Seemingly, the motivation for her poor decision was her deep desire to have a child. But let's be honest, I know women who are barren, yet it never drove them to this depth of madness. Maybe her insatiable desire to have a child was more than to have someone call her "momma."

No doubt she longed to feel the touch of her child's skin next to hers.

No doubt she too wanted to tell the stories of sleepless nights with a newborn child.

No doubt she wanted to feel the warmth as she nursed her own child.

But would this drive her to madness?

Within the context of her culture, a woman who could not birth a male child was shamed. As in our culture, it assures the passing of the family name, but unlike our culture, it was unacceptable. This pressure had to have been unbearable for her. She was held in high regard within her world, and the lack of a male child reduced her position to just an ordinary woman. And she did not want to be an ordinary woman.

Walking the streets as a barren woman brought shame and whispers within the crowd. She lived a life of unspoken despair, attempting to hold her head high in order not to give way to the shame. Carrying this cultural expectation was like a dark shadow shifting in the sand.

But there was another dark shadow that haunted her throughout her life, her beauty. It too was a curse. She wore this beauty with a cost.

Throughout the story of Abraham and Sarah, their nomadic life led them to different territories. As they would enter these territories, Abraham would make it clear with Sarah that she would be identified as his sister and not his wife. Since Sarah was his half-sister, this was partially true. But this demand he placed on her was for his protection and not hers.

> As he was approaching the border of Egypt, Abram said to his wife, Sarai, "Look, you are a very beautiful woman. When the Egyptians see you, they will say, 'This is his wife. Let's kill him; then we can have her!' So please tell them you are my sister. Then they will spare my life and treat me well because of their interest in you." (Genesis 12:11–13 NIV)

Sarah was Abraham's decoy, therefore not treasured as his wife. Her beauty became his shield. On both occasions stated in the Bible, God intervened as her protector. She was a woman who longed to be loved and treasured by her husband yet treated as a human shield for his own safety. Think about how that would make us feel as women: dishonored, degraded, disrespected, and raped, no matter the culture!

Looking deep within the heart of Sarah, we see a woman.

> We see a woman lost within her world causing her to lose her place because she had no children.

> We see a woman who had been rejected by her husband as he used her as his human shield giving her to other men.

> We see a woman who just wanted to be held in high regard receiving the love from those around her.

If she orchestrated a way to have a child, it might give her more than just the pleasure of being called "mom."

> *"If I could hold this child in my arms, I would be seen. Those around me would open their eyes and see me with the worth in which I long to be seen. Maybe I could see myself as worthy."*

You see judgment and criticism come so quickly from our mouths. When we look at Sarah and her choices, it is easy to judge her actions.

We look at other people who have made such foolish choices, choices that have caused irreparable damage. Why would they choose to do such foolish things? Such hurtful and sinful things? Why? Because they are broken! They are hurting. They are confused.

In the middle of Sarah's brokenness and pain, she made a very damaging and hurtful choice. Her pain became bigger than her God. She lost focus. She lost faith.

There are many times in my life that I too have lost focus because of my pain. And when that pain screams louder than my desire to follow God's way, I too have caused collateral damage. Some of that damage is beyond repair, causing others in my life to limp from my destruction.

My guess is that you have experienced the same. When have you lost focus? When have you lost faith? When have you acted from your brokenness and not from your wholeness?

We like to say that God is sovereign and that God is all-knowing. But sometimes that becomes just a cute little Christian catchphrase for us. It makes us appear as though we know who is in charge and that we place all things in His hands. Or is it really just a way for us to convince ourselves that we have just enough God in our lives and our speech to appear to ourselves and others that we have our Jesus all together? The truth is that we are simply broken! And because of our brokenness, we lose sight of what is right. We lose sight of Jesus. We lose sight! And in our own blindness, we make choices because we are hurting.

That is what Sarah did in this story of destruction. Her actions look foolish, thoughtless, and unthinkable. Because of her brokenness, she lost sight and created a mess with no apparent redeeming value. Jealousy rose within her, fragmenting the relationship between her and her husband, between her most cherished servant and between God. She had spun a web so thick that escaping it seemed impossible.

But God is the God of impossible. Just look at your life … okay, just look at my life. I came from a broken home that produced a broken marriage. I don't need to share the details, but trust me, it was a web so thickly woven that it made no sense that I could escape that brokenness. I made choices that could have destroyed my life permanently. But God saw beyond my brokenness, and He saw His design. He took the weak-minded choices I made and wove His purpose within them. The same happened with Sarah, and I would guess the same has happened with you.

We make choices within our brokenness. We make choices that should destroy our lives and everyone else's lives around us. We make choices that make it seem as though there is no way we will be able to escape the mess we have made.

Go back to the statement Sarah made within the argument with Abraham, a seemingly random statement, "MAY THE LORD JUDGE BETWEEN YOU AND ME." Sarah was in a rage, and she pulled God into the argument. This was a harsh statement of judgment, but what if it were a statement of reminding? A statement to remind her that somewhere amid this huge mess, God was still in the equation. God was still present.

No matter how big the mess we make of our lives, no matter how horrible the choices we make because of our brokenness, God is still there. He often waits for us to finish our fit of brokenness and then scoops us up and mends what we have broken and sets us back on the path toward Him completing His purpose, His plan.

When you act from your brokenness instead of your wholeness, remember that God is in the business of mending what we have broken.

## TALKS WITH EMILEIGH

Oh, Sarah. It would be so easy to read through this account in her season of waiting and be confused by her positioning in the Hall of Faith. It would be too easy to judge her by this poor choice, by her impatience and lack of faith, by her action out of brokenness. And yet, whether in a lighthearted avoidance to share my dessert, in my desire to simply go for a run, or in my longing to have a child, I too have allowed my own desires to cloud my vision and tempt me toward selfishness.

***What are your initial thoughts on Sarah's actions? Do you think she's selfish, or do you sympathize with her desire?***

I am a big fan of Girl Scout cookies. (Who isn't, right?!) A couple years ago, I purchased a few extra boxes for the freezer as a backup and, quite honestly, my own hidden guilty pleasure. This cookie delivery happened to line up with being pregnant when I could barely stomach consuming anything but a very specific smoothie. Cookies were not on my radar at that time. A few months later, however, my familiar craving for those frozen cookies returned. I couldn't wait to dig into my stash. I was excited that I could now consume double the cookies since I was eating for two! Those cookies were going to be the highlight of my week! When it was finally time to move aside the tortellini and frozen fruit, I unearthed the freezer's contents for my prize. I unearthed all the freezer's contents as it turned out because my cookies could not be found. After a somewhat hormonal response, my husband finally admitted that he had eaten my cookies, every one of them. He claimed he was saving me from the temptation because he knew I couldn't stomach them. I'll save you the details and simply say my response to him was neither kind nor filled with love. I wanted my cookies. They only sell them once a year! As I'm sure you can imagine, my husband felt very loved and honored by me in those moments.

No. The true result was far from it. My response was completely unjustified as I let my own desire and fixation on cookies dictate my response to the man I love dearly. I allowed my desire to dictate my emotions, my words, and my response. I let my desire distract me.

***Has there ever been something in your life you've wanted so badly you could almost taste it? Have you had a desire/want in your life you wanted so badly that it distracted you from everything else?***

Sarah also allowed her desire to dictate her emotions, words, and response. As we read in Genesis 16:1, Sarah was barren. Verses before in Genesis 15:5, God tells Abraham that his offspring will outnumber the stars in the sky. If I were Sarah, I might feel a disconnect here. If you're telling my husband he's going to have a lot of children, shouldn't we get started? When is that plan going to get started? God? Hey, God?

Sarah either got tired of waiting or thought she heard God wrong because she acted.

***Has there been something in your life you felt God calling you to, but His timing seemed off? You got tired of waiting? Maybe you thought you heard God wrong?***

I love to run. There is something freeing and uplifting about feeling the wind glide over me, about accomplishing something I didn't think my body was capable of, about the runner's high that can lift my spirits on a tough day.

This ability was one God gave me. He enabled me to run and enjoy it, which I've learned is not necessarily a normal thing. Not everyone can just lace up their tennis shoes and hit the pavement. Not everyone wants to. Not everyone's body can do it.

In recent years, I've learned my body is one of those that simply can't anymore. Years ago, I began to experience a kind of debilitating back pain that has prevented me from doing that which I love, that which I believed was a talent God had given me. I had to quit.

But then I had a plan. My running life became my prayer time.

I used it to pray for others, to talk to God, to lift up those God placed on my mind or I simply saw on the street as I ran. I believed God would give that ability back to me if I prayed hard enough. I, and though it's hard to see the emphasis on the letter I, believed this would work. Any other option was too painful. Looking back on it, I never remember hearing God tell me He'd give it back. Though my prayers were genuine, my intentions were misguided. My own desire stood in the way of what God was doing in me and the path He had.

***When have you operated out of your own accord but tried to use God to justify it? Did Sarah's plan reflect God's will or her own agenda? Did your plan reflect God's will? Who ultimately received the glory?***

I believe Sarah ignored the pause before she acted. She didn't give God the time He planned. She acted because she couldn't see past her obsession. In Genesis 16:2, Sarah states, "the Lord has prevented me from bearing children." She felt that God prevented her from what she desired, so she justified her own plan to take care of it. She didn't give God adequate time to fulfill His plan. She didn't pause to consider how the action she planned would affect those around her.

I often forget to pause to realize how fortunate I am to have completed the miles I have, the people who were lifted in prayer, and the personal accomplishment God did enable through my running. Neither Sarah nor I gave God the opportunity to weigh in on our plan. At the end of verse 16, Sarah decides that "through her I can build a family." Did you catch what I said? Sarah decided. She removed God from the equation. Her selfishness ignored the needs of those around her.

While I have plenty of extra emotions when I physically and mentally need to go for a run, I often ignore how much more I hurt my own family when I hit the pavement. My extra unjustified emotions are selfish, but being unable to pick up my children or complete household tasks due to the added pain after a run is even more selfish.

***What are some decisions you make daily that affect those around you? Your family? Coworkers? Friends?***

Let's fast-forward to the unfolding of Sarah's plan. She got what she planned, and her slave, Hagar, became pregnant. She could now build her family and fulfill God's plan to outnumber the stars.

No, wait. The planner didn't like this unfolding after all. She became bitter. Hagar began to look at Sarah with contempt. In a season that should have been a celebration for a life created, hurt was unearthed instead.

Melody states, "Her selfish choice had a ripple effect of destruction."

I would like to believe that Sarah didn't intend to hurt Hagar or Abraham and certainly not herself, but Sarah was hurting. Sarah's own hurt clouded her vision of those around her. Sarah mistreats Hagar because her own manufactured plan backfired. In fact, the blame game ensues because of Sarah's plan. In Genesis 16:5–6, Sarah blames Abraham, and he passes it back to her. No one takes the responsibility.

***Describe a time you have placed blame on another for a choice you made. What was the result? How could you have handled the circumstance better?***

Often we hurt others simply because our own heart is hurting. Sometimes we hurt others and don't even understand why. Acting in this way can hinder our ability to celebrate others who may have received a blessing that we want. Jealousy is a devious struggle, and it can lead to hurting others.

Sarah's jealousy of Hagar's blessing led her down the path of destruction and pain.

***Has your pain ever robbed you of the ability to celebrate someone else's blessing?***

I'd like to share from my own life one of the most difficult seasons I have and still do walk through. A couple years ago, my husband and I felt the Lord urging us to grow our family. We believed this was His will for us. We surrendered the plan to Him. On the day I found out I was pregnant, it was a day filled with joy. Then after weeks of the normal sickness and all the planning most women begin to do after seeing that positive result, something felt wrong. Something unexpected was about to go against my plan. We lost the baby. The plan took a new trajectory as I now needed to start planning how to grieve, how to process, and how to move past the loss. The plan I thought God had for us now looked very different to me. Did I hear God wrong?

In the excruciating weeks following, several dear friends shared with me their news of expecting. That pain is one too many know yet can hardly explain. It pierces your heart and pulls you in two different directions. While every ounce of you wants to celebrate for others, a part of you is mourning. It can break you down. Thankfully, with some friends, my heart was able to celebrate. However, on a day I thought I was okay, another friend announced her pregnancy. This unexpected announcement, this moment when I should have celebrated, my brokenness crept in like a thief in the night. My seemingly stolen desires were magnified. As a result, I acted in my brokenness and hurt my friend. I allowed my brokenness to become bigger than the blessing.

Sadly, she wasn't the only one I hurt either. My inclination when I'm hurting is to shut down. I'm not sure if Sarah talked to Abraham about how hard it was to be a barren woman, to carry the shame of that among their family and fellow travelers. I'm not sure if she even told Abraham she was hurting. He sure felt it in action though, and he certainly was affected by the consequences of it.

When I walked through this season in my life, I tried to walk it alone. I shut out my husband because I didn't want to voice my pain. In doing so, I took away his opportunity to share and grieve his own pain. It was our loss. It was our hurt. I made it about me. That was selfish. That was my brokenness.

***When have you made a decision from your brokenness, not from your wholeness? When has someone else's pain caused you pain? Have you been hurt by someone else's brokenness?***

It would be easy to stop here and judge Sarah for what we read without spending more time wondering what led her to that point of brokenness. It would be unfair to her not to consider the fragile heart that pushed her toward disobedience. It would be unwise to look simply at her flaws and disregard her placement in the Hall of Faith. Too often, we judge others by their actions and forget to look at their hearts. We don't ask what led them to their decisions and actions. At the same time, others rarely ask us this, so when our hurts rear their ugly head in destructive ways, those we hurt don't understand why. It simply causes a domino effect of hurt. It can cause the ripple effect of destruction.

***How did Sarah's plan affect those around her? Do you think it affected more than Hagar?***

Scripture doesn't tell us how those in the camp responded. Surely they heard the arguing. They inevitably saw the scowls and mistreatment between Sarah and Hagar. There was no denying that Sarah's slave now bore Sarah's husband's child. I wonder if they took sides. I wonder if they sympathized or judged the love triangle.

I would imagine the trio (Sarah, Abraham, and Hagar) would have preferred those in their camp not witness the fight, the struggle, the hurt, and the selfishness, but what if their witness of it all taught the onlookers more about who God is and how we can and should trust Him?

***What if our response to life's hurts and our willingness to share our struggles can bring others toward Jesus?***

I wanted to keep my struggles to myself. Vulnerability does not come easily for me. Transparency is too much work. The fear of appearing weak is risky. However, being selfish with my struggles helps only me. Just like Sarah, helping only me ultimately hurts even me.

***When has someone else's battle promoted growth in you? Healing? Comfort?***

Begrudgingly, I began to share my struggle for both my back and our loss. As I did, I discovered that so many others knew my same pain. My response and my next steps would reflect if I found healing or continued to walk in my brokenness. Once I became transparent though, I had support to help me navigate that battle. I had support to help me keep focused on the One who had and has a bigger, better plan.

I've grown deeper in friendships out of a shared struggle or a newfound ability to be vulnerable. Those deepened levels of friendship are a gift to me. If I'd planned it, neither I nor others would experience the brokenness of loss, infertility, abuse, and hateful words. I do know the intimacy, depth, and growth I've received as a result of my brokenness, and it's invaluable. Perhaps that makes it worth it.

Even as I've struggled to share this difficult season through my writing, God has presented me with opportunities to comfort friends experiencing the exact same struggle, friends who may not have known I was a safe space unless I'd been vulnerable. God has opened doors to use my brokenness to encourage others toward His wholeness. He's also used others who have walked through similar struggles to help me. God has used us to help each other maintain focus. He is a God who mends hearts, restores relationships, and floods souls with indescribable peace. He is a God who weaves together pain and joy for our good and His glory.

***When has your pain caused you to lose focus?***

Sarah had a great faith in the Lord. I have deep trust in the Lord. However, no matter how much we trust in Him, when we think we hear Him say no or when we experience the stinging pain of life's heartaches, we can begin to feel uncomfortable and are at risk of turning from His ways. When we do this, we lose focus.

Sarah stumbled in her need to stay focused. "Her pain became bigger than her God." She lost focus on God's greater plan and unknowingly mapped out her own darkness. She believed something had been taken from her and did everything in her own power to make what she wanted possible. She may even have felt like God told her no to what she desired. She lost focus of God's promises when her own selfishness blinded her. However, God was always present in her brokenness, and He had a purpose for her. What if what Sarah heard as no was simply God saying "not yet"? What if Sarah simply needed to wait more expectantly as God wove together His purpose?

In no way does what neither Sarah nor I walked through diminish the hurt, loss, or pain that any other individual might face. In fact, I think God has allowed each of us only a glimpse of what our sinful world's rocky path can deliver. This is simply my story and Sarah's story and the way God is still using them for His good purposes.

God has given me greater empathy and understanding of the hurt that can make us stumble and greater patience and love toward those Satan is determined to break down. God continues to give me assurance that His plan is greater and, no matter what plans I try to make on my own, He will continue to weave His purpose into them. Each struggle, each battle, and each hurt we face has the power to hurt or heal. Each obstacle along our path of life provides hurdles to stumble over or opportunities to see and hear God's voice. He can weave good purpose into your hurt. He can provide healing in your brokenness. He can redeem you from the evil that simmers within every one of our hearts.

How will you respond to your hurts? How will you use the experiences of your life? Will you keep them hidden and allow them to lead to destruction, or will you surrender to His plans that lead to life?

"I am weary from grief; strengthen me through Your Word. Keep me from the way of deceit and graciously give me Your instruction" (Psalm 119:28–29).

"Call on me in a day of trouble; I will rescue you, and you will honor me" (Psalm 50:15).

# CHAPTER 8

## TAKE A STEP BACK

Take a step back: To withdraw or remove oneself from something, often in order to consider it from a broader or more objective perspective.

—idioms.thefreedictionary.com

Take a step back. Have you ever been told to take a step back? While crowded around a table at the department store loaded with bargains, a voice in the distance says, "Ladies, ladies, take a step back. There is plenty to go around!

Standing in the aisle at the grocery store, a group of crowded onlookers takes a step back, allowing the injured person room to breathe.

Years ago, I was in Boston visiting my son when we decided to go to Mike's Pastry for their world-famous cannoli. If you have ever entered Mike's Pastry on Hanover Street in the North End of Boston, you will know when I say, "Everyone needs to take a step back!" After waiting in the extensive line that wrapped around the outside of the building, it was now time to enter the kingdom of cannoli. Pushing open the door, we were faced with a swarm of impatient customers anxious for their first bite of the creamy filling wrapped in a perfectly crispy shell. In their impatience, they have lost sight of their ability to form a single line. They crowded around the pastry counter until someone from behind the counter yelled, "Step back, people."

At some point, we have all been asked to take a step back. Whether that was a physical step, emotional step, or spiritual step, stepping back gives us perspective. It gives us a clearer understanding of our current situation. But stepping back is one of the hardest things for us to do. We would prefer to be up front and center to whatever drama is catching the eye of the crowd. We want to be "in the know" or be partied to the "well-informed." This stepping back is typically not a voluntary action. It is forced upon us by someone telling us to take a step back, or we are thrown into a situation in which the only step we can take is back.

In the book of Genesis, we read about a woman who was told to "step out" and then "step back." When she stepped back, it gave her the perspective she needed to save her own life and the life of her unborn child. The chaos of someone else's life became the chaos of her own life. She was an obedient servant, but her obedience resulted in her being pushed from her home, finding herself stepping back to allow her to gain a perspective that would change her life forever. When she stepped back, she found God.

As we completed chapter seven, we learned that Sarah and Abraham couldn't have children. Because of her hurt, Sarah makes a choice from her brokenness, therefore taking things in her own hands. Sarah then gives her slave, Hagar, as a wife to Abraham, causing Abraham and Hagar to take a walk on the wild side. And now Hagar is pregnant. "When she (Hagar) knew she was pregnant, (here it comes), SHE BEGAN TO DESPISE HER MISTRESS" (Genesis 16:4 NIV).

We don't really know why Hagar began to despise Sarah, but she did. Maybe her contempt for Sarah was brought on by Sarah's dominance of her as a master, therefore regarding her as property and not as a person. Whatever the reason was for Hagar to despise Sarah, there was a conflict that arose between the two of them. Jealousy seems to have crept in like a thief in the night, stealing their confidence as women and their kindness toward one another. As women, we know all too well what competition with another woman results in. Whether that is competition over a man, a job, or using our children as a pawn in the game, the competition can form a coating of jealousy, causing our hearts to harden and our blood to run green. The rose-colored glasses that we wore are no longer rose-colored, but green with envy, causing us to perform in ways we never thought possible. In this story, the green ran deep, resulting in disdain toward one another. Because of this disdain, life was lost, relationships severed, and hearts destroyed.

## BATTER UP!

In the previous chapter, three batters stepped up to the plate: Sarah, Abraham, and a mystery batter. As Sarah stood alongside home plate, she drew her bat, getting into hitting position. As the pitcher threw the pitch, it flew over the plate at such a speed that Sarah took a swing and missed. Walking back to the dugout, she brushed passed her husband, Abraham, with feelings of inadequacy and contempt. Abraham then stood next to the plate, positioning his feet for a home run. As he pulled back his bat, preparing for the pitch, the ball was released from the pitcher's hand. As the ball drew near the plate, Abraham swung with all his might, but to no avail. The bat narrowly missed the target, resulting in the second strike.

The mystery third batter was now making their way to the plate.

> Folks, our third batter is climbing out of the dugout. I can't quite make out their identity, but it seems as though it is a woman. Yes, folks, it is! It's Hagar! Our third batter comes from far away. Her land is not the land of her teammates. Her culture differs, as does her dress and her way of life. She is not free but enslaved to those around her. As she makes her way to the plate, her eyes show no confidence in her ability to play the game.

The pitch was thrown. Strike three and you're out!

The crowd began to roar. Contempt and anger was thrown like trash from the bleachers. Someone had to be out, and that someone was Hagar.

## SHE'S OUT, SO SHE FLED

The contempt that Sarah had toward Hagar drove Hagar away. "Then Sarai mistreated Hagar; so, she fled from her" (Genesis 16:6 NIV).

When Hagar realized that Abraham had given Sarah permission to treat her however she desired, she knew she needed to leave quickly. Sarah was angry, causing Hagar to cower in fear. As she fled to her tent to gather her belongings, her fear gave way to sadness as she gathered what little things she had. Reaching for her waterskin, she filled it with as much water as it would hold, hoping it would be enough to sustain her until she could find more. She grabbed a few small loaves of bread, put them into her sheepskin sack, and then slung the sack and the waterskin over her shoulder. As she stepped to the opening of the tent, she tried to embrace the world in front of her. How would she survive? How would she provide for herself? As she placed her hand on her stomach, she felt the small movement of her unborn child. Would she give birth to this child?

In an instant, the determination for life welled up inside her. Survival was not for her sake but for the sake of her unborn child. She had to survive!

## PEOPLE WITHOUT FACES

Stepping from the entrance of her tent, she placed her feet onto the dirt filled streets of the campground. This was a daily journey for her as she completed her tasks as a slave. But this day was different. As she made her way down the street, it was as though the people she once knew became people without faces. In her shame, she struggled to look up afraid to see disappointment staring back at her. Approaching the entrance of the campground, she knew that once her foot crossed the boundary line, she would be straddling the familiar and the unknown. Familiarity, yet brokenness shadowed her past. Unfamiliarity and fear illuminated her future.

The path she chose was the road to take her back to Egypt. With a long journey ahead, she began to process her destination. She had been gone from Egypt for such a long time that the hopes they would take her in dashed. She was now pregnant with her master's child. Would anyone want her?

So often we walk through this world with the same feelings of displacement. We want to belong, to fit in. We want a tribe or a posse, a group of friends to call our own. We will even gather people around us who are toxic because we want that feeling that we are loved.

Perhaps this is the same for Hagar. She had been placed in an environment that was not her own. She had been purchased as a slave and torn from her Egyptian family. She worked hard within her new environment to gain the approval of her owners, her new people. She obeyed even to the point of disregarding her own self and sleeping with her master. This may have given her even deeper hopes that she would be a part of her new world. But it only pushed her out to the point that she was now standing in between both worlds and yet not belonging to either.

As she tried to wrap her mind around her current situation, she realized it didn't matter if anyone would accept her in Egypt if she couldn't make it there alive.

Alive? How was she going to stay alive? If she didn't make it, then neither was her child. Somehow, she must make it!

## THE WALKING BEGINS

While stepping beyond the edge of the camp, her feet shifted onto familiar soil. She had walked this road many times to gather water for her master, so she knew if she could make it to the spring near the road of Shur, she could gather her thoughts and make a more definitive plan. Shoring up the goal gave her hope. All she had to do was make it to the spring of water.

Often, we project so far out that we become overwhelmed, causing the task or the destination to seem impossible to reach. We become paralyzed in our fear, causing us not to move. I have often learned that when I am overwhelmed with a task at hand or a season of life causing chaos, if I break it down into bite-sized pieces, then survival seems more palatable. Big pictures overwhelm!

Trying to stay focused on what was before her and shrinking her journey to reach the well, Hagar had no choice other than to move. As she stepped away from the camp, her familiar life began to fade.

Have you ever been pushed from the life with which you were familiar? Sometimes that push is so hard that it leaves your head spinning. Once your head settles, you are left feeling as though you don't belong anywhere. You can't return from where you have come from, and moving forward leaves you walking within uncharted territory. The lack of knowing which direction you need to head leaves you feeling alone and abandoned.

I am currently in a situation very similar to this one. The life in which I have known feels as though it is pushing me out. If I leave this place of familiarity, I will be forced to navigate uncharted territory. Sometimes the familiar feels best no matter how messed up it may be because I know how to navigate it. There is comfort in our dysfunction. But when I am forced to navigate the unfamiliar, my fears kick in, causing me to become stuck in the middle. I can't go back or forward. I can only pause!

## THE PAUSE

I hate pausing. I feel as long as I am in movement, that I am still alive. When I pause and quiet myself, I am afraid of what I will find. I don't want to meet my fears face-to-face, so I would rather keep in motion running from what is real.

Pausing pushes us to face the reality.

Pausing pushes us to think.

Pausing pushes us to pray.

Time and time again, God pushes us to pause at our own well so we can meet Him. If I am promised to see God as I pause at my well, what causes me to be so fearful?

Here is the fear. We live our lives trying to figure out the past and structuring out the future that a pause in the middle makes us feel as though we will fall in like quicksand. If I stay in one place for too long, then I will be swallowed up, never to be given the opportunity to move forward.

It is in the pause where we meet Jesus.

It is in the pause when we can evaluate our chaos, giving us direction and clarity.

It is in the pause when we can hear Him speak.

Pausing with Jesus is a priceless pause.

When is the last time you paused at the well before Jesus? Does your current life of chaos hold you back from that pause?

What if you paused for ten minutes and purposely turned off any noise in your life? What would you hear? Would you hear your voice continuing to gab, or would you hear the voice of Jesus calming your soul?

## HAGAR'S PAUSE

As Hagar's feet grew weary, she approached a spring of water. This well was perfect timing as her waterskin was empty and the soles of her feet were tired as well as the soul of her heart. On this journey to the well, she had pondered all the twists and turns of her current life situation.

So often in life, our waterskin sack is empty before we seek fresh spring water. The droplets of water settled into the bottom of our waterskin have grown stale and unpalatable. Instead of seeking the refreshing spring water throughout the day, we wait until there is no nourishment remaining before we cry out to God. But what if we filled our sack throughout the day, calling on Jesus, who gives us living water? It's a simple prayer, "Jesus, I need you!"

> but whoever drinks the water I give them will never thirst. Indeed, the water I give them will become in them a spring of water welling up to eternal life (John 4:14 NIV).

Hagar carefully removed her leather satchel that held her belongings. As she laid the satchel on the ground, she leaned her worn body against a rock. Resting against the rock, she slid her hand over her stomach. As she did, she felt the undeniable truth that a human life was growing inside of her. Her mind drifted to the what-ifs: What if I had refused Sarah when she told me to sleep with her husband? What if, once I was in Abraham's tent, I had convinced him that this wasn't the right thing to do? In the quiet of this moment, her mind quieted. In her pause, she heard a voice.

> The angel of the Lord found Hagar near a spring in the desert; it was the spring that is beside the road to Shur. And he said, "Hagar, slave of Sarai, where have you come from, and where are you going?" (Genesis 16:7, 8 NIV).

## WHERE HAVE YOU COME FROM, AND WHERE ARE YOU GOING?

Two simple questions:

- Where have you come from?
- Where are you going?

Two questions that changed the trajectory of her life.

When someone asks us the question, "Where have you come from?" our answer is simple. We answer with, "I came from my house," "I am from Illinois," or "I grew up in Florida." These answers are simple enough to satisfy the inquirer.

When someone asks us the question, "Where are you going?" again, our answer is simple. We answer, "I am heading home," "I am going to California on vacation," or "I am heading to the store." But sometimes these questions can have a life-altering impact.

These questions the angel asked of Hagar drove deep into a well of sorrow and discontent for her.

## WHERE HAVE YOU COME FROM?

Although this question seemed simple enough for Hagar, emotional complexities filled her answer. Does she respond with betrayal and heartache? Does she respond with confusion and hopelessness? Does she tell the angel she is pregnant with her master's child? Or does she just explain the coordinates on the map?

When we think of this question for ourselves, we too are faced with the emotional complexities that an answer may entail. We have worked hard to forget the past to live as joyous as possible in the present. So our answer to that question may also be filled with stories of betrayal and hurt, stories that we long to forget, stories that we are determined not to define us. We have chosen to build a fortress around us, convinced that a wall will protect us from our past. But does that wall protect or does that wall give us reason to deny?

## WHERE ARE YOU GOING?

The inquiry from the angel did not stop with the question, "Where have you come from?" but continued with the question, "Where are you going?"

Notice that she doesn't answer the question as to where she is going. The answer is either not recorded or she simply doesn't answer it. If she would have responded, she would have possibly said Egypt since that was her r origin of birth and it was also the direction she was walking. Egypt was her culture, her way of life therefore making sense that she would head that direction

But the truth is that she didn't know where she was going. She could verbalize her destination, but she was fearful. If Egypt were her destination, would she be accepted? The child she carried was a multicultural child. Would her child be accepted? Would her child belong? And what about her? Would she be looked upon as a traitor because she left her home? Would the slaves of the lower-class jeer at her because she was of a higher slave rank? Maybe that's why she didn't answer the angel. Perhaps she really didn't know where she was going. And she for sure didn't know if she wanted to go there.

So the perplexity of Hagar's situation is that she was stuck. Her pause at the well screamed she was stuck in the middle. Returning from where she had come from was scary, and moving forward to where she was going was not much better.

## I'M RUNNING AWAY

> "I'm running away from my mistress Sarai," she answered (Genesis 16:8).

Have you ever run away? I can think back to my own childhood and remember a funny story when my sister ran away. I was probably four and she was seven years old when my mother came home with a gift for each of us. Money was scarce, making gifts from our mother rare. On this day, Mom had brought each of us a pair of sunglasses. Sis and I grabbed those sunglasses as though someone had given us the world. We walked away with pride in our steps as the new owners of a beautiful pair of sunglasses. At some point, my sister set her glasses on the couch. When she returned to the couch, she accidentally sat on her glasses, breaking them into pieces. As I watched anxiously from the kitchen, I realized not only were her glasses broken, but so was her heart. She soon pleaded with our mother to buy her a new pair.

I am not sure what was happening within the heart of my mother, but looking back on my childhood, she was probably living in fear of my father that she had purchased the glasses in the first place. The request from my sister was met with a no from my mother. The next thing I knew, my sister grabbed her plastic bank with coins rattling inside and ran outside the door and down the street. As she walked out the front door, she looked at our mother and said she was running away.

That day, in her anger and hurt, my sister left our house, hoping to never return. Not long after her departure, my mother discovered she was about two houses down playing at our neighbor's house.

In attempts to survive the abuse of our father, departure or running away became a regular thing for me. But since I had nowhere to go, I would find myself returning to heartache and confusion.

In the same way, Hagar was running away from the pain and hurt she was experiencing in the abuse of Sarah. She was running away from the confusion and rejection. She was running away from humiliation and hatred.

But Hagar was not the only character in this story with deep emotional pain. We see Sarah as the bad guy (girl), but bad guys hurt too. That is why they are bad.

These are not simply characters in a play acting out a story for our pleasure reading. These are real women with real hurts: women longing to be loved, women longing to be honored and respected, and women longing to matter in this world. Yes, their culture surrounding them is different from ours, but just because their culture was different doesn't mean that their need to be loved is any different than our need to be loved.

Two women are reacting out of their brokenness, not their wholeness. We can point and shoot, but we need to be aware of our target.

Hagar knew there was more to her story than simply a coordinate on a map. So she responded with, "I'm running away."

## MY STORY

As the abuse in my home worsened, I found that running away provided safety for me. I would often grab my bicycle, attempting to escape the pain. This is an excerpt from one of my journal writings written in January 2018. It is titled "Share the Road."

> The day I chose the left turn (at the end of my driveway), I rode (my bike) miles from my home. It was new territory for me but a lovely ride of new discoveries. As I was riding down a hill on a busy street in South County, St. Louis, I was forced to stop at a stoplight. As I was waiting for the traffic light to give me permission to cross the intersection, I noticed an elderly woman walking along the sidewalk, carrying a sack of groceries. She was attempting to get my attention.
>
> My response was quick. I was a young girl who longed to be noticed. And that day, this woman noticed me. I loved that feeling.
>
> Once I crossed the street to see what I could help her with, I realized she wanted me to help carry her sack of groceries to her home. This should have made a young girl feel unsafe and guarded. But there was nothing unsafe or guarded for me that afternoon. I leaned my bicycle against the light pole, fiddled with the combination on my lock, and attached my bicycle safely to the pole.
>
> As we walked up the hill to her house, I carried her bag of groceries, and we talked about life. It was a sweet, innocent conversation between an elderly woman and a young girl. I never told her about

> the dark cloud because in these moments, that dark cloud no longer existed for me. As we approached her humble home, I handed her the sack of groceries. I was going to be on my way back to my bicycle to continue my journey when she invited me into her home. I was a little hesitant in doing so but was also starving for conversation. The simple fears I had quickly dissipated.
>
> As I entered her home, we stepped into her small yet immaculate kitchen. She sweetly asked for my aid to put away the groceries. Once I completed the task, I proceeded to excuse myself from her home when she asked if I would like some cookies and lemonade. Little did she realize how hungry and thirsty I was. I graciously accepted her invitation, and we sat aside her 1970s Formica top table with matching metal chairs, continuing to talk about various topics as I enjoyed the homemade cookies and lemonade.
>
> Once I had finished, we said our goodbyes. I had a spring in my step as I made my way down her concrete stairs.
>
> At this moment, this woman had "shared the road" with a hurting, lonely cyclist. I would never see her again, but she was an angel who not only provided nourishment for my physical body in the form of lemonade and cookies, but this angel provided much deeper nourishment. She provided nourishment for my soul. God had given her the opportunity to "share the road" with me that day, and she obliged.

If my angel had asked me that day, "Where did you come from?" I would not have been able to answer that question with deep clarity of the hurt and pain I was suffering in that season of my life. I would not have been able to tell my angel that I was running away to find safety. I simply would have replied with a finger point in the direction of my house.

There is a chance that Hagar may not have been able to answer that question with deep clarity either. When hurt and confusion overtake our lives, survival is all we have. The ability to clearly state or process our current state of being is impossible. Choices from brokenness take center stage. We should never expect that we will make the wisest choices during this time of crisis. I once heard a statement that I captured and tucked in my pocket, "We do the best we can with the resources that we currently have available."

When those resources are hurt and pain, we still do the best we can. If other people judge the choices we make, remind them that they are not "walking in our shoes." Destruction and despair filled Hagar's shoes. That was the only way she knew to walk.

## GOD SPOKE AT THE PAUSE

Pausing at the well brought Hagar physical relief, but as she paused, it brought to reality the circumstances she was in. Her life seemed hopeless and left her feeling lost and alone.

Sound familiar? Often God brings us to a pause at the well. Within this pause, He brings us nourishment for our physical bodies. But also within that pause, we are faced with the reality of the hurt and pain our souls are in. As Hagar paused at the well, it gave God space to speak. And sometimes those words bring fear for our future.

Pausing at the well reminds us that we don't like where we have come from, and we for sure don't like where we are going. But we know we can't stay where we are. As we pause at the well, we ask, "God, why can't I stay here at the well? I have everything I need: plenty of water for my refreshment, no one I feel enslaved to, and the opportunity to raise my child on my own."

As a young girl, sitting in the kitchen of the elderly woman with my cookies and lemonade, I felt safe. I wanted to stay because she was sweet and kind. I loved her cookies, and the lemonade was refreshing. But I knew I must return to my bicycle chained around the pole. I couldn't stay in the safety. I either needed to move forward or return to my home.

God looks at us with eyes of compassion. He knows we feel safe by the well, but He wants more for our lives than just the feeling of safety. He knows for Him to use us; we must go somewhere. We must move.

## GO BACK

> Then the angel of the Lord told her, 'Go back to your mistress and submit to her' (Genesis 16:8 NIV).

*No way, God! I can't go back! I just can't go back!* I know that is how I would respond. The thought of going back and facing the woman who drove me from the camp would be the epitome of anxiety for me. So why does the angel tell Hagar to go back? Again, it is not clear. But there are times when we cannot move forward until we take a step back.

I know this goes against everything society tells us. It goes against what we often think God is telling us. But there are situations when the best and deepest healing comes from a backward move. A backward move means there are unresolved issues. Unresolved issues equal pain, pain we have often shoved deep into our soul because dealing with it means more pain and we are tired of hurting.

There are times when God moves best when we move most.

In 2014, I took on the challenge of my life. I had paused at the well after running away from my hurt and brokenness. My life was in complete chaos. I was running because the pain of a hurting marriage, but as I ran from that pain, I found myself in a pool of pain from the abuse of my father. The spiral was real, and I had made a mess of things. Amid my destruction, I knew God was saying, "Go back."

*"Go back to the pain and heartache from your childhood. Go back to the memories you have buried. Go back to the emotions. Go back to the broken relationships in your family caused by the abuse of your father. Go back."*

I cried out to God to not make me go back because I was afraid of what I would find. But God made a promise to me. He promised me that no matter how deep I had to go for healing, He would never let go. And He didn't. Because I chose to follow God's path back, I am now able to take my movement forward. I am no longer stuck in that pain of a little child, but I live triumphed from the healing God has done within me. If I had never gone back, I would have never healed.

The running and escaping that we do in life only accomplishes exactly that, running and escaping. In my running, I became a very guarded woman. I filled myself with religious piety and a critical spirit to ward off anyone who wanted to get close. My marriage was breaking, and so was my soul, but no one knew. I used scripture and my role as a pastor's wife as the concrete blocks around my heart. No one could get in, and I, for sure, would not allow myself to be revealed so I could protect the abused little girl within me.

When God told me to go back, I crumbled to the floor. My body shook in fear. With each step back, I was faced with memories of abuse and the emotions that ran alongside those memories. But as I allowed my wall to be taken down piece by piece, healing became the path I chose.

Is it worth it to go back? Absolutely!
Is it difficult to go back? Absolutely!
Will you heal when you go back? Absolutely!

Is God telling you to take a step back today? Is He trying to tell you to hold on tight, knowing the other side of healing is worth the journey? I can't answer that for you. But I know that I can say with all integrity that it is worth the walk.

## TALKS WITH EMILEIGH

"9-1-1. What's your emergency?"

"My son and his friend are missing."

"Can you tell me your son's name, ma'am?"

"Lucas."

"Can you tell me what he's wearing?"

"I … I don't remember."

On August 31, 2021, my son, Lucas, and his friend went missing.

Who can even think about stepping back when you're stopped dead in your tracks? I remember the first time my Spider-Man-loving son, Lucas, saw his favorite superhero at Disney World. He was starstruck, dead in his tracks, unable to take his eyes off the hero he asked to read about daily, the superhero he not only dressed like but also imitated as he shot webs everywhere. When he turned three and asked how old he was, he would hold up his thumb, pointer finger, and pinky, palm up, to show you three fingers in the pose of a web-shooting hand. When the workers at Disneyland urged the extensive line waiting to meet Spider-Man to "take a step back," no one moved. It's almost as if they couldn't hear the direction being given to them because they were hyper-focused on the goal in sight. Lucas's eyes were set on his hero, and little else around him mattered. He had to get to Spider-Man, but to do so, we all had to take a step back, primarily to give the man some breathing room and then collectively make a move forward one painstakingly long step at a time.

***When have you been asked to take a step back? Have you ever needed to tell someone else to take a step back?***

Genesis 16:4 tells us that Hagar begins to despise Sarah. This response intrigues me. It makes sense to us as readers that Sarah became bitter toward Hagar for receiving the blessing she wanted. For Hagar to revile Sarah though is quite another story. Hagar, now impregnated by her master, was likely now even closer to the inner circle than before. Perhaps now she was too close for comfort. She's part of the newfound love triangle, target of Sarah's earnest desire to build a family through any means necessary and the victim to the little regard of collateral damage. Hagar's very life, any sense of freedom she may have clung to, was collateral damage. Perhaps once this close, she couldn't see past what was right in front of her. She may have stopped dead in her tracks, and her new forced future clouded peripheral vision. Given the circumstance, it would be easy to be hyper-focused on the new predicament and struggle to process much of the surrounding factors.

Just like Lucas couldn't see past his need to meet his favorite hero, Sarah couldn't see past her need to start a family, and Hagar couldn't see past her need to live her own life and make her own choices. She held a deeper need to be seen.

***Why do you think Hagar despised Sarah? Have you ever had a disagreement with another female friend and felt no resolution? How did you respond? Flee? Confront? Avoid?***

My inclination leans toward Hagar, blaming Sarah for her current situation. Sarah took the first swing. Sarah missed because she operated in her own strength. What Sarah thought she wanted turned out to be a double-strike. (Yes, I'm aware that's not a real thing.) Not only did Hagar now have the baby in her womb that Sarah wanted, but Hagar also had been given Sarah's husband. The odds weren't looking good for Sarah. Sarah's brutal strike put Hagar directly in the game, whether she wanted to be or not.

***Have you ever blamed someone else for your problem? Did playing the blame game make the situation better or worse? How did that person respond?***

Scripture gives us minimal detail about Abraham's role in this narrative. Upon the surface, we see that he takes Hagar as his wife and gets her pregnant and then essentially tells Sarah to deal with the resulting problem on her own. Abraham certainly isn't earning an RBI here! Even Hagar, now his wife and mother to Abraham's unborn first child, receives no support, at least none that is recorded.

***When have you ever felt unsupported during a crisis? When have you shown or someone else shown you support even after a poor choice?***

My husband loves ham and beans. I'm not a fan and rarely make them, so it's not a perfected recipe for me. Several years ago, I decided to make them for him and our friend. I was so proud of myself for soaking the beans, adding the additional spices, and putting in that extra effort and love to do something kind. I would later discover that I hadn't soaked the beans long enough prior to cooking and they were completely undercooked. They both tease me to this day, and to be honest, it's a happy memory. Why? Because I discovered the beans were undercooked. Both men ate every bite of their meal without saying a word! They ate them not because my meal was delicious or because I had done something right. Truly, my mistake was innocent. They ate the meal because they support and love me, even in my failure. I gladly take the teasing now because their support meant so much. Their silence was them supporting me.

***Did Abraham's lack of support intensify the exchange between these two emotion-filled women? What impact did Abraham's lack of support have when Sarah made a poor choice, when Hagar needed her child's father to stand up for her, or when the love triangle's dynamic was spiraling out of control?***

I happen to believe Abraham was a godly, righteous man and would like to believe he heeded God's lead as often as he was able. Thus, I wonder if Abraham's silence in this narrative were simply part of God's plan. Was Abraham silent in this exchange because it wasn't his game to umpire, but God's intentions and plans were much bigger than any of the three could realize?

***Do you perceive Abraham's silence as a lack of support or as part of God's bigger plan?***

Poor Hagar was the final strike, and she took ownership of the failure and shame. She felt like she was out of options and the situation had become too great for her to see clearly. She needed to take a step back, but in the thick of the tension, it was too hard to do.

Just like Sarah, life wasn't going as planned, so Hagar hatched her own plan and stepped out on her own and away from her problems. She could no longer bear the shame.

***When have you bore the shame for someone else's choice(s)?***

Hagar stepped away and set a new goal, the spring. Sometimes small goals are the only moves we feel capable of making; small goals are more attainable when so much stands between us and the end. For Lucas, it was the never-ending line of other fans standing in front of him. For Hagar, it was the uncertainty of everything weighing on her. It was the unknown gripping her in place.

***Have you ever been in a circumstance so overwhelming that you felt paralyzed by fear?***

The playdate was over, and his friend needed to go home. They weren't done playing yet, and thus a final game of hide-and-seek ensued. It was a game until the hiding lasted just a little too long. The search began, and the search party gradually increased. Kids checked their usual play areas. Parents checked the best hiding places in their homes. We made phone calls and divided up. There were two strong-minded yet beautifully innocent five-year-olds officially missing.

There was no hide-and-seek game for Hagar's growing belly. There was no hiding her fear. Did they even notice she'd gone missing? She couldn't focus on that though when there was a spring in sight, a spring that was attainable for her. This spring would provide temporary relief in her overwhelming circumstances. She just had to get there.

***What or where do you find your spring? Your refreshment? Refueling to keep moving forward?***

I looked down to see my husband calling on his way home from work, so I answered and robotically said, "We can't find Lucas. I don't know where he is. I can't talk." Then I hung up.

I cannot even begin to imagine the paralyzing fear that came over him after that phone call. For me, those were the only words I could muster up. I was becoming paralyzed by my fear.

And yet somehow amid the excruciating trial, I saw hope as I stood at the end of my driveway, panicked by the unknown. As I looked, I saw kids, neighbors, and friends stepping up for me, my friend, and our missing boys. The emotion it provoked was almost too much. Seeing that level of support, seeing so many drop what may have been in front of them to step in for our circumstance, was a spring of refreshment. It was the encouragement needed to keep moving forward.

Have you ever run away from something? Why and how did it feel?

As Hagar reached her source of refreshment at the well, the big question posed was, "Where do you come from?" For me, the big question became, "What is he wearing?"

Hagar felt the need to be vulnerable in this scenario. She didn't say Canaan or Egypt. She didn't mention her physical whereabouts, but in what I imagine to be a relieved sigh, she shared with this stranger a glimpse into her emotional condition. What she received in response would change the trajectory of her life. When she paused at the well for physical rest, it gave God the opportunity to step in.

***Have you ever experienced God's presence in a powerful way?***

As my frazzled mind tried to make sense of the fears and worries circling around me, I heard a still, small voice. That voice placed a sense of calm over me that I still struggle to explain. I paused. I listened. I took a step back from my circumstance. I stepped out of my emotional constraints. In that pause, I received peace, and in an instant, I remembered exactly what my son was wearing that day.

Hagar was met in her pause by an angel of the Lord. Melody was met in her pause by a kind woman bearing cookies. I was met in my pause by a newfound sense of peace. For us all, God was present.

When the angel of the Lord met Hagar, she was tired. Melody was hungry and starving for conversation. Both women wanted physical nourishment, but God knew they needed something more. They needed spiritual nourishment, and only the Lord who continues to show up could provide that. His presence holds the power to provide everything we need. "The Lord is my shepherd, I lack nothing" (Psalm 23:1).

***In what ways does God nourish you spiritually?***

In my moment of panic, I wasn't sure how to pray. The words simply wouldn't come. In those moments, I invited others to pray for me. When they did, I felt it. When we forget how to pray, God can use others He's placed in our life to do it for us. On this afternoon, He used the prayers of friends to nourish my spirit.

I could have easily missed this opportunity. I could have easily forgotten to pause—pause and remember others who could help, pause; and let God step in.

If Hagar hadn't paused at the well, she would have missed an encounter with God and the chance to walk in His plan for her. Little did she know that He had a plan for her bigger than her nearsighted, hurting heart could see. Her "pause at the well" presented two uncharted roads, paralyzed by all that had happened and the hurt she now carried or rest in His plan for her and her unborn child. She had to pause long enough to determine if she would choose to simmer in her brokenness or take a step in learning to trust. She had to determine if she would move forward where she felt she would be safe or where God told her to go.

***Have you ever stayed where it was safe instead of going where God called to go?***

When Hagar set out on her journey, I assume she was fearful of the unknown, yet now she is being told to return where her hurts began. Perhaps this induced more fear. Maybe it felt more comfortable to rest at the well in her despair than to risk even deeper hardship. Melody wanted to stay for more cookies, but she had to return home. Both chose to follow God's lead, and both could have missed His grander plan if they hadn't paused long enough.

### Sharing the Road

The moment I was told our boys had been found, all I could do was look up and say, "Thank You, Jesus." Fear, worry, and the voice of Satan trying to drag me into a pit were replaced by the resounding voice of God's promises for peace. I later reflected on this verse, "You will keep the mind that is dependent on you in perfect peace, for it is trusting in you. Trust in the Lord forever, because in the Lord, the Lord himself is an everlasting rock" (Isaiah 26:3–4).

The mom of Lucas's friend missing with him that day is a dear friend of mine, and on that afternoon, we were united in a new way. I can't speak for her emotions or potential takeaways from the day, but I do know we walked a road together that will stick with us for years to come. I'm certain we both would have preferred to avoid this experience, but where would the life application for Hagar's decision to run away be then? That day, we shared the road God paved for us, and we are both grateful He protected our boys.

As it turns out, our boys shared quite the journey together that day as well. They were found inside my friend's car after having walked about a mile. They'd been sharing Oreos and drinking milk from whiskey glasses with no awareness of the dangers that lurked or of the many individuals who'd been searching for them. In their innocent minds, they weren't lost at all. Their growing friendship is a precious gift, and I believe God intends for them to share the road of life for many more adventures. One day, they may be clinking those glasses again with a stack of Oreos in hand, thanking God for the road He paved for them.

The outcome of the day reminds me now of a beautiful promise. No matter how lost we may feel, no matter how scary or desperate our circumstances may become, we are never lost to God. He has a path paved for us, perhaps even with Oreos and milk to dip them in at the end. He had eyes on our boys as we searched for them. He led Melody toward the temporary nourishment she needed. He grasped a hurting Hagar and held her tightly.

***Do you feel lost now?***

Reach out to the Lord. He's standing with open arms, anxious to welcome you home and willing to provide the spiritual nourishment you need. If you've never surrendered your heart to Him, you can do that right now. He's just waiting for you to choose the right road.

I'm certain as readers you want to know how we reacted when our boys returned home. Well, just as the Lord rejoices in Luke 15:1–7 when His lost sheep is found, our boys were welcomed home with open, rejoicing arms (and quite a few tears from me). Lucas was also put under Mom's constant surveillance for an extended period of time!

When Hagar chose to heed the Lord's guidance back to her mistress and chose to trust the Lord's plan, I can just picture the Lord rejoicing for his sheep, once feeling lost, now found.

***Take a step back and walk away refreshed.***

Silence can be part of God's plan. It can be an opportunity for God to speak into our circumstances. Silence without a true pause though is simply silence. To heed God's lead, we must fully pause and wait for Him to fill the void. In it, fears can dissipate, and healing can begin. He invites us to bring our pain and brokenness to His feet so that in His presence, He can replace it with peace.

He's seeking you with open arms, and if you're feeling lost, I pray His all-consuming love will nourish you. Your soul is never lost to the One who created you.

# 9

# BEFORE YOU WALK BACK

Leaning against the well, Hagar heard the words, "go back." Just two words caused deep angst inside her. As she focused on those two words, it caused a near-miss in hearing the following words from the angel, "and submit to her" (Genesis 16:9 NIV). Hearing the word *submit* caused Hagar's stomach to twist and turn. Grateful that her stomach was empty at that moment, she began an internal conversation with herself.

> *Submit? I have already submitted to that woman and look where it has gotten me. I submitted to the point that I have lost control of my own life. It has driven me from my surroundings, as oddly comforting they were, and has caused me to face being the mother of a child that Sarah will abhor from her jealous soul. I don't want to go back, and I definitely don't want to submit to her.*

Submission to our enemy is an unfair notion. They are our enemy for a reason, causing feelings of betrayal and hurt. To submit to an enemy is like writing a death sentence for our soul. But for some reason, God felt as though that was the best move for Hagar at that point in her life.

Submission to my enemy is an oxymoron in my books. I submit only to those I trust for my own emotional health. I can even adjust to the idea of loving my enemy because I have learned to love my enemy from afar, reaching an understanding that I can pray for them but I don't have to hug them. I'm all right with that. But submission is an entirely different approach. Submission pushes me to be near my enemy to know what I need to submit to. And I prefer to stay far away from those of distaste.

Scripture speaks otherwise. Scripture after scripture speaks about loving our enemies, and most of these come from the New Testament, as Jesus turned our world upside-down with the "enemy loving" concept. But one of the hardest scriptures for me comes from the Old Testament. "If your enemy is hungry, give him food to eat; if he is thirsty, give him water to drink. In doing this, you will heap burning coals on his head, and the Lord will reward you" (Proverbs 25:21–22 NIV).

What does *heaping burning coals* mean? To be honest, it would give me great satisfaction to place these coals on the head of my enemy. That might teach them to be nice to those around them, including me. But as I looked deeper into this coal thing, I learned that heaping burning coals on the head of their enemy was an act of kindness and submission. Years ago in Bible times, hot burning coals were needed to cook food for their family. These coals were often carried on top of their head in a vessel as they were transferred to the hearth. If they passed a neighbor in need and their coals were burning low, they would graciously place some of their hot coals in the pan for their neighbor. This was a gesture of kindness and an opportunity to let their neighbor know they were cared for.

The same was true if you chose to do this for your enemy. If you heap burning coals on your enemy's head, it would communicate to your enemy that you cared for them in spite of the treatment you had endured. It would communicate the need for repentance, not the need for revenge.

Recently I wrote a blog titled "Take Your Enemy a Casserole." It was based on this scripture of "heaping coals" on your enemy's head. Through growth in my own life, I learned that the equal to this for me was to take food to my enemy when they were in need. So I set out on a mission to make my enemy a casserole and drop it off on their doorstep. This was my way of letting them know they were cared for, even in my books they didn't deserve it. Try it. It is a simple gesture and fairly easy!

When the angel told Hagar to submit, he was saying it was time to make her enemy a casserole. It was time to gesture to her enemy there was a bigger protector, a bigger presence in her life that is going to conquer her fears. God had a bigger purpose, a bigger cause.

I, of all people, would never suggest we return to abuse. That is not the story here. When someone is a toxic abuser in your life, it is time to take a stand and walk away. Read Genesis 21 of Hagar's final exit. But we need to see God as bigger than our enemy. There are times when God says to show them kindness and be that bigger person. Showing kindness should never be for their sake, but for ours. The times I have shown kindness to my enemy brings me confidence in my relationship with my Maker. It allows me to see that I can do this through the strength of Christ. My gesture of kindness has been a meal when they are sick or a prayer for their wellbeing. But in this story, it was made clear that Hagar was to return and to submit. This was not an easy task.

## THE STORY IS NOT OVER

But the story was not over. There was more to come.

> The angel says, "Hagar, before you go, there is one more thing I would like to say. You may want to listen closely to this because it will change your world and your perspective for your return."
>
> The angel added, "I will increase your descendants so much that they will be too numerous to count" (Genesis 16:10 NIV).

As the angel made this statement about Hagar's descendants increasing, a curiosity grew within herr. Somehow her submission to Sarah would allow her to prosper. This added statement from the angel gave Hagar courage to return to where she had come. It gave her hope that God did care for her and was not going to leave her.

I believe that this should be a lesson for all of us struggling with submitting to our enemy. Living with the anchor that our acts of obedience to God will always result in prosperity should remind us that there is so much more than saying yes to God. The results of our obedience may not be an "increase in our descendants," but obedience to God in submitting and learning to love those we hate will allow us to prosper and grow in our trust in God.

## KNEELING BEFORE GOD

Hagar was no longer leaning against the well as I envision her now kneeling before God. In the quiet of the moment, the posture of standing gave way to her brokenness, causing her to kneel in her submission. The angel had told her two things that changed the trajectory of her world, two things that were not things that she had laid out in her plan.

"Go back ... go back, Hagar, to the place of hurt and disappointment. I will increase ... I will increase your descendants so much."

> *"But, God, I didn't sign up for this. I am struggling to figure out how I am going to take care of this one child, and now you are telling me that I will have more descendants. This is too much ... this is too much!"*

At one moment, she thought her life was about to take a hard turn and she was returning to her home of Egypt and now she must return to the land of Canaan.

In the craziness and confusion, her mind must shift to returning to those who mistreated her and to growing a nation. "God, I can't grow a nation ... I just can't!"

Tired,
Worn,
Confused,
Scared.

Hopeful,
Surrendered,
Encouraged,
Comforted.

These emotions within her battled for center stage. Does she give way to the pain and suffering she has endured, or does she hang onto the hope for a better tomorrow, a brighter forever?

In the posture of submission before God, she looks up and gives God a name. This was a name no one had given before. This was a name that crept up from the depths of her soul.

With her knees bent before God, with a tear making way down her dirt-stained cheek, with the dryness that had settled in her thirsty throat, she states in a gentle voice,

"You are the God who sees me …" (Genesis 16:13 NIV).

You are the God who SEES me!

YOU are the God who sees me!

You are the God who sees ME!

YOU SEE ME!

*"I kneel before the God of the heavens, the God of creation. I see my life as rags, and He sees my life as riches. I see my life as over, and He sees my life as beginning. I see my life as invisible, and He sees my life as a beautiful light in this vast existence."*

Why would she name God "the one who sees"? This was not the god of her culture. This was not the god with whom she was raised. What made this God any different from any other god with whom she was familiar?

## THE SPIN

Because this is the One true God who sees.

God had the ability to look deep into her soul and love her for who she truly was. He looked beyond this tattered and worn servant and saw her beauty. He saw her as someone who mattered in this world. He saw her as His child.

*"For some reason, God, Your eyes are fixed on me. There is nothing I have done to deserve even a glance from You. Yet You fix Your eyes on me."*

Disbelief. Pure disbelief! Her life had spun out of control, leaving her alone in this world. Why would anyone care for her? Why would anyone see her?

## LET'S GO PLAY ON THE PLAYGROUND

Do you remember the old playground equipment called the merry-go-round, the round, metal one typically with peeling paint and rusty bottoms? If you are too young to remember this, just Google merry-go-round playground equipment to get a visual.

As a kid, this round metal apparatus provided a great place to sit and rest if it weren't spinning. But once someone stepped to the edge of the round metal disc and grabbed one of the bars, it was too late. This intruder stood safely with two feet firmly planted on the ground and a big smile on their face, knowing they were about to throw your life into chaos. Seeing the intruder's face, you are keenly aware your life is about to spin out of control. Scrambling as quickly as you could, you would try to escape. But it was too late. You found yourself stuck in the center of the merry-go-round while the maniac grabbed the outside bar and began to spin the apparatus. Closing your eyes, you prayed to God that it would end. You also prayed you wouldn't throw up on the floor of this thing and make a fool of yourself.

There are times in our lives when life spins so quickly out of control that we are about three spins behind before we even know it's spinning. This is how Hagar felt. Her life had spun out of control at the very point when Sarah stepped up to the edge to give her a spin, telling her to sleep with her husband. Sarah stood on the edge of Hagar's world and grabbed the bar that controlled Hagar's life. As she grabbed hold of that bar getting it ready to spin, she said, "Go have sex with my husband." One command given from master to slave put Hagar's life in a spin that had no hope of stopping. No hope … until she paused at the well.

Pausing at the well was the moment God reached out, grabbed the bar, and stopped the spin!

## FOR GOD'S EYES ONLY

When the spin stopped, Hagar paused. Stunned and dismayed at the command to return to where she had come from and the declaration from the angel that she would mother a nation, she knew her life had taken a turn far beyond her ability to navigate on her own. In her despair, disbelief, and dismay, she gave God a name. But naming God was only one part of her transformation.

Hagar went on to explain why she gave God that name. "FOR SHE SAID … " (Genesis 16:13 NIV). This statement gives us the reason she gave God this name, "for she said, I have NOW seen the God who sees me" (Genesis 16:13 NIV).

At this very moment when God saw her, she also saw Him. They were no longer ships passing in the night. They had now collided, bringing them face-to-face.

Was she aware throughout her life that there was a God who watched over her, who cared for her, who loved her? Why would she say the word *now*?

Before this moment, she had been blinded to His presence. Her life had been a chain of events connecting to one another with no real purpose. At this moment when she opened her eyes to see Him, her life went from black-and-white to full color.

As she slowly opened her eyes, she saw God compassionately looking into her eyes, into her soul. Once she realized she was safe and the spinning had stopped, she quietly spoke in a feeble and broken voice, "You are the God who sees me."

> *"God, everything in my life is wrong. I'm in such despair. I have tried and tried to make things right, but I keep getting it wrong. I have displeased so many people in my life. I have made some horrible decisions. I have made a mess of things, things I can never undo. And now I have a child growing inside of me that needs me. And truthfully, I need him too. My hurt and confusion run deep. And now I must go back and face it all. When I walk back to the camp of my master, I know I will feel lonelier than how I feel now. I don't think I can do this … I really don't think I can do this! But as I sit here on the edge of my spin, You see me. You aren't looking at all the bad choices I have made; You are looking at me. I am overwhelmed because I have never felt as though anyone has seen me … never! But You see me!"*

## EYES WIDE SHUT

Often in our lives, we traverse through life's journey with our eyes wide shut. Even as believers, we become so inundated with life, even church life, but we do not see Jesus. We lose perspective as to why we do what we do. We only see what is closely surrounding us, the trials of the day, the hurt from yesterday, or the lack of hope of tomorrow. Our eyes are wide shut.

As we are tossed from moment to moment, activity to activity, or ministry to ministry, we have a choice to either open our eyes and see the Jesus who sees us or walk blindly, hoping that when we land, we land firmly in His grace and His purpose.

But just as Hagar had a choice in her focus, so do we. The eyes of God are never lost on us. He sees us, He knows us, and He loves us.

When we navigate through life with closed eyes, we can rest assured that His eyes are and always will be opened toward us. But how much more beautiful will this union be when we return the gaze? When our eyes open and we can see the God who sees us and has always seen us, we are joined together with Him to follow Him, obey Him, and love Him. Don't let this be a one-way gaze.

When Hagar opened her eyes, her eyes locked eyes with the One who sees her! When she looked into the eyes of God, she knew at that moment that she could go back. Knowing that God saw her gave her the courage and strength she needed to go back and face the destruction she had left.

Often in our lives, we are faced with returning to face our destruction and pain, but unfortunately, we choose to take this journey in our own strength. But when we see the One who sees us, a supernatural strength wells up within us, giving the courage to know we will be okay. I believe this divine appointment between God and Hagar at the well gave her the strength to return. God's gaze upon her allowed her to return in confidence only found in Him.

## IT'S TIME TO WALK AWAY FROM THE WELL

Hagar then placed her hands into the dirt, steadying herself to stand once again. As she regained her balance, she felt the confidence of God in her to return. Grabbing her satchel, she brushed the loose dirt from the sides and placed it over her shoulder. Staring at her surroundings, she couldn't believe the encounter that had taken place. Just moments before, she had approached the well to replenish her body so she could continue on her journey. Now she is returning to her heartache, but this time she is returning with the gaze of God on her and her gaze on the God who sees. There was so much more that took place at the well that day … so much more!

As she stepped away from the well, her feet paused. Turning around to take one last look at the well, she saw the rock where she had rested. The pause at the well changed her life. The angel was no longer visible; God was no longer visible with her human eyes, but the message that was brought to her was very much in her heart.

On that day, Beer Lahai Roi became the name of the well,

"The Well of Him that Lives and Sees Me."
Tears began to roll down her dirty and dusty cheeks. As
those tears gave way, she knew she had seen God that day.

This is an incredible story, one that gives us comfort and hope. But there is a critical lesson that we could easily miss: For Hagar to see God, she had to open her eyes! Please hear this: For Hagar to see God, she had to open her eyes!

Look at the different translations of Genesis 16:13.

- "I have now seen the One who sees me." (NIV)
- "Have I truly seen the One who sees me?" (NLT)
- "Truly here I have seen him who looks after me." (ESV)

We have moments and times when we think we see God, but our eyes are still closed. We know the stories of God. We tell the stories of God, but we are still blind to His holiness, His healing, and His wholeness!

We are aware of His presence, His existence, and His movements. We tell our friends about the miracles of God. We even say, "God is good all the time … all the time, God is good."

But have we really opened our eyes? We talk about the wonderful things He does, but do we truly know the God who did those wonderful things? We keep those things at a distance like a trophy on a shelf but never allow them to impact our lives to the point of change.

We love the comfort that God always sees us! "He knows when we are sleeping; he knows when we're awake. He knows when we've been bad or good, so be good for goodness' sake." But He is not Santa Claus waiting to put us on His naughty-or-nice list. He is a God who watches over us, loves us, and longs to be with us.

But so often we rest in that feeling of comfort like a pair of thick, fuzzy socks on our cold feet.

And yet our eyes remain closed.

## BACK TO THE PLAYGROUND

Let's go back to the merry-go-round on the playground. It is spinning, spinning, and spinning. We have reached the point of discomfort, causing us to lose our sense of reality.

Will this ever stop? Stuck in the middle of the chaos, there is no power within us to stop the movement.

Finally it does stop. Someone grabbed the edge, causing an abrupt cessation of motion, therefore stopping the spin.

As it comes to a halt, we sit on the apparatus with our eyes closed until we feel better ... until the spinning in our head stops. With our eyes closed, we scoot to the edge, plant our feet on solid ground, and then push ourselves up to a standing position. All the time, our eyes are shut. When we finally open them, our savior is gone. The one who stopped the spinning waited for us to open our eyes and see who saved us, but it is too late. We felt the presence of that person, we felt their comfort, and we felt their care for us as they halted our spin. But when we don't open our eyes, we don't acknowledge them as the one who saved us.

The same is true in our relationship with God. We often walk through life enjoying all the comforts of God. We love to tell His stories, His greatness, and His love, but we don't see Him! We don't stop long enough to open our eyes in the moments He wants to connect with us. We become too busy or overwhelmed with life to open our eyes and see Him. We love the stories but miss the Storyteller!

What will it take for us to open our eyes?<br>What will it take for us to say, "I have now seen God"?

Let's try this. The next time we see the workings of God, His beauty, His miracles, and His blessings, we open our eyes, and we see him! We pause and SEE HIM!

When you see the wind and enjoy the pleasant breeze, open your eyes and see the Creator of the breeze. See God!

- When you experience the salty waves of the ocean, praise the One who made this possible.
- When you touch the finger of a newborn baby, thank the God who was and is.
- When your life is struck by tragedy and you exist through life, open your eyes and see His mighty hand holding you steady.

A deep relationship with our Creator is as
simple as the opening of our eyes!
"And NOW I see the God who SEES me."

Meet God at the well today. Pause for your drink of water and the opening of your eyes. You will not be disappointed!

## TALKS WITH EMILEIGH

- *Enemy:* a person who is actively opposed or hostile to someone; a thing that harms or weakens something else
- *Submission:* the action of accepting or yielding to the authority of another

Many of us can relate to the term *enemy* in a variety of ways. We read in the history books of enemies fighting wars against one another. We read books about enemies providing the action in the story. We even hear of socioeconomic factors posed as enemies that threaten our world. For some, even food can be your enemy. To understand the emotion that raged inside Hagar when she was told to submit to her enemy, we need to identify our own. I have had friends I care about unexpectedly end our friendship or loved ones use hateful words when expressing their emotions. I have experienced the pain of another looking me in the eye and saying they hated me. I have felt the loss of a child. I have seen my children be bullied. In those moments, I certainly felt like there was an enemy present. My spirit and emotions were unquestionably weakened. In none of those times did I think I was capable of submission. In none of those moments did I consider that Satan was my true enemy.

For Hagar, she was weakened and opposed to Sarah for a good reason. The two were at odds with one another and felt no hope of resolution. I believe Satan was at work in the hearts of both these women, instigating their weakened spirits. Satan took a foothold but was halted when Hagar paused at the well.

At that point in her life, God said that submission to her enemy was the best option for Hagar. God told her to humble herself and return to the same abuse she'd been suffering under. He was telling her more than to be kind. In Proverbs 25:21–22, He is telling us to bless our enemy with more than just simple kindness. We are to love them like Jesus would.

***Read Proverbs 25:21–22. Do you have someone or something in your life you consider your enemy? Do you find it easy to bless your enemy, or is simple kindness all you can muster when in their presence?***

I cannot begin to imagine how difficult it was for Hagar to be in Sarah's presence, wondering if at any given moment she may taunt her or simply give her that look; yet God was telling her to not only withstand it but yield to it. When I am in the presence of someone I know who doesn't care for me or who has been unkind, my instinct is to avoid them. My strong-willed personality wants to defend myself, especially when I feel attacked. I can recall one instance when I felt strongly justified to defend myself, and my wise husband told me that sometimes it's more important to be wrong than right. I believe the Lord would have agreed that Sarah's actions toward Hagar were wrong; however, He wanted to look past the need to point out Sarah's wrongdoing for Hagar's soul to be right with Him. At this point, it wasn't about Sarah. It was about Hagar's heart and a choice only she could make. Sometimes it takes submission for our hearts to reach that right posture.

In the face of the adversity He called her back to, the Lord promises Hagar a great blessing. He tells her in Genesis 16:10 that her offspring will be too many to count. Can you just feel Hagar's inner struggle weighing her options? The angel wants her to humbly walk back into a weakening situation, a painful circumstance, but in return, her offspring will be plentiful. Does she choose the hard life for the greater reward? Does she surrender to this new hope? Does she allow this newfound hope to propel her forward? This promise wouldn't fix the circumstances. It wouldn't take away the pain. It would, however, give her courage to move forward. It would give her the strength to face her enemy.

***When have you felt hope and encouragement amid trial and despair?***

My dad recently returned from a transformational mission trip to Africa. He shared a story with me that struck me and gave me a new appreciation for the account of Hagar. One day as my dad and his friends were sharing their testimonies and the gospel in a slum, they encountered a man who wanted to hear about the man named Jesus. He quickly decided that Jesus was someone he wanted to follow. As the men began to pray together, they prayed repentance for this man and surrender of his life. In the middle of this prayer, unexpectedly and in a moment of beautiful submission, this man dropped to his knees. He kneeled before the God he had just encountered. Despite poverty and poor conditions, in the dirt streets around him, He submitted to a God He now knew loved him. He surrendered to a God who loved him so much that He sent a team of men halfway around the world to prepare and help posture his heart.

"Come, let us worship and bow down; let us kneel before the Lord our Maker" (Psalm 95:6).

***Have you ever truly surrendered to God?***

Sometimes this heartfelt surrender is dropping to your knees in desperation like this man in Africa. Other times, this surrender can be an outcry when pain becomes almost too much to bear. When we faced losing a child, my pain was almost unbearable. My heart ached with sadness, confusion, and despair. In those moments, I felt no choice but to surrender my pain to the One I trusted was and is in control. I chose to cling in desperation to His good and perfect plan. In a journal entry dated during our uncertain days when we didn't know what the outcome would be, I wrote, "I hear You telling me to be patient. You are holding me. You have a great plan. Strengthen my spirit to endure patiently as You work out all the details."

At that point in my life, I was being asked to endure. Hagar and I both had to make a choice when life felt like it was spinning out of control.

***Have you ever felt like life was spinning out of control? Where or who do you turn when life feels out of control?***

Sometimes in life, especially when we feel at odds with an enemy, life has the potential to spin out of control. As the rivalry intensified between Hagar and Sarah, life was feeling hopeless for her. Hagar was feeling unwanted, used, abused, and unseen. No one seemed to understand Hagar's pain, and I can imagine it felt like no one cared. When we feel that our pain or our worries are unseen, our enemies tend to weaken us more. Our feelings of worth and value tend to be damaged. These feelings can cause the spinning to feel faster and deeper and like a season that will never end.

***When have you felt unseen?***

Though in this book I share many personal details of my life, this is not my normal inclination during trials. When I struggle, I tend to keep to myself and, sadly, shut others out. In these moments, I'm my own worst enemy because when I'm hiding my pain, others don't see it. While this releases me from the need to share, it carries the ability to wound my hurting heart further. When we feel our brokenness is unseen, we are allowing Satan an opportunity to lurk where he doesn't belong. But Melody says, "He looked beyond this tattered and worn servant and saw her beauty."

God saw past Hagar's pain to her heart. He saw beyond her circumstances and asked for her trust. He sees beyond our circumstances and asks us to trust Him with our hearts. When we take steps in trusting the Lord, He uses us, and we ultimately prosper. Hagar was told to return, and if she chose obedience and pursued the plan He offered, she'd receive the promise to prosper.

As Hagar's life began to spin out of control, out of desperation or exhaustion, she paused at the well. Sometimes when we get to the other side of our merry-go-round spin, we can pinpoint a moment we should have paused. Hindsight can be 20/20, and we come out seeing markers of hope, but other times, we stay on and continue to spin. In Hagar's desperation, in my despair, and in your moments of brokenness, we have a choice: continue to spin in disarray or step off the ride and stumble forward, choosing to trust one step at a time.

***When was the last time you paused at the well?***

"The Lord is gracious and righteous; our God is full of compassion. The Lord guards and protects the unwary; when I was brought low, He saved me" (Psalm 116:5–6).

Hagar paused at the well in the depth of her darkness. Even in my deepest, darkest moments, God can and has pulled me through. You see, desperation in our darkness can be powerful if we allow it to become a desperate dependence on the Lord. He uses our brokenness to show us His compassion and hope. If we're not pausing to see His goodness, we'll miss that compassion. If we're not pausing when life is spinning around us, we will simply continue to spin and miss seeing who God truly is. When Hagar paused, she not only had the opportunity to see who God was, but she felt truly seen by Him.

***Describe a moment you felt genuinely seen by God.***

When God met me and I felt seen in the loss of a child, He transformed my faith. I journaled my feelings at that time in response to a verse He'd placed on my heart. "When I said, 'my foot is slipping;' your love, O Lord, supported me. When anxiety was great within me, your consolation brought joy to my soul" (Psalm 94:18–19).

*The only thing that stops my desperation, the uncertainties, and the insecurities is for the Spirit to cover my heart and make it still. This season has brought confusion, fear, uncertainty, and worry. It's brought sadness I don't understand and am struggling to process. The flesh invades my mind with anxiety and hurt. You, Lord, offer me joy and promise and a perfect will that knows no bounds. You are in control of it all. You see me and offer me a release from all of it. This healing process is simply that, a process. As I heal, reassure me, Father, of Your perfect plan. Help me to rest and find You in the stillness, in the quiet, in the pain, and alongside me every step of the way.*

Whether Hagar could comprehend the peace God was offering her or if she simply were compelled to take a step of obedience, she chose the God who saw her. For what may have been the first time in her life to feel truly seen, I imagine her releasing a sigh of surrender on her knees. When her anxiety was great, El Roi brought her hope, and I believe it brought her joy.

"El Roi" is the name Hagar gives Him. She would walk away with a story, hope, and a promise. El Roi also saw me in my pain, and with every passing trial I face, this name Hagar gave Him gives me hope too. Scripture gives God many names. Perhaps you haven't felt truly seen by El Roi, but He's spoken to you in a different way, in a different season.

***What names of God do you most intimately connect with?***

As Hagar walks away from the well, we can picture her turning to see the rock where she'd rested, where she'd felt seen, where her life had been transformed. This rock would become a rock of remembrance for Hagar. She could look upon it as a reminder of what God had done in her life. We can carry our own rocks of remembrance. These rocks can remind us of heartache but also of times when God showed up and saw us. These rocks can help us remember His goodness.

We can't all position boulders along our path in life, but for me, my journal entries serve as rocks of remembrance. My children are rocks of His mercy. My husband is a rock of His grace. My family, my friends, and my Bible are all rocks of His goodness.

***What rocks of remembrance do you carry or have?***

For much of my life, I've known God is good, but in my moment of heartache, I needed to believe it. I needed to feel it. I needed to live it. I needed to learn to trust God with my heart all the way. And when our third child was admitted to the NICU and I encountered a fork in the road of spinning or trust, my husband simply said, "We are not in control." When life threatened to take me for another spin and Satan was lurking for another opportunity, my rock of a husband reminded me of the Rock our faith is built upon.

***Do you find yourself knowing God is good or truly believing it and living it out?***

We all face enemies that look different in this life, but we all share a common enemy. That enemy wants to blind us from all that God is doing. He wants to blind us from truly seeing God. He wants to distract us with all the enemies we face. That common enemy wants to hold us in our doubts, hardships, and fears. But there is a God who sees you, and He sees me. He sees our struggles and pain, and when we're feeling lost or hopeless or simply worrisome, He's reaching out and begging us to open our eyes. When we do, we'll discover that He's transforming us one rock at a time.

***Who is God to you?***

Storyteller. Healer. Provider. Savior. Redeemer. Creator. Open your eyes and see who God desires to be for you. Pause now. Record three things God has done in your life. Reflecting on His goodness can help you feel seen. I challenge you to make a habit of writing down a way God has moved in your life each week and sharing with someone you trust.

# 10

# WALK BEFORE ME

As Hagar returned to the camp, she shook with fear and apprehension as she entered the gates. Tucked deep within her heart was the memory of that moment when she saw God. As she departed from her place of surrender, she had reached down to pick up a smooth stone that had fallen from the well. Now returning to the camp, she reached into her pocket. As she did, her fingers rubbed the stone, reminding her that this is "the well of him that liveth and seeth me."

Not long after returning to the camp, Hagar gave birth to a son, calling him Ishmael. After giving birth, Hagar was reminded what the angel had said, "He will be a wild donkey of a man; his hand will be against everyone and everyone's hand against him, and he will live in hostility toward all his brothers" (Genesis 16:13 NIV).

The stone in her pocket remained as that reminder that no matter what was ahead, God was with her.

## EL SHADDAI

Thirteen years after the birth of Ismael, God spoke to Abraham. "I am El Shaddai."

"I am God Almighty" (Genesis 17:1 NIV).

God simply said to Abraham, "I AM GOD ALMIGHTY!"

God was declaring not only a name but a statement of who He is. He was and is the God who is almighty, absolute power over all, unlimited power, and great power.

It is interesting as we look at the moment in which God spoke to Hagar versus the moment He spoke with Abraham. With Hagar, God spoke in His gentleness, but with Abraham, God spoke in His strength.

So often, God reveals Himself to us in accordance with the need of our current situation. When we hurt, He is gentle. When we doubt, He is truth. When we are weak, He is strength.

Serving a God who sees us and speaks to us through our current needs assures us of His deep love for us. Many times, I have needed God's gentle voice, but then there are times when I need God to speak strength and power to me, reminding me that the same resurrection power that is within Him is the same power that resides within me.

As God spoke to Abraham that day He said,

> I am God Almighty; walk before Me faithfully and be blameless. THEN I… (Genesis 17:1 NIV).

So often we focus on the "Then I," what we are going to receive because of obedience?

The rewards become our focus of hope. But we forget or ignore what our responsibility before God is. The continuation of that verse explores once again the covenant between God and Abraham. "Then I will make my covenant between me and you and will greatly increase your numbers" (Genesis 17:2 NIV).

God wanted to do great things through the life of Abraham. God had chosen him to be the father of all nations, therefore making it through the bloodline of Abraham that the Israelite nation would be born. The weight of that responsibility was enormous, but the joy that would come to Abraham's heart was beyond words.

As we saw in the previous chapters, Sarah's obsession to mother a child blinded both her and Abraham. But even after they falsely orchestrated God's will, God was not done using Abraham to accomplish the promise given to him by God.

Our ability to walk back to Eden comes through the obedience of Abraham. Through him, God would provide our Savior, our Messiah, our Redeemer. Since the fall of Adam and Eve, this was God's plan. But Abraham was asked to do something, to be something for God. And if he were able to do and be this, God would then complete His covenant through Abraham.

... walk before me faithfully.

... be blameless!

## A FAITHFUL WALK

Between the end of Genesis 16 and the beginning of Genesis 17, there were thirteen years of silence. Abraham had heard from God many times that he would be the father of a nation, yet his only son was Ishmael, whose mother was an Egyptian slave. Was this the beginning of God's plan? Was Ishmael the first of this nation?

Abraham had questioned God before about this plan. In Genesis 15, Abraham is frustrated with God because of God's continual declaration that Abraham would birth a nation. Abraham had waited long enough and had heard God make this declaration enough that it became time for Abraham to question God's next move.

> Sovereign Lord, what can you give me since I remain childless and the one who will inherit my estate is Eliezer of Damascus? You have given me no children; so a servant in my household will be my heir. (Genesis 15:2–3 NIV)

Out of frustration, Abraham felt the need to figure out God's plan. Abraham had no heir because he had no children; therefore logic for him was that his favorite and loyal servant, Eliezer, would be his heir.

I am confident you can think of times in your life when God was slow to act, so in your lack of patience, you devised your own plan. If God doesn't move fast enough, then I will move on my own. We all know all too well how that logic plays out.

This is God's response to Abraham's plan, "but a son who is your own flesh and blood will be your heir" (Genesis 15:4 NIV).

Fast-forward to the current situation. Ishmael had been born. Ishmael was Abraham's flesh and blood; therefore, logic tells us that Ishmael would be Abraham's heir and God's plan for a nation. But this is still not God's plan or desire. Look closely at this conversation between God and Abraham as they discuss God's plan.

> God also said to Abraham, "As for Sarai your wife, you are no longer to call her Sarai, her name will be Sarah. I will bless her and will surely give you a son by her. I will bless her so that she will be the mother of nations; kings of peoples will come from her."
>
> Abraham fell facedown; he laughed and said to himself, "Will a son be born to a man a hundred years old? Will Sarah bear a child at the age of ninety?" And Abraham said to God, "If only Ishmael might live under your blessing!"
>
> The God said, "Yes, but your wife Sarah will bear you a son, and you will call him Isaac." (Genesis 17:15–19 NIV)

God is speaking loud and clear to Abraham that he will have a son through the womb of Sarah. But even though God is speaking very clearly, Abraham still laughs at this possibility, using his age as the obstacle to God's sovereignty.

As believers, we beg God to speak. We long to hear His voice to give us direction and a plan. But how many times is He speaking loud and clear and yet we respond with laughter or disbelief? The plan that God lays out for us is incredible, yet we discredit the credible. We don't believe that God can move in the way He wants to move so we laugh and look for another plan; a plan that makes more sense, calling it the "Ishmael plan," not perfect, but good enough!

God said no to Abraham's plan and yes to His plan. God had allowed Sarah and Abraham to devise their plan through the birth of Ishmael, yet bringing to light that their plan was faulty and unreliable. But once Sarah and Abraham had driven their plan into the ground, causing heartache and pain, God stepped in and said, "Now let's do it My way."

God said, "Abraham, I have allowed you to try this apart from Me. You and Sarah were determined to figure this out for yourself. I watched you choose things through your own human eyes, not allowing the sovereignty of Me to shine. But because it wasn't My plan, it failed. Now if you will walk alongside Me in My presence and My sovereignty, I will show you when and where to walk. Walk before Me faithfully, Abraham. Surround yourself with Me and live a life pleasing to Me, loyal to Me, committed to Me."

This command of God seems simple if Abraham would just walk before God.

## WALKING BEFORE GOD

What would it mean to walk before God? Is that walking in front of God so we can see what is ahead of us? So we can shine our own light on the path? Does it mean to walk behind God so we can follow in His steps? Does it mean as we walk behind Him, we are blinded to the path and only see Him?

I believe it means to walk right alongside Him. We see the path, and He sees the path. We see the path together. But as we see the path together, we can talk about the path. We can chat about what is in front of us. We can identify the obstacles together and navigate them as one. When we get distracted on the path and begin to take a wrong turn, God can gently grab our hand and guide us back to His path. We don't go in front or behind; we walk alongside, allowing us to see each of His moves and choosing to move when and where He does. Moving when and where He does is called "faithful."

Steadfast …
Constant …
Loyal …
Determined …
Dyed-in-the-wool …
Fervent …
Steady …
Unfaltering …
Trustworthy …
Tried-and-true …
Passionate …

## OUR FAITHFULNESS TO GOD DETERMINES OUR OUTCOME

Looking at the life of Abraham, we see his faith. It took faith for him to leave his homeland of Haran and move his family to Canaan, the land of the unknown. It took faith for him to part with Lot, giving Lot the "good land" while he took the "leftovers." It took faith to offer his son on the altar before God, a story we will address in chapter 13. Every time Abraham responded with big faith, God responded in big outcomes.

But the moments when Abraham's faith waned, it resulted in destruction. His faith lacked when Sarah devised the plan for him to have a child through Hagar. Abraham's faith lacked when he entered Egypt, telling Sarah to pose as his sister and not his wife. In each of those situations, the outcome was poor and painful. Let's look at the story of the "bags of gold" from Matthew 25 and see a beautiful illustration of this.

> The master handed out a certain amount of "bags of gold" to three different people. To one he gave five bags of gold, to another two bags. And to another one bag, each according to his ability. (Matthew 25:15 NIV)

But as this story unfolds, we see the person with five and two bags used their abilities wisely and produced more bags, doubling their worth. It says in verse 16 that they "put their money to work." But the person with one bag buried it in the ground, waiting for the master to return. When the master returned, the men with five and two bags were rewarded according to their faith. This was the master's reply, "'Well done, good and faithful servant! You have been faithful with a few things; I will put you in charge of many things'" (Matthew 25:21 NIV).

To the man who buried the gold producing no growth, the master did not reply with such joy and admiration. This was the master's reply, "'You wicked, lazy servant!'" (Matthew 25:26 NIV).

The conclusion of this story is this.

> "So take the bag of gold from him and give it to the one who has ten bags. For whoever has will be given more, and they will have an abundance. Whoever does not have, even what they have will be taken from them." (Matthew 25:28–29 NIV)

What we do with what God gives us is our responsibility. Whether the outcome is big or small in comparison to others, it is our faith that needs to be big in order for God to move accordingly to His story and His desire. Our faith is not measured by the size of our story but in our willingness to listen to our heavenly Father. Faith can be small acts of obedience that grow into a bigger availability to God.

## STORY FROM MY LIFE

Recently my husband and I resigned from the church we had started in 1991. We had been serving God through this church for thirty-one years. We had seen growth and life change beyond what words can communicate. But on a Wednesday in January 2022, both my husband and I felt as though God was encouraging each of us to "let go." The turmoil and disbelief within both of us were overwhelming. Was God asking us to leave this church of thirty-one years? Was God asking us to leave the safety and security of this place we loved and called home? And where was God asking us to go? We had no idea, but we both had a peace in God.

The next Monday, I went to my counselor and told her about this. As I left her office, she looked at me and said, "It took a lot of faith thirty-one years ago for you to move your family to a place of unknown. It is going to take as much faith, if not more, to leave this church that you love." Tears began to roll down my cheek.

A few weeks later, we resigned, having faith that God would provide. We had no idea what God was doing. We had no idea why God was allowing this. But because of our small acts of obedience throughout the course of our lives, our faith had grown large enough to handle this disruption. A few weeks after our resignation, my husband was hired at a job he loves. We have more time together, which has been wonderful for our marriage. The stress of pastoring is no longer existent, we laugh more, we talk more, and we relax more. My husband now has the opportunity to meet and work with pastors starting new churches in our state. We went from impacting one church to affecting almost a thousand churches for His kingdom.

You see, the fear and trepidation that causes our faith to be small keep us from the outcome being big, big by God's standards, not the world's. Our faithfulness to God determines our outcome.

What act of faith or obedience is God asking you to do? Why are you stuck? Why is your faith not moving you forward? Ask Abraham what it felt like when he was faithful. Ask him how it felt when he was not.

God was speaking to Abraham, telling Him, if he walked beside Him, then they could navigate this path as one as Abraham's faith grew to God-sized faith.

"Grab my hand, Abraham. Let's walk side by side, allowing your faith to grow with each step we take together. It will take a lot of faith to accomplish what I have set out for you, but as your faith grows alongside me, I will give you everything you need for this journey."

We limit God when we limit our faith!

## A BLAMELESS WALK

"...walk before me faithfully and be blameless ... " (Genesis 17:1).

Why did God use the word *blameless*? We all know that is an impossible feat. I could not walk blameless if I tried. No matter how hard I try, I will stumble and fall.

Years ago, my husband and I were heading to Europe for three weeks and five countries. We were locked and loaded for the journey. Since most of our trip was going to be hiking and jumping from one train to the next, we packed as light as possible with only a backpack and one small case. As we were heading into the Chicago airport entrance doors, my husband was several steps ahead of me. I was doing the best I could to keep up with him. Seeing him in the close distance, I was moving my feet as fast I could when suddenly I found myself falling face-first onto the concrete sidewalk. People looked at me with disgust as though I was some strange woman just choosing to sit in the middle of the sidewalk groaning from pain. As my husband turned around, he realized I was no longer keeping up with him and found me bleeding and in pain, sitting in the middle of the sidewalk. When he approached me, I soon realized what had happened. I fell flat with no warning and no stumbling, just face-first, catching myself with my hands and arms, causing two sprained wrists and a bloody arm. Observing the damage and the cause of the fall, I realized the lace from one of my hiking boots had gotten caught in the eyelet of the other boot because I had not laced them all the way to the top. When that happened, I fell with no warning.

I tell you this story not just for your pleasure at my nonsense, but to illustrate that so many times in our lives, our intentions are good. We are walking along the path, doing the best we can to keep up. But things happen. We are caught off guard, causing us to fall flat with no warning. Our desire is to be blameless, but we don't "lace up our boots" all the way to the top because we get lazy or let our guard down. It is in those moments of vulnerability that we fall with no warning.

Was God commanding Abraham to never stumble? Was He giving him an ultimatum that if he didn't walk perfectly, Abraham would not be the recipient of His covenant?

Absolutely not! Taken within the context of the entire Bible with God creating Adam and Eve with choice, God knew that was not possible for Abraham or anyone. And as we look at the past behaviors of Abraham with his slave Hagar, it is obvious that Abraham was not going to be able to heed this call.

God was talking about the intention of Abraham's heart. God needed a man whose heart's desire was to be faithful and to walk blamelessly before God, not perfectly!

It is so easy for us to get caught up in perfection that we misconstrue the blameless. Perfection becomes something within our own control. It is the portrayal of our outer world speaking to others that we have it all under our control. But blameless comes only from the heart.

Perfection drives each of us differently. Some pursue perfection as though it is a target to hit or a goal to achieve. Some give up on perfection, allowing themselves to be defeated and quit. But perfection is not the target here. Blameless is the target.

Stay with me, blameless in our pursuit.

As I was making my way into that airport, I was blameless in my pursuit of keeping up with my husband and catching that plane. But my laziness in not lacing my boots all the way to the top caused me to fall. That did not change my heart any. It just paused me a bit in my journey, not to mention an extremely painful flight to Ireland.

God was telling Abraham,

Make your heart good!

Focus on Me!

Desire truth!

Be blameless in your pursuit!

Perfection? No!

Blameless? Yes!

Blameless in our heart's desire to walk alongside God on this path.

## THEN I ...

"Then I will make my covenant between me and you and will greatly increase your numbers" (Genesis 17:2). When we pursue God in faith and a heart's desire to be blameless in our pursuit, there will always be a "then I."

God told Abraham two things He desired of him: faith and blameless in his pursuit. These two things rested on the shoulders of Abraham, were not controlled by God or the responsibility of God and were Abraham's responsibility.

The importance of walking faithfully before God and walking blameless were critical for God to use Abraham to carry out His purpose of bringing His people back to Eden, to peace and relationship with Him, a reclaimed paradise!

We often forget that God's design and purpose will happen no matter our response. If God can't use us because our faith is lacking or our desire to be blameless in our pursuit is waning, He will simply choose someone else. It is not that God's purpose will not be fulfilled. It will always be fulfilled. It is simply a matter if it is fulfilled through us as a willing servant or fulfilled through someone else. You choose!

In the story of Esther in the Old Testament, Esther's cousin, Mordecai, presented the option for Esther to be the one God used to save her people. Esther was faced with a choice. We often think she was just a good girl and an obedient servant of God. But she too questioned greatly if she wanted to be the one to put her life on the line to save her people. She could have walked away. But walking away was not going to change God's plan. It just changed God's instrument of purpose.

When Mordecai was trying to persuade Esther to be obedient, he said, "For if you remain silent at this time, relief and deliverance for the Jews will arise from another place" (Esther 4:14 NIV).

Your life and my life have been filled with opportunities lost. When our eyes are not fixed on Jesus, we cannot see what is before us in our faithfulness to Him. We are preoccupied or fearful in our obedience, causing missed opportunities to purpose ourselves for Him. But what if God has knocked on our door of opportunity with no answer from us, causing Him to stop knocking and to move on? What if He has wanted to use us for something great but the measure with which we are faithful only warrants something small? Our lives being used by God is on us! We choose how big that is by choosing how big our faith is!

As Abraham learned to walk beside God in his faithfulness and pursuit to be blameless, the finishing of God's story in his life resulted in big things. God's "then I" for Abraham was the covenant to save His creation. It is through Abraham's obedience that a path was provided for us to reclaim the paradise God designed from the beginning. Abraham's obedience gave way for God's covenant to take us to the new covenant in Jesus.

## ABRAHAM FELL ON HIS FACE

Abraham then fell on his face before God. At this moment, Abraham felt the weight of what God was calling him to do and to be. At this moment, God spoke once again, "As for me, this is my covenant with you. You will be the father of many nations" (Genesis 17:4 NIV).

Little did Abraham realize what that would become. God had laid the foundation for Abraham in the years leading up to this moment. God had called him out of the land of Harran to the land of Canaan.

God had showed Abraham the land of promise and purpose. God had allowed Abraham to stumble and fall, only to get back up, pursuing God's purpose in him. It was through the seed of Abraham and womb of Sarah that a nation would be born. It was through this nation, the nation of Israelites, that a Savior would be born. It was through the death of that Savior that we would be born into a new and reclaimed relationship with God. It was through that reclaimed relationship that we can walk back to Eden and experience God's perfect paradise in eternity with Him.

## WHAT IS YOUR "THEN I"?

What is your "then I" statement? If God were speaking to you, which I believe He always is, how would finish that statement? If you pursued blameless living and stood before God as faithful, what do you think His finishing line would be?

Would He make you a great nation? Probably not! That has already been done. But what would He do that would be great in you and great for His kingdom?

Let me ask this a different way. If your life were right before God and failure were not an option, what would you desire to do within the kingdom of God to make a kingdom difference? I believe if you could answer that question, it would change your life!

When we sell ourselves short in faith, then we will sell ourselves short in opportunity! Often we get so stuck on the "then I," on the results and privileges of our faith, that we forget that the "then I" is God speaking His purpose and His story. We think that when our faith is good and that our pursuit of blameless is on target, then our "then I" is our reward from God because of our good behavior. It's kind of like God owes us a great "then I." But remember, the "then I" is God speaking His design, His purpose, and His glory.

Our obedience is not for our pleasure but for God's purpose!

What is your "then I"?
Make it for God's glory!

## TALKS WITH EMILEIGH

Melody prompts us to dive into this chapter remembering again. She takes us to Hagar at the well, and we imagine her stone of remembrance, the stone that would remind her of El Roi, the stone that would help her continue moving forward. This reminder for Hagar would help her face the rocky path that still lies ahead for her.

When I wrote about my children being rocks of remembrance for me and shared our second experience in the NICU, I had no idea how God would later use that trial. He would use the blessing of our son, Samuel, who had helped heal our pain after miscarriage, to prepare us for yet another trial. God would use this stone of remembrance to give me the courage to face the next step in my story.

***Has one of your stones of remembrance helped you face a trial? What was it and how?***

Hagar didn't let her brokenness keep her from embracing her blessing with Ishmael. She clung to El Roi and the tenderness in which He had met her. He saw her trial, and therefore she could trust Him with the next step. Abraham also needed El Roi to see his trial and to meet him in it; however, tenderness wasn't an option with Abraham. Abraham needed El Shaddai. Abraham needed to see and feel God's power.

Melody said, "God reveals Himself in accordance with the need in our current situation." The Lord knows our needs (often far better than we know ourselves) and meets us where we are, not where we want to be or even where He thinks we should be but exactly where we are. This ability of the Lord enables us to then trust Him in situations as they come.

Look back at the names you felt intimately connected with from our last chapter. Ask yourself why you chose this name. Was it due to a particular season you were walking through, and does the name of God (for you) change with the seasons? At the risk of being redundant, we're revisiting these names. Often in Scripture when we feel it's redundant, it's actually just important. I believe the names of God we connect intimately with are incredibly important.

***Make a list of three to five names of God found in Scripture and how each name may help you in a particular season.***

I took the liberty of asking several dear friends for their favorite name of God and why it resonates with them to get you started:

- Heavenly Father: He is a constant even when my relationship with my earthly father was not.
- Heavenly Father: I am showing Him respect/love/devotion in a personal way.
- Heavenly Father: He is my ultimate Provider and Protector.
- God the Father: He encompasses everything a good father should be: compassionate, forgiving, and loving.
- Elohim: This is my reminder that He is strong and in control.
- El Roi: He sees the good, the bad, and the ugly. I am known by the Creator of the Universe.
- God Almighty: He has absolute sovereignty in His universe. Evil cannot advance or stand against Him!
- Father God: I sometimes think of Him as Daddy because His great love for me reminds me of the encouraging protection, provision, and loving discipline my earthly father provided.
- Shepherd: He guides me with His staff but also corrects me as needed with His rod.
- Yahweh: He is Creator of all things and in control of all things.
- Savior: It reminds me of all the good things God has done for me.
- My Lord: This feels familial to me
- God: His name God perfectly embodies the Trinity—Father, Son, and Holy Spirit—making this name powerful and

all-encompassing; the three letters alone remind me of the perfect Trinity.
- Defender: I see so many times how He has defended and fought for me when I didn't even realize it.

These examples give reasons my friends (and even my young daughter) resonate with these names. I have not included their names for privacy reasons but can tell you how much I enjoyed their willingness to share these answers. Sharing these intimate connections with the Lord can be an illuminating insight into deeper friendships. I believe we often take for granted how uniquely the Lord connects with us and, more so, the unique way our loved ones need to see and feel God's presence. As you consider the name God reveals to you best, challenge yourself to discover why and share with trusted friends who may need to discover Him in this same way.

Because God met Abraham exactly where he was, Abraham was able to trust God with the next step in the plan. To clarify, the plan turned out to not be what Abraham had planned nor what he expected. In fact, Abraham seemed quite frustrated with God's timing because he didn't understand God's plan. This interaction between Abraham and God reminded me of John 13:7 when Jesus says, "What I'm doing you don't realize now, but afterward you will understand." You see, God has never asked or expected us to understand His plans. He just asks us to trust Him.

***When have you been frustrated with God's plan not aligning with your own?***

After having Samuel, our third child, we felt confident our family was complete. We even recently have found pleasure in small parenting freedoms with older siblings to help, the ability to leave all three with a trusted sitter, sleeping all night. Then a few short months ago, our world was turned upside-down. I will share the struggle I faced with great sensitivity to my many friends who yearn for or struggled to have children; yet my story is my own. My story is what God is using to grow me.

The positive pregnancy test was not only unexpected but incredibly unplanned. It brought me to tears, and in all vulnerability, they were not the typical happy tears I had shed four times before upon seeing those tiny two lines. Those tears were quickly followed by guilty tears for not having the proper reaction. The reality I now faced was certainly not part of my plan. I was upset and confused. I didn't understand. Quite frankly, I didn't like God's plan.

In this life, there will always be an obstacle or a reason that God's plan seems unimaginable. Those fleeting and even sometimes debilitating moments will always threaten to stand in the way of God's path. They can give us reason to forget His consistent faithfulness. My emotions and my misunderstanding were pushing me away from El Roi.

By the grace of God, He led incredible friends to meet me exactly where I was and to even confront me with some hard truths about what I knew to be true. I am convinced those friends were speaking on God's behalf because He is the God who sees me and speaks to me in accordance with my needs.

***When have you faced an obstacle that forced you to lean on His faithfulness?***

A short week and a half after my positive result, I was sitting in my doctor's office awaiting more unexpected news. I would soon discover that I was not only pregnant but thirteen weeks along. My busy life with three had distracted me enough to miss an entire trimester. Talk about feeling out of the loop with your own life story! Then within five short days after this news, I landed in the emergency room. I was spending far more time at the hospital than the content mom of three had planned for. I learned in the emergency room that I had just as much chance of continuing with a healthy pregnancy as I did chances of losing the baby. As my husband and I processed this new set of plans for our life, we had to choose to live in fear of the unknown or to embrace an open-handed approach.

***Does the seemingly impossible encourage you to live more open-handed or guarded and fearful?***

As I sat down to write this chapter a few days ago, my son experienced a Lego dilemma. We typically construct Lego sets together as I select the specific Legos in each step as he assembles. On this day, he'd decided to construct on his own. He came downstairs, upset that a certain piece wouldn't fit correctly. After looking, I realized he had skipped a step and placed one upside-down. Immediately, Lucas was worried his entire construction was ruined and would have to be redone. I asked him to trust me as I removed only a few pieces and got him back on track. I reminded him to follow the directions and asked why he hadn't. "I just wanted to do it on my own," he'd said. After he allowed me to make the adjustment, he allowed me to work alongside him. A few minutes into further construction, he said, "Mom, I need help." I responded simply, "That's what I'm here for."

The moment the words left my mouth, I heard God whisper in my heart. You see, my favorite part of doing Legos with both my older kids is that even if they are fully capable on their own, they choose to let me be part of the construction. They choose to do it together. Our Father God feels the same. So often I attempt to plan life on my own, and I get frustrated when things go awry. When I let God walk alongside me and I invite Him to be part of the building, part of my story, the construction is much more seamless. Every time I have a setback or need redirection, He's right there reminding me, "That's what I'm here for."

***Has God ever spoken to you unexpectedly but exactly when you needed it? What is one specific area of your life you can invite God to be part of with you?***

I must choose to let my fear fuel my faith. As we walked out of the emergency room to our car, I began to cry. My heart seemed to be on an emotional roller coaster, and the new twist added an extra obstacle. I now carried a heavy feeling of guilt over my initial reaction to this pregnancy and a fear that I couldn't see the other side. "What is God trying to teach me?" I'd said to my husband. His hard-truth response, which I've been reminded of before, was simply, "He's teaching us that we're not in control." We made the decision in that moment to live open-handed and to trust the next step, one day at a time, no matter the outcome. Making this decision, for me, didn't remove the fear, guilt, anxiety, or uneasiness. It just made taking the next step and opening my hands to His plan something to which I could cling. Living open-handed is scary. Learning God's plan is taking the place of our own selfishly constructed plan is trying. Not knowing the results or next twist of the roller coaster in life causes worry. But to trust God, to walk blamelessly, and to keep moving forward, I must let my fear fuel my faith. Walking into and out of that emergency room transformed my perspective, shifted my prayers, and fueled my faith. I had a choice.

***When have you let a trial halt your faith? When have you let your fear fuel and ignite your faith?***

"… walk before me faithfully and be blameless …" (Genesis 17:1).

Blameless, not perfect. As I began to share my prayer needs and even the pregnancy itself, I had a choice to feign excitement of an obvious blessing, or I could be honest about the struggle and the emotional roller coaster I was walking through. It became time for my faith to be put on display by sharing my heart.

My plan was no longer our reality, and that was tough for me, but in it all, my faith did not waver. My heart, though tender, was steadfast. Many reading this book would assume my personality is an open book for others to see, but that's far from the truth. Until this book, my struggles stayed snug in my comfort bubble. As I've written more and opened deeper with you, our reader, I've learned how incredibly important it is to be honest in the joyful and the difficult. My propensity to keep struggles snug allowed me to maintain an aura of perfect faith; yet perfect faith is an illusion and not an accurate depiction of my walk. I can appear to have the perfect life and the put-together faith to outsiders, but even living that perfect life doesn't mean I'm walking blamelessly. My tender heart needed to display God's unwavering faithfulness. He invites me to walk blamelessly in an effort to display his glory, to stay focused on His truth, and to walk with Him through each step of the process. Living a life of perceived perfection is burdensome, but living blamelessly before a sovereign God is freeing. The Legos of our lives don't have to fit together perfectly, but we do need to follow each step of the plan to achieve the best possible result.

***When have you hidden your struggle to appear perfect?***

I share none of this season of my life to engage in the very sensitive topic of family size or fertility challenges because every child the Lord blesses our world with is a blessing, including those born to us and those lost along the way. I share because I know the struggle of having my plans changed, my heart conflicted, and my choice to seek perfection or blameless set before me.

My life being used by God is my choice. If the opportunity to write this very book had knocked and my fear or preference for privacy had won, He would've used another willing writer. When this opportunity knocked, that plan seemed just as unbelievable to me as having a fourth child, but I made a choice to take a step of faith. With each small step I've taken, He's proven His faithfulness again and again. This process of writing has been a work in progress, continually halted by life's busy schedules or my lack of motivation. However, almost every time I feel stuck about what to write, God has been delicately preparing the next story and text you're reading. He's preparing me for the task I chose to be part of with Him. He's beside me, asking me to trust Him.

***Read Isaiah 30:21 and 2 Peter 3:14.***

Whether your plan has been altered, an opportunity is knocking, or you're just feeling disheartened with your lack of perfect faith, He is nearby, waiting for your invitation. He wants you to hear His voice, and He wants to reveal Himself according to your need. He yearns to guide you in His way. We just have to choose to walk along the path blamelessly with Him.

***What is one way you can stop reaching for perfect faith and embrace blameless faith?***

Melody wrote, "The weight of that responsibility was enormous, but the joy that would come to Abraham's heart was beyond words."

Each day is full of new emotions lately. I stress about how we will juggle a large family. I shake my head, thinking we had our life all planned out. I laugh reading of Abraham's astonishment to bear a child in their old age each time another medical professional refers to my geriatric pregnancy. I pray earnest prayers of dependence on Him to show me what I should be learning and how to choose blameless faith day after day. The responsibility I feel knowing I will one day be mom to another precious blessing is enormous, but I know the joy each of our children has brought us. Each of our stones of remembrance teaches me. I know the joy that will come from this unexpected change in plans will be beyond words.

***What responsibility in your life can you start looking at joyfully?***

# 11

# IT'S A CIRCUMCISION PARTY

Have you ever been promised something, and you are still waiting for the fulfillment of that promise?

Over time, those promises mean nothing. They simply become like watered-down lemonade with a hint of flavor diluted by stale water.

Throughout the life of Abraham, God repeats His promise over and over. His promise is clear: land and babies! Two and a half kids, white picket fence, and a place to call home.

As we continue in Genesis 17, God says again, "Abraham, I am going to make you a nation, and the land on which you are standing will be yours forever."

> I will make you very fruitful; I will make nations of you and kings will come from you. I will establish my covenant as an everlasting covenant between me and you and your descendants after you for the generations to come, to be your God and the God of your descendants after you. The whole land of Canaan, where you now reside as a foreigner, I will give as an everlasting possession to you and your descendants after you; and I will be their God. (Genesis 17:6–8)

## I PROMISE YOU LAND

Have you ever had land promised to you? I have met several people in my life that have been given land from their parents or grandparents. I personally have never received land from someone, but I can imagine that if you are standing on soil that your grandfather and his grandfather once stood, there would be great significance to where your feet would beplanted.

Just recently, my husband and I purchased a small acreage of land in the country. This property is densely wooded, causing our clothes to be peppered with thorns as we walk through the underbrush. But every time we stand on our land, *our* land, we are filled with excitement of the possibilities of joy and laughter that will take place once our house is built.

Owning property provides a sense of stability. Because we own, we will always have a place to call home.

God was giving Abraham that same sense of stability. But this was not solely for Abraham to have a place to call home. The land of Canaan was also the land for God to bring His children home as they exited Egypt escaping slavery. This land was God's covenant, His promise!

## I PROMISE YOU PEOPLE

"I will make nations of you and kings will come from you" (Genesis 17:6).

By now, you are probably tired of hearing about God's promise to Abraham for land and people. It is repeated over and over again throughout the beginning of Genesis. Once again, this is the promise to Abraham: he would be the father of nations and he will possess land-- lots and lots of land. But until the birth of Ishmael, Abraham was childless. Yet God made it clear the nation Abraham was promised would only come from the womb of Sarah, not his purchased slave, Hagar. God stated that "kings will come from you." This was serious business. God had planned for great people to come from the line of Abraham, so great that their lineage would save the world!

## MEN, LINE UP! IT'S A CIRCUMCISION PARTY! WHAT?

Land and people… God's covenant with Abraham!

But in return for God's covenant, God desired something from Abraham. This thing or action God required was a mark to prove the covenant between God and Abraham.

> Then God said to Abraham, "As for you, you must keep my covenant, you and your descendants after you for the generations to come. This is my covenant with you and your descendants after you, the covenant you are to keep: Every male among you shall be circumcised." (Genesis 17:9–10 NIV)

The mark desired of God was for every male to be circumcised!

Each one of my boys was circumcised at birth. At the hospital, the nurse would take away my newborn to perform this simple surgery. This is obviously not something you typically talk about amongst your friends and family, but these were some of the hardest moments for me as a new mom. When the nurses returned my son, he lay in the bassinet in obvious discomfort and pain. But soon the pain was forgotten, and the trauma he had experienced was a faded memory. Why? Because he was a newborn.

When God commanded Abraham to be circumcised, he was a grown man. I can imagine the PTSD that this caused for him!

Tempted to skip this section in scripture because of how bizarre it is, I decided to pause and take a closer look. I just couldn't shake the question why. Why would this be necessary? In my research, I soon realized the significance of this story. Circumcision is significant for our salvation!

So let's talk circumcision. Let's look at the circumcision party on behalf of Abraham and his men.

"Everyone, form a straight line! Today we will have a party like none you have ever seen. Once you have participated in the festivities, punch and cookies will be served. And you might want to grab a few pain pills on your way out."

According to Webster's Dictionary, to circumcise is defined as "to cut off the foreskin of a male." I share this definition to make sure we all understand what we are talking about. This is not the piercing of the ears or belly button. This one requires a much larger and sharper instrument.

In Genesis 17, it is made clear this is what they are to do in order to mark the covenant between God and what will now be His people. This was to be a part of every male born to this nation from this point on and anyone living within the same household.

> For the generations to come every male among you who is eight days old must be circumcised, including those born in your household or bought with money from a foreigner—those who are not your offspring." (Genesis 17:12 NIV)

Let me paint this picture for you. Abraham is ninety-nine years old! He is not a newborn who will soon forget the trauma. His son, Ishmael, would be circumcised as a thirteen-year-old boy. Folks, I raised three thirteen-year-old boys, and if I would have told them that today's list of activities included a knife and their special part, they would have freaked out and run away.

The list of men continues with "all those born in his household or bought with his money." Grown men are lining up to have their foreskin removed. I will let your imagination draw your own conclusion as to what that day was like. It was a party gone bad. Were they offered punch and cookies for their suffering? Or did they limp home for days of recovery? I don't know, and I don't want to know! But what I do know is they obeyed immediately.

> Abraham and his son Ismael were both circumcised on that very day. And every male in Abraham's household, including those born in his household or bought from a foreigner, was circumcised with him. (Genesis 17:26–27 NIV)

Why circumcision? Why did God decide that would be the sign of the covenant between Him and His people? Couldn't it have been something a little less invasive, like clipping off an earlobe?

Here is a possible reason: circumcision was actually a familiar practice to Abraham. In Egypt, circumcision was used by the people to show devotion to the god they worshipped. This rite was reserved only for the king and those within his household. (ps.edu; Seth Trout). I have to say that this still baffles me as to why they would choose this procedure to mark their territory. I can think of many other ways to show your loyalty.

Why would Abraham be familiar with it if he didn't live in Egypt? Egypt was known for being a land rich with natural resources. The Nile provided a way for trade and a way for the resources to grow. Abraham had lived in Egypt for a short time, escaping famine in the land of Canaan, therefore relying on these resources that Egypt could provide. It would then make logical sense that while in the land of Egypt, Abraham would have learned of the practice of circumcision. Just think about it: this was not something that people would keep to themselves, at least not the women. I imagine the women bragged about how clean-cut their men were and the men of higher rank agonized over their day of doom!

God was speaking the language of Abraham. He was aware of Abraham's familiarity with the procedure when he asked Abraham to circumcise himself and the men in his household. But the significance of this for God's nation went far beyond what it meant to the leaders of Egypt. Circumcision for the One True God was an act of worship, an act of devotion.

To get a deeper understanding of this, we must look at the context of the entire Bible. Circumcision was a word used throughout the scripture. But as the scripture progresses from Genesis 17, it takes a turn. Even though the physical practice continued as a sign of devotion to God, it became more of an act of the heart. Throughout the Old Testament and into the New Testament, people continued this practice more of a tradition following the Mosaic law. Unfortunately, they became more devoted to their law than to their God. Because law replaced heart, God desired to get their attention once again through the word *circumcision*. By sheer definition of this word, the people knew it was cutting away needless flesh, the flesh of the heart. "The Lord your God will circumcise your hearts and the hearts of your descendants, so that you may love him with all your heart and with all your soul, and live" (Deuteronomy 30:6 NIV).

"Circumcise yourselves to the Lord, circumcise your hearts, you people of Judah and inhabitants of Jerusalem …" (Jeremiah 4:4 NIV).

In the New Testament, the writers and Jesus often refer to "the flesh." The flesh is our earthly being and desires. When we are living in "the flesh," we are living in our human brokenness involving ourselves in things of the world. The New Testament refers to stripping ourselves of our flesh and living according to the Spirit.

> The mind governed by the flesh is hostile to God; it does not submit to God's law, nor can it do so. Those who are in the realm of the flesh cannot please God. (Romans 8:7–8 NIV)

> Whoever sows to please their flesh, from the flesh will reap destruction; whoever sows to please the Spirit, from the Spirit will reap eternal life. (Galatians 6:8 NIV)

As we all know, the desires of our flesh get in our way of truly following God. Every day, we are torn between the two. For instance, if someone hurt me, I may give in to my fleshly desires and respond to them in kind. A hurt for a hurt! My fleshly desire to be liked and noticed by others may give way to me spreading a rumor just so I can fit in with the others in my work environment. My fleshly desire to have a man really love me may give way to a lingering look at one who is not my husband, or an extended conversation while walking to our cars after work.

We are bombarded daily with the battle of our flesh. But in Colossians, circumcision and our fleshly desires are brought together to give us a deeper understanding as to why God chose circumcision, the cutting of the foreskin of the male, to be the symbol of our hearts for Him.

> For in Christ all the fullness of the Deity lives in bodily form, and in Christ you have been brought to fullness. He is the head over every power and authority. In him you were also circumcised with a circumcision not performed by human hands. Your whole self ruled by the flesh was put off when you were circumcised by Christ … (Colossians 2:9–11 NIV)

> When you were dead in your sins and in the uncircumcision of your flesh, God made you alive with Christ. He forgave us all our sins, having canceled the charge of our legal indebtedness, which stood against us and condemned us; he had taken it away, nailing it to the cross. (Colossians 2:13–14 NIV)

The cutting of the foreskin is the removal of needless flesh in a very practical way. There are benefits to this. When the foreskin is removed, it allows for better hygiene and decreased possibility of infection.

These same benefits apply to our spiritual life. When we allow the circumcision of our hearts, the removal of our fleshly ways given to us by the death of Christ and the sacrifice He made for us, we will experience a clean life free from infection from the world.

God chose this illustration to show us His perfect plan. We disregard this practice because of the lack of understanding. For the male, it is a very painful thought. But from the beginning, God chose a tradition that we carry on to today to show us that the cutting out of needless flesh, no matter how painful that might be, is what needs to happen for the saving of our souls. Jesus came to this earth to "circumcise" our hearts. He "canceled the charge of our legal indebtedness" (Colossians 2:13), meaning He did away with the legality of this practice because this legality "stood against us and condemned us" (Colossians 2:13) and He nailed it to the cross. This makes me want to stand up and shout! God has stripped me of my needless flesh so I can follow Him and be redeemed by Him!

So what about you? Have you allowed Christ to circumcise your heart? Or do you walk through this world with needless flesh following the ways of this world? Allow Jesus today to purify your heart, cutting out the ways of this world to find peace and hope that only He can give.

## THREE MEN AND STILL NO BABY

Sitting in the shade protecting himself from the sun, Abraham could hear his wife inside the tent as she continued preparing for the day. Abraham would often find himself sitting on the same tree stump positioned perfectly under the trees outside the tent. As he would sit, many things crowded his mind. He was so grateful to God for what He had done for him: a new land he loved and could call his own; his son, Ishmael, whom he loved so deeply; his wife, Sarah; and so many things.

But as he sat counting his blessings, there was still an undefined emptiness. The promise by God to bless him with a child from the womb of Sarah was unfulfilled. Abraham and Sarah were now past the childbearing years, so the reality of this seemed impossible. Would this ever come into fruition? God had promised, but Abraham was still waiting.

So often this is the truth for our own lives. We hear, read, and claim God's promises, but we are still waiting. What we do in the waiting defines who we are in our faith. We wait for the results from the doctor, we wait for the job offer, we wait for God to shine through the darkness of evil … we wait! But what do we do in the waiting? Do we pace or do we prosper? Do we ponder or do we produce?

This next verse is the words of the apostle Paul in the New Testament. He was speaking to the church of Rome, pleading with them to live in peace with one another as believers. He says, "Never be lacking in zeal, but keep your spiritual fervor, serving the Lord. Be joyful in hope, patient in affliction, faithful in prayer" (Romans 12:11–12 NIV).

Imagine with me that the apostle Paul is sitting on a tree stump next to Abraham. He knew Abraham was afflicted in his waiting. Abraham's heart's desire to have a child through the womb of Sarah and to believe the promise from God that he would birth a nation was weighing heavy on his heart. He had lived day after day, trying hard to be faithful. He had followed God in obedience to the best of his human ability. He had followed in God's command for circumcision for himself and his household, but now he waits. He is sitting broken in his heart and broken in his waiting.

If the apostle Paul could have spoken to Abraham that day, he would have said …

Don't lack …<br>
Keep the fervor …<br>
Serve the Lord …<br>
Be joyful …<br>
Be patient …<br>
Be faithful!

Be patient … be patient in affliction. These are the words of a man who knew affliction as though it was his best friend. He had been beaten, robbed, and imprisoned because of his faith. He had plenty, and he had nothing. He was loved most, and he was loved least.

Paul would have said, "Abraham, I know you are hurting in this waiting. I know you do not understand why you must wait. I know that waiting causes you to question the promises of God. But I want you to hear that it is in the waiting where your faith will grow. God wants us to be patient in our affliction. But truthfully, whether we are patient or not, God's promises are out of our control. We cannot move this mountain, we cannot orchestrate this change, we cannot … we cannot!"

If the apostle Paul were sitting next to you today, encouraging you to be "be patient in your affliction," what would that look like?

When we are stuck in our affliction, the last thing we want to endure is patience. We want it to be solved swiftly and thoroughly. But many times, the affliction hangs on like an unwelcomed in-law. Hope to move beyond the affliction not only wavers but can be nonexistent. I do not want affliction, and I don't want to be patient in it.

The apostle Paul's words take an unexpected turn. He said that instead of looking within yourself, look at what is around you, what is outside of your affliction. It could be someone else who is in affliction. Busy yourself in caring for others, and it will make this afflicted time more tolerable and more productive.

I am a sitter, not a server! I would rather sit in my comfy chair and wait for God to move. Once He starts to move, then I will move. But what if God desires us to move in our waiting? What if "patience in our affliction" looks more like the first part of those verses from Romans 12? "Don't lack … Keep the fervor … Serve the Lord …" Our waiting would no longer look like waiting. There is no reason we can't prosper in the pause.

Look further to what the apostle Paul says. In the next verse, He gives us a to-do list while we pause. "Share with the Lord's people who are in need. Practice hospitality" (Romans 12:13 NIV).

Pain and affliction stop us dead in our tracks. Our natural tendency is to hide until it goes away. Let's just wait it out until we feel better. But the apostle Paul says something different.

Get up on your feet and serve! While you wait, serve! Find

someone in need and serve them. Be hospitable to others around you. That is exactly what Abraham did.

> The Lord appeared to Abraham near the great trees of Mamre while he was sitting at the entrance to his tent in the heat of the day. Abraham looked up and saw three men standing nearby. When he saw them, he hurried from the entrance of his tent to meet them and bowed low to the ground.
>
> He said, "If I have found favor in your eyes, my lord, do not pass your servant by. Let a little water be brought, and then you may wash your feet and rest under this tree. Let me get you something to eat, so you can be refreshed and then go on your way—now that you have come to your servant." (Genesis 18:1–5 NIV)

And then there were three. As Abraham sat quietly in the shade, he noticed three men approaching the campground. He hurried out to the field to greet them. When Abraham approached them, he realized there was something different about these men. Were they marked with the deity? Were they dressed as royalty?

Whatever the sign, Abraham's response to these men was to bow down low to the ground. Abraham immediately called them "lord" and positioned himself as their servant. The cause for this immediate reaction is unknown, but as you read further, you will see that at some point the three separated, leaving one with Abraham and two heading toward the city of Sodom.

So who were these mystery men, and why did they come? Again, reading within the context, you will see that scripture itself identifies them. Scripture will interpret scripture. One is presumably God because as the other two left for the city, Abraham addresses the remaining man as "the Lord." "The men turned away and went toward Sodom, but Abraham remained standing before the Lord" (Genesis 18:22 NIV).

Some scholars identify this man as Jesus, God in human form. This could be, but it is not stated clearly here. But what is stated is that this is the Lord God. And in the continuation of this story, Abraham addresses him as such and has an extensive conversation with God.

So who are the other two? Again, often scripture interprets scripture. "The two angels arrived at Sodom in the evening, and Lot was sitting in the gateway of the city" (Genesis 19:1 NIV).

According to the scripture, they were angels who had accompanied God when they met Abraham at his tent. So we have two angels and the Lord. No wonder Abraham bowed immediately when they approached him. We have answered the "who." Now let's take a look at the "why."

Showing the men hospitality, he had asked Sarah to fix a meal for the three men. After the meal had been prepared, Abraham stood close under a tree while they ate. Then the men asked, "Where is your wife Sarah?"

"There, in the tent," he said.

"Then one of them said, 'I will surely return to you about this time next year, and Sarah your wife will have a son'" (Genesis 18:10 NIV).

She laughed in disregard at "and Sarah your wife will have a son."

> Now Sarah was listening at the entrance to the tent, which was behind him. Abraham and Sarah were already very old, and Sarah was past the age of childbearing. So **Sarah laughed** to herself as she thought, "After I am worn out and my lord is old, will I now have this pleasure?" (Genesis 18:10–12)

Let's sit with Sarah a bit and listen to her laughter. Eavesdropping on the conversation, she laughed at what they had said. This time next year, she supposedly would have a son.

By this time, Sarah was so over having a child. Or was she? Her laughter was a strong indication that the desire and pain were still present. Laughter is that mask covering our disappointments.

Sarah, being keenly aware she did not have a child, had spent years of her life living in the pain of disappointment. She had orchestrated a plan years ago, hoping to ease the pain and suffering. Maybe if Abraham would have a child with another woman, she could call that child her own. But no matter how hard she had tried, she was still without a son. Her arms were empty, and her body was old.

Standing at the edge of the tent, Sarah could hear the words of these men;en who were strangers yet dared to enter her private world of infertility; men who made a promise that she dared to believe would ever be true; men who were strangers yet made a declaration as though they were deities. Within this declaration, emotions flowed. Could this be true, or was this another one of God's empty promises?

The emotions of Sarah are all too familiar to us. Waiting for God's promises feels empty and unattainable. As we look for any sign of hope, our expectation is dashed once again by disappointment. Disappointment blinds us, leaving us empty in our disbelief. Why would God promise and not fulfill? Maybe we are looking in the wrong direction.

There are promises and hopes that we hold so tightly that if we get one glimpse of hope for fulfillment, we become the straw sucking up the last of a delicious milkshake. We close our eyes, hoping that magically the glass will refill. But when we open our eyes, our reality settles in. The thing we hoped for is still empty and unfulfilled. Our well is dry, as dry as our glass of milkshake.

I believe this is how Sarah felt that day. Her well of hope was dry. Year after year, her hopes to hold a child in her arms made her feel dejected. Her young hope to feel the soft skin of her newborn child had vanished. The longing to experience a toddler's grasp no longer existed. Over time, she had to put these hopes aside, knowing the pain of being childless was more than she could bear. She had become callous to the thought of being a mother. As she stood hearing this news, her calloused heart responded in laughter, in disregard. Letting down her guard and feeling this hope again was out of the question, so she laughed! Treating this news as unworthy of notice, she laughed to protect her broken heart.

I can see in my own life how I have held onto an unfulfilled hope until that desire no longer lives. To guard my heart, I have set that desire aside, denying its very existence. But all it takes is just one mention of it or something that triggers that thought, and that desire comes rushing in like an unbridled wind. My thoughts become so overwhelmed that I spend my energy trying to capture them, putting them back in the jar where they belong. If someone were to tell me that my dream was going to come true, I too would have laughed in disregard.

## SHE LIED IN HER LAUGHTER

> Then the Lord said to Abraham, "Why did Sarah laugh and say, 'Will I really have a child, now that I am old? Is anything too hard for the Lord? I will return to you at the appointed time next year, and Sarah will have a son."
>
> Sarah was afraid, so she lied and said, "I did not laugh."
>
> But he said, "Yes, you did laugh." (Genesis 18:13–15 NIV)

When I was a young child, my father asked me to empty the trash can in his restroom. As a typical child, I got caught up in something I wanted to do and forgot about the trash. When he came home, he asked if I had done what he had asked. My quick response was yes, a lie. I lied because I was afraid.

Sarah responded in the same way. She did not want to admit that she had laughed, so she lied in her laughter. Did she think that lying to God would cover up her disbelief? Did she think that her lie would protect her heart? Maybe! But truth be told, it didn't matter what she thought. She had lied about her laughter.

Lying to God is like running on a treadmill with no stop button.

It will get you nowhere in your pursuit. To tell the God who knows all that you did not do something is pointless and frivolous. Our image of God determines how honest we are with Him. When we see God as cold and indifferent, we hold our truths tightly to our chest because we don't trust what He will do with our heart. But when we see God as kind and loving, a true friend, is doesn't matter what our truth is. We will feel safe with Him in our anger, disappointment, and hurt. He will be the first one we run to in order to find peace and tranquility.

Sarah was angry and hurt, but instead of pouring her emotions out to God in the safety of His arms, she laughed and pulled away in her hurt. She had a skewed image of God, therefore not trusting Him.

What is your image of God? How do you see God? Our image of God often rests on our experiences with God. And our experiences with God are determined by us. God is always present, always working, always desiring. But we pick and choose how much God we want. Do we want all of Him or just enough to make us feel good? Are we experiencing Him daily, or are our experiences determined by our mood?

When we choose to experience God for who He really is and who He desires to be in us, when promises seem as though they will not be fulfilled, our faith gets stronger; when God seems slow to speak, our faith gets stronger; when God chooses a no, our faith gets stronger! We measure our image of Him by how we measure our experiences with Him. How do you choose to experience God today? Picking and choosing what you would like, choosing from a dinner menu or choosing all of Him like a full-course meal? If you choose to experience God to the fullest, tell Him that. Then allow your actions to show that decision by spending time with Him and getting to know His heart.

## ISAAC'S FIRST STEPS AND HAGAR'S FINAL WALK

As the story progresses, the fulfillment of God's promise came into fruition one year later.

> Now the Lord was gracious to Sarah as he had said, and the Lord did for Sarah what he had promised. Sarah became pregnant and bore a son to Abraham in his old age, at the very time God had promised him. (Genesis 21:1–3 NIV)

So this is a fun part of this story, or should I say funny? The laughter from Sarah didn't stop, but it changed. Her laughter went from disregard to design.

> Sarah said, "God has brought me laughter, and everyone who hears about this will laugh with me." And she added, "Who would have said to Abraham that Sarah would nurse children? Yet I have borne him a son in his old age." (Genesis 21:6–7 NIV)

Through the delight in her soul, Sarah could now see God's design, which caused a deep belly laugh, a laughter of joy and design.

But when Sarah and Abraham's child, Isaac, was taking his first steps, Hagar was taking her final walk.

## TALKS WITH EMILEIGH

Some of you may not remember the original *Land Before Time* movie, but as a child, my brother and I watched this movie often. My grandparents had a Ziploc set of cups with all the characters on them, and I can still remember fighting for the Little Foot cup with my brother and cousins at their home. Little Foot was the timid but kind longneck dinosaur, and he was my favorite. Spike and Petrie were great too, but even now I gravitate to Little Foot when pouring juice for breakfast. Those cups were a treasured memory from visiting my grandparents' home. A couple years before my grandmother passed away, she gave them to me, telling me she wanted to be sure I received the cups she knew I loved so much. These cups are used frequently in my own home now. My daughter has grown to love Little Foot, and my son always uses Spike. Even my nephew will ask for the dinosaur cup when he visits. To many and likely even to my cousins who may not remember them, they're just cups. To me, they're important. They're not valuable in the monetary sense or take up much space, but someone I love dearly passed them on to me. She loved me enough to pass along something she knew I would love.

***Do you have possessions that have been passed down through your family?***

"And to you and your offspring I will give the land … as a permanent possession … " (Genesis 17:8).

Our family recently purchased five acres of land. Right now, it sits. We paid for the land and love the potential it holds, but there isn't value in it like I hold for my *Land Before Time* cups. The cups were given to me with intentionality and purpose. We use them regularly. I don't yet know what our land will become, but I trust the purpose and future for it that I cannot yet see.

Abraham also could not see all God had planned for the land He was given as a possession. God had great purpose beyond any plans Abraham himself could have constructed or imagined. God was planning and preparing stability not in something temporary like plastic cups or even lush pastures but in something long-lasting and flowing with milk and honey. (See Deuteronomy 11:8–9 and 26:9.)

***Have you ever held onto something in hopes it would reap great purpose? Did you hold on too long, or did you see it prosper?***

We believe the land our family purchased holds purpose, and our kids (and prayerfully even our grandkids one day) will enjoy its beauty. For now, we hold onto it as life throws obstacles in the way of that opportunity. It would be easy to be frustrated by life's constant challenges, changing plans, the rising building costs, or even our hesitancy to leave our current neighbors we love. Even so, if we allow the setbacks to hold us back, we'll miss the purpose. We'll miss the enjoyment of the journey, the details preparing us for the destination. One thing is certain for our family: We believe God wants us to take this step.

***When have you taken a step of faith without understanding the purpose?***

Let's be honest here. There's no easy way to transition into discussing circumcision. I can't help but wonder if Abraham hesitated just a moment as he thought, "You want me to do what now?" I wasn't quite prepared the day Melody told me the topic of this chapter, and yet I can remember vividly the two days we were faced with it, and the feelings it evoked in me are still raw.

As mentioned, two of our boys were NICU babies. They were poked, prodded, tested, and visibly uncomfortable for the first several vulnerable days of their lives. Both circumstances were different, but with both, I was hard-pressed to leave their side. With Samuel in particular, I remember the nurses forcing me to take cafeteria breaks just for some fresh air and scenery change. Despite this, when the time came for each boy's circumcision, I had no desire to be nearby. I couldn't bear the thought of more pain being inflicted on my son.

In my experience with circumcision, I escaped immediately to what has become a familiar practice in hospitals. We'd decided to have the procedure completed, but I steered away from the potential pain it would inflict. For Abraham, he didn't escape or even attempt to; he simply obeyed.

***When faced with a difficult decision, do you avoid, or is it instinct for you to pray/listen/obey?***

As I prayed over and considered my reaction versus Abraham's, it prompted me to wonder: How often do I avoid my own need to cut away needless flesh? When there is a need in my life to shed "needless flesh," I'm certain God doesn't shy away from the process. Even when the necessary circumcision of my heart is or will be painful, its removal is honoring to Him. He stands by to guide and strengthen me through its process. Like the Israelites who circumcised themselves as an act of devotion of God, we now circumcise our hearts in the same way for the same purpose, to devote ourselves more intimately to Him by living more purely by the Spirit, not according to the flesh.

***What needless desires of the flesh do you need to remove?***

Consider a few of my struggles as you contemplate that question. Sometimes when I hear something intriguing about a friend, I am tempted to share it with another. I find myself jealous of the mom who seemingly has it all together. I struggle to forgive the family member who has caused pain to myself and others I love. I can even struggle to pray for that family member if I let the hurt simmer too long. I yell at my kids if my patience runs too thin. The growing division in our society on so many different topics prevents me from showing love and grace freely. I don't honor my husband when my exhaustion is overwhelming. I resist the need to apologize when my pride wins over.

***Read Galatians 5:19–21.***

This scripture concerning the desires of the flesh is not restricted to the more evident sins of drunkenness or sexual immorality. We often narrow in on the more evident sins when considering these types of conversations. In truth, there are actions and temptations every day standing in the way of our walk with and devotion to the Lord.

Jesus died once to atone for all the needless flesh we insist on being burdened by. Yet the removal of it, the circumcision of the heart, is a process, a continual and consistent action toward progress. Our effort to remove each fleshly desire is a step toward honoring He who made you. He who commanded the original circumcision has purpose to purify and cleanse our hearts, and He loves us enough to point out the need to circumcise our fleshly desires. Our response to obey His command is a choice we make daily to worship Him and devote our hearts toward His purity.

***Give an example of a time you shed needless flesh. Was it difficult or easy? Do you have someone in your life you trust enough to challenge you when you need to remove needless flesh?***

Sometimes the removal of needless flesh can be painful. Sometimes it can be exhausting. Always, it takes time, strength, and enablement from Him.

I've written before that it's not always the details of our story that matter but how we allow God to use them. In relation to our need to cleanse and discard our fleshly desires, our sinful ways, it isn't always about the particular struggle or circumstance we're facing but about what we do with the time it takes to move from afflicted to faithful. How do we allow God to use the time and write the details with us? Where do we focus our energy? Where and how do we lean into Romans 12:12?

***Read Romans 12:12. Which command do you find most challenging? When facing affliction, are you joyful, patient, or faithful?***

While Melody proclaims to be a sitter, I am a do-er. When affliction hits, I do my best to avoid it. However, because I don't sit well, affliction can become exhaustion. Whether it be sitting in a NICU, on bed rest, the unknown future of our land and future home, the desire to be the perfect wife/mother/daughter/friend, or feeling out of control fuels my affliction. Therefore, pooling my energy into comforting a friend navigating rough waters, making a meal for another, or simply listening to others' affliction provides an easy distraction. It brings me joy to serve others in this way, but it certainly doesn't aid my level of patience with my own affliction.

Abraham served wholeheartedly when their visitors arrived, but Sarah, while active in her task to prepare a meal and serve, was focused on her own affliction. As I glean from my own life, it's possible Sarah was focused more on what she could do than why she was doing it. She accomplished the task. She served even in her affliction, but she was still hurting and seemed to initially miss the joy Romans 12 calls for. Too often, I can be caught up in doing things for others and distracting myself that I lose sight of my true reason for serving. I can miss the joy serving can truly offer.

I believe Sarah was patient. Goodness, she was at least ninety years old, waiting on her earnest desire to have a child. We know from Hebrews 11:11 that she clung to Hall of Faith-level trust in the Lord. She needed to rediscover her joy. By the Lord's beautiful plan, her laughter she would expel in disregard would soon turn to pure joy.

***Have you experienced the adage "laugh so you don't cry"?***

An unending day of unfortunate events, a seemingly hopeless situation, a struggle to find the joy, I believe Sarah laughed so she wouldn't cry. She desperately wanted a child, but she was old. She and Abraham were beyond childbearing years, so when the Lord promised she would bear a child and name him Isaac, she laughed in disregard.

As my husband and I continued to process the expectant arrival of a fourth child, we shared the news with our children. They experienced immediate joy and gratitude. We were honest with them about both the unexpected news as well as the ER visit and risk of still losing the baby. One evening at dinner, our two older children shared with us their grand plan. They wanted to name the new baby Isaac. They said, "Isaac means laughter. When Sarah found out she would have a baby, she laughed. Mommy thought she was done having babies. Then God gave us one more, and she probably laughed too." In all honesty, I was doing more crying than laughing. In fact, I think God may have been doing a little laughing of His own at my desire to constantly be in control and write my own plans. Their hearts' joy for this new sibling, their pristine ability to bring light to the true blessing of our circumstance, and their trust in God's design turned what once felt like affliction in this unexpected season into joy. I needed to be patient while God used my children to write some of the details.

God used Sarah's fear, her brokenness, and her disregard to write the details for her ultimate joy. He boosted her faith because sometimes the best way to grow our faith is for it to be stretched. As she processed her affliction, as He stretched her faith, she learned to trust the Lord more with her heart. When we don't trust someone with our hearts, it's easier to lie, to laugh in disregard, and to cling to the fleshly desires. But when we see God for who He wants to be in our lives, we learn to trust Him with the details of our affliction and turn that frustration, confusion, disappointment, and hurt into a patient, joyful faith.

***Read Psalm 139:13.***

He knows my heart because He knit me together. He knows my heart better than I know myself. He knows your heart as well. Through affliction, joy, patience, and trust, we can learn to trust

Him to tend to our hearts and work with us to write the details of our story. As Sarah took steps to trust the Lord with her heart and to surrender her story to His design, her disregard turned to joy. Her once-pained laughter became a laughter that glorified the Lord.

***When has something brought you joy to the point of laughter?***

One day soon, our family will welcome our baby Isaac. I can't predict the future. In fact, you'd think by now, I'd learn my lesson and stop trying to plan altogether. I do suspect I'll do some laughing with his arrival though. I suspect I will laugh out of joy for the precious blessing he will be. I suspect I will laugh, remembering when our older children chose his name. I suspect I'll even laugh recalling how I once felt stuck to begin writing these chapters about Abraham and Sarah's Isaac as the Lord unknowingly prepared me for my own Isaac, as He prepared the details of this chapter in our family's life.

Purpose, circumcision, and laughter, these three words don't seem to correlate, and yet the book of Genesis brings powerful meaning to God's design and application for our lives. The Promised Land held purpose, given by One who loved those He passed it to and those He gave it to loved Him. It held value because of its inherent purpose. When we circumcise our heart, our flesh for the One we love, it also holds purpose and value. Though sometimes arduous, the process is refining. When we devote our hearts toward true joy, expectant patience, and relentless faith, our Father unearths purpose and His ultimate glory. For that reason, we can cry and laugh with exuberant joy. We have opportunities to inherit His purpose when we circumcise our hearts for Him and enjoy the laughter in the details written with Him.

# 12

# ISAAC'S FIRST STEPS, HAGAR'S FINAL WALK

A short recap: As the story progresses, God's promise was brought into fruition.

> Now the Lord was gracious to Sarah as he had said, and the Lord did for Sarah what he had promised. Sarah became pregnant and bore a son to Abraham in his old age, at the very time God had promised him. (Genesis 21:1–3 NIV)

At the birth of Isaac, the laughter of Sarah changed. Her laughter was no longer rooted in disregard but in design. She was beginning to see God's design for her to be the mother of a nation.

> Sarah said, "God has brought me laughter, and everyone who hears about this will laugh with me." And she added, "Who would have said to Abraham that Sarah would nurse children? Yet I have borne him a son in his old age." (Genesis 21:6–7 NIV)

Laughter could be heard throughout the camp, a deep belly laugh, a laughter of joy, and a laughter of design.

For three years, joy filled the camp as the son of Abraham and Sarah learned to walk and talk. People were amazed at the joy that

Sarah's only son brought her. Laughter that had once been held captive within her was now a familiar sound to those she encountered. As Isaac toddled in his new world, Sarah rejoiced in a happiness that she had never known.

But as Isaac took his first steps, Hagar was taking her final walk.

## HAGAR'S FINAL WALK

Thirteen years prior to Isaac's birth, Hagar had been kicked out of the camp because of the hatred Sarah had for her. But in that dark moment as she stood by the well seeking refuge and refreshment, Hagar had a moment with an angel of God.

Looking back at that moment in Genesis 16:9, the angel made it very clear to Hagar, "Go back!"

"Go back," these words shattered Hagar's world. These two simple words from the angel placed Hagar on the road, returning to the person she feared the most, Sarah. God said, "Go back to where you have come from and allow Me to work out what I want worked out in you. I will not only provide for you, but I will provide for your unborn son."

As Hagar returned to the camp of Abraham and Sarah, there were many things that she was witness to: the circumcision of men; the continued promises from God to Abraham and Sarah that they would have a son who would produce a nation; the three visitors; Sodom and Gomorrah destroyed; and then the birth of Sarah and Abraham's son, Isaac.

For thirteen years, she and her son, Ishmael, formed a bond that no one could separate. For thirteen years, Ishmael also bonded with his father. Within these critical years for Ishmael, beliefs and morals were spoken into him as father and mother carved into him the man they desired him to be.

The son of Abraham and Sarah is often our focus as we watch Isaac grow up to become the chosen nation. But the relationship between Abraham and his son, Ishmael, was also significant. Abraham loved his firstborn son more than life itself, causing his heart to break in millions of pieces as he waved his final goodbye.

As parents, we know full well the critical years of parenting, the young years where the bond is formed, instilling morals and the foundation for future life. These are the years our children build their morals and beliefs according to our morals and beliefs. We instill these in our children in hopes that they will mature into an image similar to us. But as our children grow into their preteen years, that bond is challenged by their desire to be independent. This independence is met with many challenges as they form their own belief system. I once read that as our children grow, we give them blocks to build their castle. These blocks have been carefully chosen by us and then handed to our children to strategically place them as they build their structure. Our young children accept these with gratitude and trust, placing them within their castle. In their young life, their castle looks similar to ours. Then it happens. They become teenagers! And they become strangers living within our own homes!

In their teenage years, a large machine called independence enters the scene and bulldozes each and every block they have strategically placed within their castle. The castle we once took pride in as parents is now unrecognizable. We begin to panic, fearing what our children will become. I once feared my son would end up in jail because I couldn't get him to clean his room and do his homework. That is called extreme parent thinking.

As our teenagers continue in their pursuit of independence, eventually they grow tired. In their exhaustion, they begin picking up the blocks that once formed their castle. As they pick each block up, they examine that block, determining if they want that block to return to their castle. The scary part for us as parents is to watch which blocks they pick up and which blocks they discard. As the fear sets in, it is important for us to step aside and be patient, trusting the foundation we have laid. If we have given them a firm foundation, they will pick up each block, keeping the blocks they feel are important. The rebuild of their castle may be shaped a bit differently, but more than likely, they will have selected several of the blocks we were able to give them when they were young. They will add a few here and there, but the castles will look similar. As a mother of grown sons, I can testify this to be true. I have watched each of my sons knock down the castle we built for them. As each one knocked it down, there was a point in which their dad and I walked in to see the castle destroyed. We felt devastated and fearful as to what they would become. But looking at their lives today, we can see blocks that have been used from the foundation we laid. But we also see blocks we do not recognize. Those are blocks they chose for themselves. But that is okay. This is their castle now and no longer ours!

Within the thirteen years that Ishmael got to spend with his father, Abraham, his castle had been built by a man who loved and followed God. This exposure was priceless. If the angel had not told Hagar to return from where she had come, she and Ishmael would probably have returned to the land of Egypt, which is not a land built on the foundation of the One True God. Perhaps God was showing Hagar and Ishmael His deep love for them, allowing Ishmael to receive a foundation built by his father, Abraham. And perhaps Hagar also got the opportunity to learn these principles during her thirteen years at the camp.

## ALL EYES ON ISAAC

After the birth of Isaac, things for Ishmael and Hagar took a turn for the worse. All eyes were now on Isaac. Isaac was now an adorable toddler. He was almost three years old when the time to wean him from his mother arrived. Tradition wrote that a celebration of this occasion was in order. And because this was the child of the king and queen of the camp, this party was rather large.

Since Isaac was almost three, his brother, Ishmael, was approaching seventeen years old. Ishmael was still designing his castle, and baby brother became the intruder in the room, threatening Ishmael's design.

As the party for Isaac raged on, Ishmael thought it might be fun to taunt his brother. Now if you have ever taunted a three-year-old, you will know that the taunt never ends well. This is nothing new between brothers, but because of the complexity of the situation, two moms and one dad, Sarah would not tolerate her precious son to be teased by the other woman's son.

When our youngest son was still a baby, I remember our middle son telling me he would never taunt his younger brother because he loved him so much. You can guess how long that lasted! It lasted until his little brother became a toddler tyrant and was no longer so adorable. I imagine the same thing happened in this story between Ishmael and Isaac. They may have been brothers, but they would never be friends.

As the story continues, Sarah was enraged when she saw her baby boy being teased by the other woman's son. Truth be told, she never liked this arrangement. Yes, she was the one who devised this nasty scheme, but she was not enjoying the outcome. So the taunting was her perfect excuse to rid Hagar and Ishmael once and for all. And that is exactly what she did.

But Hagar was also in need for an escape clause, and she had the perfect one. Because Hagar was a bought slave, she was mere property. She had no rights as a human; she was owned and controlled by Abraham and Sarah. But here was her escape clause: Ishmael, her only son. Because of Mesopotamian law, Ishmael, being the firstborn, had first dibs on the inheritance of Abraham. But as the escape clause states, Hagar could sell those rights.

> Early the next morning Abraham took some food and a skin of water and gave them to Hagar. He set them on her shoulders and then sent her off with the boy. She went on her way and wandered to the Desert of Beersheba. (Genesis 21:14 NIV)

Another morning of sadness and departure for Hagar and Abraham. I can imagine Sarah peeking through the blinds of her tent, assuring herself that Abraham would complete the plan. With her three-year-old on her hip, she smiled her heart whispering, "vengeance is mine sayeth Sarah."

As the sun began to rise, Abraham approached Hagar and Ishmael's tent with sadness. He had gathered some food for their departure and a skin filled with water; he laid them on the shoulders of Hagar. She felt the weight of the provisions, but even more, she felt the weight of the journey ahead of her.

Abraham was sad: "The matter distressed Abraham greatly because it concerned his son" (Genesis 21:11 NIV).

God assures Abraham that Ishmael would be taken care of. Ishmael had become a pawn in the hands of both Sarah and Hagar. In the end, the final movement of this pawn benefited both Sarah and Hagar, leaving Ishmael to lose in so many ways.

Sarah resisted,
Abraham mourned,
God spoke,
And Hagar walked!

> The matter distressed Abraham greatly because it concerned his son. But God said to him, "Do not be so distressed about the boy and your slave woman. Listen to whatever Sarah tells you, because it is through Isaac that your offspring will be reckoned. I will make the son of the slave into a nation also because he is your offspring." (Genesis 21:11–13 NIV)

## GOD KEEPS HIS WORD

Have you ever considered that God keeps His word even when it wasn't His original word?

Some call this God's permissive will versus His perfect will. But truth of the matter is that it doesn't matter what you call it; it is still God's will.

Because we live in a imperfectworld, God's perfect will very rarely touches us, if at all. We are navigating through His permissive will brought on by a choice we have made or a choice that someone else has made. If we were in His perfect will, we would not be residing on our current streets. We would be living in the land of Eden, and there would be no need for a walk back to Eden because we would be walking within Eden. Life is filled with imperfect navigation of God's will, so let's agree to join hands and walk together as imperfect vessels.

The story of Isaac and Ishmael was imperfect. But even in this imperfection, they were both products of a word given, and a word kept by God. Throughout the story of Abraham, God promised a nation. But as we have looked closely at the story, that promise took a side road, producing Ishmael. Ishmael was not God's original promise; he was more God's provision. But since Ishmael was from the seed of Abraham and God had promised that from the seed of Abraham would come forth a nation, God kept His promise. Even though Ishmael was the right seed coming from the wrong womb, the promise was still the same. God promised a nation! "I will make the son of the slave into a nation also because he is your offspring" (Genesis 21:11–13 NIV).

It would be easy to dismiss God's original promise to Abraham to birth a nation because God's original design took a side road journey due to the sins of Sarah and Abraham. It would be easy for us to skip Ishmael. But God never skips His creation. He has a plan and purpose for each and every one of us. So now, instead of one nation being born, there will be two. Granted, the nation that came from Isaac was the chosen nation, but nevertheless, Ishmael also became a successful and prosperous nation.

> The angel added, "I will increase your descendants so much that they will be too numerous to count." (Genesis 16:10)

This was the promise that God gave to Hagar as she leaned against the well some seventeen years ago. Her child growing within her womb would become a great nation and increase in numbers and be fruitful.

When you look at these promises from God for Ishmael and Isaac, they are uncanny in their similarities. The future story within the Old Testament shows us the twelve tribes of Jacob. Jacob was the son of Isaac; therefore, the promise of a nation through Isaac came through the twelve tribes of Jacob. But we also have the twelve tribes of Ishmael.

> This is the account of the family line of Abraham's son Ishmael, whom Sarah's slave, Hagar the Egyptian, bore to Abraham.
>
> These are the names of the sons of Ishmael, listed in the order of their birth; Nebaioth the firstborn of Ishmael, Kedar, Adbeel, Mibsam, Mishma, Dumah, Massa, Hadad, Tema, Jetur, Naphish and Kedemah. These were the sons of Ishmael, and these are the names of the twelve tribal rulers according to their settlements and camps. Ishmael lived a hundred and thirty-seven years. He breathed his last and died, and he was gathered to his people. (Genesis 25:12–17 NIV).

These similarities posed a curiosity within me that I could not shake. The parallels between these stories begged for a deeper story told.

So I asked myself, "What does God want to say to us through this story? Why was it important for God to communicate that His promise would not only be for Isaac, his chosen one, but also for Ishmael, which by human standards was a mistake?"

This truth touched my heart. What is stuck between these promises? Why am I stuck between these promises?

Two sons,
one father,
similar promises …
but two outcomes.

The product of Isaac was the great Israelite nation, the chosen Israelite nation. It is the nation we continue to read about in scripture, the nation in captivity, the nation saved from captivity.

The twelve tribes of Ishmael were Arab tribes from which the earlier tribes of the Muslim community descended from. Therefore, the nation born to Ishmael was the Islamic nation who have fought and struggled against one another throughout time.

As I looked closer into my heart for the why, the question of who became more relevant than the why. Who did I identify with? Isaac? Ishmael? Or was it more Sarah or Hagar? Why did I wrestle with this part of the story?

Recently I was having a conversation about this with a friend. I told her that I was stuck in my writing. I could not figure out why the contrast or likeness of these two stories stuck to me like flies on honey. I couldn't shake it, and I didn't want to rewrite this chapter. Often when I am stuck in my writing, I will ask God what He wants me to communicate to my audience. What do these people need to hear? But I found myself no longer asking that question but more the question of, "God, what are you trying to say to me?" My heart began to break with the truth of how these characters wrestled within my own heart.

On the surface, there are incredible lessons to be absorbed:

- Lessons that teach us that God keeps His promises, which provides tremendous comfort.
- Lessons that there are no favorites in God's world.

Looking at the comparison of Isaac and Ishmael, it would be so easy to conclude that playing favorites would make sense. I mean, who played the main stage here?

Yet God knew that their lives were in stark contrast to each other.

He stated it.

He prophesied it.

He warned against it.

He completed it …

He completed His promise for both men, His promise of a nation and a fruitful life. God knew His story before it was written. Yet He loved both equally and gave both the same opportunities. Raised by Abraham, it was the beginning of two nations.

## I AM ISHMAEL … I AM HAGAR

Who did I identify with? There are ways in which I can see myself as Sarah. I am often filled with distrust and manipulation. I have wanted my life to go a certain direction and have manipulated in order to find some semblance of that path.

Abraham? Well, he is just out of my league!

Honestly, I saw myself as Ishmael and as Hagar. I related to their life as castaways and torn from their world.

Here is my story written amongst the pages of Hagar and Ishmael.

Growing up, I felt alone and different in my world. I navigated my world aimlessly, lost yet oddly connected. Hindsight allows me to see that as a young teen, I felt lost and disconnected because of the abuse I was surviving. I would quietly peer into my world whether that was at school, my neighborhood, or church feeling cast out, feeling odd and different as though I didn't belong. I lived in secret fear of bringing my friends to my home for a sleepover or hang-out night because I feared what my father would do. I was determined that his abuse would stay restricted to my world and not the world of my friends. All of this weight convinced me that I was different. No one knew why I was different because that was my secret.

When I look at Ishmael and Hagar, they too were different. They did not fit into the world in which they were placed. Ishmael was the child that shouldn't have been, and I am convinced he knew that no matter how hard he tried. Hagar was an unwanted slave who birthed a troubled child. They navigated life as best they could, but never felt as though they fit in. So they escaped into the wilderness. Day after day, I escaped my world. It wasn't to the wilderness, but it was to the streets of my neighborhood, the streets of my community. The only place I felt truly loved was when I was no longer trapped within the walls of my home. My escape seemed innocent and without regard, but my escape brought peace and tranquility that did not exist within the walls of my home. Each morning I would go to our immaculately clean garage and pull out my escape. As I pulled my bike from the garage, I would head down our steep driveway. As soon as my tires touched the street, I knew I was free. As long as I pedaled the streets, I would feel peace. I no longer felt cast out, but I felt like I belonged, me, my bicycle, and the street below. We were connected in a way that cannot be described.

Maybe that is how Ismael and Hagar felt. Maybe they felt release from rejection and pain. Perhaps once their feet hit the dirt road heading to the wilderness, peace overcame them. Obviously, that cannot be answered. But when I connect my heart to their hearts, I know that feeling of release, release from abuse and ridicule. As I allowed my heart to connect to their story, I saw me.

There was a moment while they were in the wilderness that the lack of food and water overcame their bodies. God once again swooped down to provide for their bodies and to provide for their souls. God too provided for me. In my hunger and thirst, He provided a gentle woman who offered me cookies and lemonade.

The parallels between the story of Ishmael and Hagar and the story of me explains why I was stuck between those two promises. I could feel the despair for Hagar and Ishmael because I could feel my own despair. I could feel the provision of God for them because I could feel my own provision given by God. I could feel the hope that God laid out for them because I could feel my own hope.

In my search for healing, I could see time after time how God kept His promises for me, promises for hope, promises for provision, and promises for peace! I have often seen my life as a mistake and not wanted by anyone. As a result of the abusive environment, I struggled with seeing myself with any value to others. I saw myself as an Ishmael, wondering where I belonged. I see God's promises within me that brought about the hope of healing that flows out from me each and every day. I am confident that some may ask how God provided in my abuse. To be honest, I too have asked that question. Why did He allow this? This is one of those things that is very difficult to navigate in this earthly world. But I can shout from the mountaintop that what Satan meant to destroy, God meant to heal. There is no battle won by Satan when God leads the army!

As a writer, I do not know the stories of my readers. But I do know the heart of humans, and our hearts are often met with the same feelings and emotions met with Ishmael and Hagar's story, mother and son walking into the wilderness with hearts depleted from the harshness of this world.

Is your heart depleted? Have you lost your hope within the world you are surviving? Do you too feel stuck between the promises? If so, read this story as though it is your story. And as you read, you too will feel a sense of belonging because the one we truly belong to is our Father, our heavenly Father, the Father of hope!

> God heard the boy crying, and the angel of God called to Hagar from heaven and said to her, "What is the matter, Hagar? Do not be afraid; God has heard the boy crying as he lies there. Lift the boy up and take him by the hand, for I will make him into a great nation."
>
> Then God opened her eyes, and she saw a well of water. So she went and filled the skin with water and gave the boy a drink. (Genesis 21:17–19 NIV)

Open your eyes today and allow God to provide!

## TALKS WITH EMILEIGH

From disregard to design. From sadness and bitterness to laughter and joy.

Sarah's transformation was notable, not only by those in her camp but even by readers today. The fulfillment of God's promise to her fueled her faith, but the process and journey she walked before that fulfillment deepened that faith.

Without that depth to our faith, we would be shallow vessels grasping at each obstacle and challenge we encounter, hoping and praying for strength to overcome. With depth, we experience a reliance and firm trust in His promises.

Sarah didn't keep this growth to herself. In fact, she said that "everyone who hears will laugh with me" (Genesis 21:6). She wanted her joy to be known throughout the camp. She wanted to share the work He'd done in her life, the transformation He'd enacted to her faith, and the goodness of her God.

***Do others know the good things God has done for you? Are you prone to share or keep private when exciting things happen?***

In all our lives, we have friends who know Jesus and those who don't. For those who don't have a relationship with Him, our story of God's goodness may be the only opportunity they have to get to know who He is. For those who do, our story could serve as inspiration to dig deeper in their own walk with Him. For all, our story and the way He moves in our lives is worth sharing. If we don't share it, how can He use it?

You see, when I hear one of my children laugh, it brings me joy. It makes me smile. When that laughter catches and we're all laughing together, it breathes life and love into our home. Laughter is contagious, and its joy is meant to be shared. Sarah knew this and wanted others not only to hear but to feel the same joy God had evoked in her tent.

***Read Psalm 34:3. What good thing has God recently done in your life that you're willing to share with those around you?***

For Sarah, she had a physical reminder of God's answer to her prayer. She had Isaac to show off and share her laughter. Sometimes, even quite often, the goodness we can share isn't tangible and is even more important to bring notice to. The intangible answers can instill just as much laughter, joy, and contagious hope: a new job to provide a way out of the challenging work culture you or your spouse is in; a friend made in the town you just moved to; an unexpected source of income to pay the hospital bill; an answer or even sense of relief from the chronic pain you've been living with; a warm, sunny day that gives you a glimmer of hope after what's felt like weeks of gloom; a soft breeze during a long run; or an atmosphere of peace during a season trodden with schemes by Satan.

Too often, our society accuses us of bragging or putting on a front when we share the good, the exciting, and the noteworthy. We should be building camps around us filled with others who support in the tough and celebrate with us when God brings us our own laughter. We need to stop censoring our celebration for the sake of society's criticism and simply celebrate His goodness.

***Have you ever felt society or even those in your camp squash your joy, preventing you from sharing the good things God has done in your life?***

From the small to the large, tangible to intangible, the way God is working in and through you can deepen your faith and breathe life into the faith of others. Allow your laughter to be heard throughout your camp!

I still consider my parents to be part of my camp. As an adult now with kids of my own, yet still in the trenches, as they say, I lean into their wisdom and share both celebration and many of life's challenges with them. There have been countless calls of "what did you do when I did this?" or "did I really do this?!" or even simply reflection on the way they raised me. I have been blessed with parents who helped lay a foundation of His Word early in my life, and I pray my husband and I are doing the same for our children. That early foundation and ability to celebrate His goodness and question His plans in a safe space have been pivotal for me as I navigate life's challenges, but it certainly is not a shared attribute of all who reside in my camp.

***Was your faith founded at a young age, or did it develop later in life?***

It's incredible how much we can learn from others who may have lived much of their life following Jesus or much of their life before Jesus transformed them. We too often characterize the depth of a person's faith by the time they've known the Lord, but this is far from truth. Some of the wisest people I know range from those with powerful stories of redemption during adulthood, solid lifelong followers who have read the Bible countless times, brand-new believers hungry for understanding, and even the nuggets of truth from my own kids that have brought me to my knees.

***Who is one of the wisest people in your life? Or from whom do you glean wisdom?***

Sometimes I've felt I write too much about my children. Then one day recently God showed me why. I realized the stories I write about my children are much more about how God uses them to grow me and deepen my faith. In a sense, He uses my children to strengthen the mortar holding my castle of faith together. As God uses me to help them build their own castles, He uses them to strengthen mine.

***Who does God use to strengthen your castle? Whose castle do you help build or strengthen?***

You don't have to be a parent to help build or strengthen someone's faith castle. We all have a camp or sphere of influence we can invest in. I love this terminology Melody uses. Buildings need to be solid structures to withstand weather and abuse. Castles, however, need to be fortified to withstand war but refined enough to house royalty. I look to my kids as those I am helping contribute and strengthen blocks for a firm foundation. I desire a solid infrastructure to withstand the spiritual and physical war at play throughout their lives. I pray what they ultimately build for themselves will glorify the King they choose to follow.

Ken Chism, a.k.a. my dad, said, "You are building a foundation you may never see until you get to heaven. You know you typically don't see the foundation of a house, but everything is held up by it."

Abraham was told to let Ishmael go, to trust that the thirteen years he'd invested in him was enough, to believe that God was in control and would guide him toward a prosperous life. Abraham didn't know if he'd ever see his firstborn son again, but he could rest assured of the promise God gave to care for him and of the solid foundation he'd helped lay in Ishmael's life.

Goodness, I cannot help but marvel at how much purpose Ishmael held. His very life catalyzed growth in Hagar, Abraham, Sarah, and surely many in their camp. God used the son of a mere slave woman to affirm promise and solidify castle foundations. Abraham may have never known the value of the role he played, but he surely knew Ishmael's heavenly Father was directing the building process.

I may never see the fruit of the labor I'm investing in my children's lives. I may never see their completed castles. I have zero control over which blocks they will ultimately choose in their building process, but I am taking the time, listening to His guidance and unique direction for each individual child, and trusting the One who has chosen me to help lay their foundation. It's a heavy responsibility and a tremendous privilege. I'm tirelessly investing and ultimately trusting that their foundation will be built to hold up everything else they face.

***Is the faith foundation in your life strong enough to withstand spiritual warfare and worthy of serving the King we call Jesus? If not, what are ways or people who can help you fortify your infrastructure?***

Ishmael sounds to me like a typical brother who would instigate and provoke, simply seeking attention. Surely within the same camp, with the same dad and two different yet similar mama bears, there was a fair share of squabbles, until Mama Bear Sarah couldn't take it anymore.

There's little that disrupts the peace more in the Ziebka home than when a sibling deliberately destroys a Lego infrastructure. I say deliberately because of course there's no possibility that something so mean could have been done without motive whether you're nine, six, or one. I'm a firm believer in letting siblings work it out unless there's blood or serious injury, but sometimes Mom has to step in. When this is necessary, I admittedly do so sometimes without gentleness or ample grace. I too often react with the emotions their sibling squabble evokes. Sarah's reaction to Ishmael's mocking strikes as similarly familiar. Just as I often do, Sarah reacted in her emotions rather than responding with love.

God, however, can take even these unjustified reactions of frustration rather than rightful responses in love, and He redeems them. God doesn't miss chances to refine us when we pause enough to look to Him. In the matter of Ishmael, Abraham looked to Him. Instead of reacting in emotion, God responded to the circumstance with promise.

***When have you reacted in your emotions rather than pausing long enough to respond according to God's guidance?***

I'd like to parallel this feud in the camp with scripture God recently used to penetrate my heart.

***Read Joshua 9.***

Joshua was leading God's people. They were defeating enemies and faithfully seeking God's will. But then, read verse 14 again, they "did not seek the Lord's decision" (Joshua 9:14b).

Joshua and the men of Israel reacted based on what they saw and felt was right. They didn't pause long enough to hear God's input before responding. One might then expect consequences, failure, or it to even anger the Lord. God doesn't hold our poor or even rash decisions against us though! He uses them to sharpen us.

For the Israelites and Gibeonites, He responds with provision. He provided a way and reinforced the need to seek His discretion in all things. The Gibeonites were certainly deceitful, but it was the Israelites who didn't seek God's wisdom; however, both needed rescue.

It was Mama Bear Sarah who reacted in jealousy of her baby boy's mistreatment. It was Ishmael who did the mocking. It was Hagar who dared to bear Abraham's firstborn son. It was Abraham who sought the Lord for a way. It was all parties involved who needed His provision and redeeming love. It is me who sometimes makes rash decisions, reacts in impatience to sibling rivalry, and asserts my own plan as superior. Yet it is the Lord who always makes a way. He is the provider, promise-keeper, and passionate lover of our souls.

***When has God provided a way or extended grace and forgiveness despite you ignoring the need to seek Him first?***

God provides a way … always. Sometimes it doesn't look the way we want it to or come in the time we'd prefer. This was the case with Isaac and Ishmael. Both were given a way. The promised descendants of Abraham extended, but the path of each son was different. God's promises stood and sustained. God's promises remain today too, and yet each of our paths will look different from those around us.

Both men had different stories, but their similarities rest in the value and purpose God placed throughout their lives and along each of their unique paths. We often lose sight of the value and purpose from God when the noise around us gets too loud, when the voices in our camp fog the clarity of God's voice, when society again tells us to stifle God's design.

Melody was led to believe she didn't belong. Hagar and Ishmael were forced out. Their surrounding camps filled their minds with lies to isolate them and distract them from what God truly had for them. Just as Hagar finally heard God clearly in her desperation, in the desert, in the quiet, Melody felt God's presence on her bike. Both needed to escape the noise of lies to clearly hear the voice of promise. Sometimes to hear that voice of promise, it requires discovering an escape before we can truly embrace God's unique way and will. We need an escape from the noise, from the pressures, from the barrage of schemes Satan cleverly poses before us. When we discover that escape, we can find rest and true peace in His uplifting voice.

***Where do you escape to?***

My escape used to be going for a run. These days I have still not been healed from back pain to enjoy that escape. Some days, the inability to enjoy that particular escape can be suffocating. The need to find alternate escapes can leave me feeling frustrated and defeated, or it can propel me deeper into my pursuit of Him. It leaves me with a choice.

As society fills all the silences and leads me to believe I'm on my own to figure it out, God's voice gets progressively dimmed. Those unfilled silences leave room for society and Satan to fill with lies. Society and sometimes even those in our camp can whisper lies of isolation as well. They can leave us feeling left out, just as Hagar, Ishmael, and Melody were led to believe. I've felt left out myself when friends make plans without me, when my kids were new to a school with established friendships, when I felt like I was the only one choosing God's way.

***When have you felt left out?***

Despite this, when we choose to escape into His arms, we realize we are never truly left out. God always makes a way and always has a place for us. Whether cast out as Hagar by a jealous Sarah, shut out by an absent parent or abusive spouse, or left out (even unintentionally) by friends or acquaintances, He makes a way. Even in the times we neglect God's plan, attempt to pave our own way, and find ourselves lacking, He offers to redeem us and extends a path back to Him. He offers us refuge in the isolation, on the bike ride, and in the despair to whisper His truth and promises. Even in those times when we feel like we don't belong, it never negates our belonging to God. Our awareness and sometimes blatant disregard of that fact doesn't change His unrelenting pursuit of our hearts and His invitation to be fully part of His plan.

***When have you seen God pave a way amid isolation or despair?***

# 13

## WALKING UP THE HILL OF SACRIFICE

"This is a test. For the next sixty seconds, this station will conduct a test of the Emergency Broadcasting System. This is only a test."

Back in the 1960s, an emergency system was developed during the Kennedy administration, allowing President Kennedy to address the entire nation in case of a national emergency. This test was broadcast through your television and was transmitted once a week on each television station at random times. It lasted sixty seconds and totally disrupted your favorite television show. My favorite watch was *Gilligan's Island*. I watched with intensity, cheering on the Skipper and Gilligan, hoping they would escape the deserted island. So when that high-pitched obnoxious tone blared on my box television, I was truly annoyed, fearing I would miss their escape. But if the system had never been tested, when a true emergency arose, we would not be confident that we would be informed. Disaster could strike with no warning. So with that in perspective, I guess I could endure sixty seconds of no Skipper and Gilligan shenanigans.

In Genesis 22, Abraham endured such a test. The difference was that he had no idea it was just a test. If so, he would have ignored the signal just like I did every time the sixty seconds of test showed up on my television. When Abraham was tested, his response was quick and obedient. Nowhere in his mind did he speculate that "this is a test … this is only a test."

"Sometime later God TESTED Abraham. He said to him, 'Abraham!' 'Here I am,' he replied" (Genesis 22:1 NIV). The simple calling of his name alerted Abraham to God's voice. Abraham never wavered or questioned the test God was about to put him through. Even though he did not know what the test would be, he still agreed to it. There is no indication of a question.

If God were to inform me that He was about to put me to a test, I would change the channel as quickly as I could, just like when the Emergency Broadcasting System blared its obnoxious warning on my television. Or I would ask God for clarification and details before agreeing to the test. A quick-to-my-feet response of yes would not describe my typical response to God. But Abraham agreed to the test before knowing any details.

## HERE IS THE TEST

So often I have heard people referring to things in their lives as though God was testing them as He tested Abraham. And I have often agreed with those statements, for instance, "Wow, I guess God was testing me just like He tested Abraham. God wanted to see if I would really give this up, but in the end, it was just a test."

When I process what they have said, I realize how absolutely absurd those statements are. If we think we can compare any test or any potential sacrifice to the sacrifice Abraham was asked to give, we missed the depth of this request. There has never been anything remotely close in our lives that compares to this.

"Take your son, your only son, whom you love—Isaac—and go to the region of Moriah. Sacrifice him there as a burnt offering on a mountain I will show you" (Genesis 22:2 NIV).

Let's pause here and think about what God is asking. Replace an unknown boy with your own child, nephew, or cousin. When we make this request personal, it makes this real. We easily become emotionally disconnected from what has been asked of Abraham, therefore not feeling the depth of this request. This is preposterous, absurd, and sickening, and it was God who made the request.

## WHAT DID GOD ASK?

What is God asking here? Abraham was asked to slaughter his son with a knife on a hot bed of coals. He is asking Abraham to take his son, his only son, and kill him.

Now, we have come far enough along in this story for you to know that Abraham was father to two sons, Isaac and Ishmael. But when Hagar sold Ishmael's rights for her freedom, Ishmael was no longer considered a son of Abraham. So it is true in what it states that Isaac is now Abraham's only son.

Do you remember how long it took for Sarah and Abraham to have a child? Abraham was one hundred years old when Isaac was born. The wait for this child was a grueling wait with twists and turns along the path, causing destruction and deceit. The mountains that needed to be climbed for Abraham to hold his son in his arms are mountains that none of us would be willing to climb. This is the only son he had, and God was asking him to do the absurd and sacrifice him. And what is even more unbelievable is that Abraham said yes! Do we have a God who has lost His mind and a follower of this God who has done the same?

## WHY DID GOD ASK?

Let's continue in the story. The story of the sacrifice of Isaac is a familiar story to most. It causes confusion and, to be honest, a bit of distaste for God. Why would God ask any parent to do this? As we filter this through our human minds, our perspective is limited, very limited. But limited as it may be, this story is still about child sacrifice.

The sickness and sadness is that child sacrifice was not unheard of in the days of the Old Testament. There is nothing more despicable to us than to kill our own child. We despise the thought of it, and interestingly, God also despised child sacrifice, as stated in Jeremiah 7:30–31,

> The people of Judah have done evil in my eyes, declares the LORD. They have set up their detestable idols in the house that bears my Name and have defiled it. They have built the high places of Topeth in the Valley of Ben Hinnom to burn their sons and daughters in the fire—something I did not command, nor did it enter my mind.

Or as stated in Deuteronomy 12:31,

> You must not worship the LORD your God in their way, because in worshiping their gods, they do all kinds of detestable things the LORD hates. They even burn their sons and daughters in the fire as sacrifices to their gods.

So this brings us great confusion as to why God would ask Abraham to do something He detested. Maybe there are no answers, just questions. But I believe there are answers to this, so let's start by looking at what sacrifice is according to the Old Testament. Why was this such an important part of the story?

We have all experienced sacrifice at some point in our lives. Sacrifice to us is typically for something or someone we love. It often is to show our deep devotion to them or a cause. It can be as simple as sacrificing or offering the last Twinkie in the house to our little brother because we love him. Or it's as complicated as offering or sacrificing our paycheck to a cause greater than us. Whether it is the last Twinkie or money for our own living, the sacrifice is great and not without pain.

Sacrifice within the Old Testament was common amongst all of creation. It was not just within the world of the Creator of Heaven and Earth, but it was also used by those who worshiped other gods. It was a very common response to worship.

Within the Levitical law, God instructed His people to offer sacrifices to Him in many different ways. There are five main sacrifices within the Old Testament. Three are voluntary; two are involuntary. The type of sacrifice God was asking of Abraham was a voluntary offering. The burnt offering was a voluntary sacrifice to express devotion to the One True God. So when God told Abraham to offer his only son as a burnt offering, this was a voluntary act. Abraham could have said no to God's command. But Abraham's love for God was deeper than any of us have reached in our faith. Or at least I would think that to be true. Abraham was voluntarily offering his only son to show God how deeply devoted he was to Him.

If sacrifice to God were a voluntary choice and I could choose anything within my private world to offer Him, what would that be: my new car, my new house, or my job? What do I have within my possession that would show God how deeply I love Him?

We want to say we love God deeply and would give up anything to show that love, but would we really? Would we move, sell, or give of our own possessions or time or money? I look at my own world and my own life and would like to think that I would or even that I have. But have I really? Have you really? What are you holding onto so tightly that you would keep instead of sacrificing it to God? What blessings have you missed because your grasp is too tight?

Abraham held his son loosely and was willing to give exactly what God asked. But we still have not answered the question why, and truthfully, I am not sure we will be able to do that. I believe these are those moments when we have a choice and a decision to make. Do I trust this God, or do I discard Him because He asked too much? The truth of the matter is that this is the question we ask ourselves often, not just in the story of Abraham and Isaac. Do I trust God, or do I discard Him?

Abraham was not just any parent, and Isaac was not just any son.

Within Abraham and Isaac, God desired to carry his covenant, His promise for His people. It was through this covenant that the world would be saved, so this test was big!

If Abraham said no, would the covenant be lost? Would the hope for the world be gone? If Abraham said yes and killed his only son, would the covenant be lost? Would the hope for the world be gone? There is a lot at stake here not just for their lives but for ours. Could this have been the catalyst that destroyed hope for the world? We don't know because the story doesn't end that way. And for that I am grateful!

This is where the promises of God are staggering. Stay with me!

## WHY DID ABRAHAM AGREE?

So now we have to contend with the question, "Why did Abraham agree?" Faith ... yes! Trust ... yes! Belief... yes! I believe the statement of this faith is written within one word spoken by Abraham, *we*.

> Early the next morning Abraham got up and loaded his donkey. He took with him two of his servants and his son Isaac. When he had cut enough wood for the burnt offering, he set out for the place God had told him about. On the third day Abraham looked up and saw the place in the distance. He said to his servants, "Stay here with the donkey while I and the boy go over there. We will worship and then we will come back to you." (Genesis 22:3–5 NIV)

WE will worship, and WE will return.

At the point in which Abraham was following through with his obedience, at the point in which the donkey was loaded and the wood had been cut, Abraham believed. He believed that there would be a "we" upon the return. There was a confidence and a faith that when he returned, Isaac would be returning with him. He knew, and he believed! But what made Abraham so confident that there would be "we" upon returning to his servants?

That answer is found in the book of Hebrews. The answer to "we" is found in the word *could*. Read this verse carefully as we learn more about Abraham's bottomless faith. "Abraham reasoned that God *could* even raise the dead, and so in a manner of speaking he did receive Isaac back from death" (Hebrews 11:19 NIV).

It says here that "God could even raise the dead." Wait a minute! Didn't Abraham mean to say that "God would" raise the dead? When I declare from my strong faith that God IS going to do something, I am labeled a deep, strong believer with unshakable faith. If I state it, declare it, and shout it, then God will do it, right? But what if God just needs for me to know that He COULD? Faith is the hope of things not seen. From all my reading and studying the Old Testament, up to this point in history, we have seen no story of God raising anyone from the dead. There are accounts of people dying as in the story of Cain killing Abel and in the slaughter of Sodom and Gomorrah, but nowhere do I read that anyone had been brought back to life … not yet. The stories of the dead rising are stories we read post-Abraham.

So how did Abraham see that this was a remote possibility? How does a man who has never seen or heard of anyone coming back to life think this would be possible?

Go back and reread this scripture. Abraham reasoned. Or in other translations, it says Abraham "considered it possible." Abraham did not know that God was going to or would raise dead people. He just believed that He could! "Abraham reasoned that God could … " (Hebrews 11:19 NIV).

Abraham's faith in God was so grounded that it wasn't a matter of whether God was going to do something; it simply was grounded in the fact that God could do something. Nothing was impossible with God, even things that had never been seen.

Our faith so often rests on what has been seen, miracles that have gone before us. But what if God wants to create something that has never been seen? What if God wants to use us to show that

He is not finished creating the wonderful things He can do? Would our faith be that strong? Would we believe so deeply that whether or not God was going to or would, we just believe that He could? What mountains would be moved? What lives would be changed? What anxiety would be released? What peace would be found simply because we "reasoned that God could"? Not that He will, but simply that He could! The fact that He will is up to God. That is why it is called God's will. But the believing that He could rests solely on our shoulders.

Do you believe that He can?

## ABRAHAM HEADS TOWARD THE MOUNTAIN

As the story continues, Abraham follows through with what God asks him to do. He heads up the mountain to sacrifice his only son.

As Abraham's knife was readied for the kill, God says, "Stop. Put your knife down!"

"'Do not lay a hand on the boy,' he said. 'Do not do anything to him'" (Genesis 22:12 NIV).

While Abraham was putting down the knife, God says, "Now I know that you fear God, because you have not withheld from me your son, your only son" (Genesis 22:12 NIV).

This was a test. This was only a test!

## YOUR ONLY SON

When we look at this story, there are lessons to be learned: lessons of obedience, lessons of faith, and lessons of devotion. But the story presented here goes much further than the lessons learned.

There is a reason for this test that takes us far beyond a story we can relate to or a faith measure for ourselves. This story takes us to the cross!

Listen to what God says.

> I swear by myself, declares the Lord, that because you have done this and have not withheld your son, your only son, I will surely bless you and make your descendants as numerous as the stars in the sky and as the sand on the seashore. Your descendants will take possession of the cities of their enemies, and through your offspring all nations on earth will be blessed, because you have obeyed me. (Genesis 22:16–18 NIV)

I wonder if God breathed a sigh of relief at this point. Looking at this through my human perspective, what if this plan had not worked out? What if Abraham had not heard God tell him to put the knife down and completed the killing of Isaac, the hope for nations? I am grateful this was only a test.

Did you know that Jesus was a descendent of Abraham and Isaac? Because the life of Isaac was spared, the lineage of Jesus is traced back to the Father of Nations.

God spoke to Abraham long before his son, Isaac, was born. God promised Abraham that he would be the father of a nation. He promised this not because God wanted a lot of children, but because it was through His children that He longed to carry his covenant of salvation. Salvation that we so desperately need today because of the sin in this world. If God would have allowed Isaac to be killed that day, the hope of the covenant would have also died. Now, what we don't know is whether God would have orchestrated another plan. But what we do know is that He chose to keep Isaac alive to carry this covenant forward.

When you look at this story of sacrifice, the similarities to the sacrifice of God's only Son is uncanny. I'm not saying that this is the story of Jesus foretold. But I do know both fathers, Abraham and the heavenly Father, faced the sacrifice of their only son. They both placed their son on a hill. And both sons carried the hope of salvation. But within this story of Isaac, God was not ready to offer the ultimate hope for salvation. It wasn't time!

Within this story, God made provision for us! He tested Abraham to see if his faith was strong and worthy to carry the covenant of old to the covenant of new. It is through the covenant of new that we can find our salvation through the sacrifice of death in Jesus Christ. God took his only Son and laid Him on the altar of sacrifice. God did not swoop down in the final moment to save His Son from an excruciating death on the cross. Unlike the story of Isaac, Jesus was killed. When Jesus died, the world went dark. The world lost all hope of salvation. How can a dead man save my soul?

In the days of Abraham, Abraham "reasoned that God could even raise the dead." This was the hope that Abraham clung to as he laid his son onto the altar. He reasoned that God had the power to raise the dead even though he had never seen it nor heard of it.

In the days of Jesus, the reasoning of Abraham proved to be true. Something that seemed impossible became possible. Through the death of Jesus Christ came the resurrection of our souls. What Abraham reasoned, Jesus portrayed! Through His resurrection, life was claimed. Life for us in Christ, the hope for our world.

Two fathers …

Two only sons …

Two sacrifices …

ONE DEATH!

One hope of our salvation!

## TALKS WITH EMILEIGH

Life was going well. It seemed life was at peace, which is usually when Satan strikes. It's prime opportunity for him to disrupt the peace.

Like a whirlwind, dominoes started to fall in my peaceful bubble I'd been enjoying. Satan began nipping at my heel. "My plan" had been rerouted. Our property and future building plans hit a major hiccup. Our extended family was walking through some muddy waters that seemed to inevitably ripple our way. My hormones and stress levels had me experiencing way too early contractions. Our kids were asking hard questions and feeling heavy emotions. Steve and I were battling trust and boundary concerns. Then if hitting me head-on wasn't proving successful enough, I began to watch Satan attack many we love and use it to wear me down. Often, I feel him using those I love to distract me as I tend to carry their pain in addition to my own. I had become utterly weary.

Could my faith weather this storm swirling around us? Could I face what felt like a test on my faith and stand strong in defense?

Then I paused, and I heard God say, "TV broadcasts are tested so we can be confident in emergency we will be informed." If my faith is never tested, how can I be confident in its disruption that I'll stand firm?

***When have you felt tested (by God, your spouse, kids, employer, and so forth)?***

As a parent, I am tested daily. I feel that struggle to my core. When my husband forgets to empty the overflowing trash can on trash pickup day, when my coworker fails to complete what seems to be simple tasks required before I can complete my own work, when a relative is passive-aggressive, or when an acquaintance says something contrary to my belief system, I feel tested. As a Christ-follower, I feel tested, judged, and scorned in my walk, my demeanor, and my spirit. When Satan taps my shoulder with someone cutting me off in traffic or he breaks me down when I see someone I love being harmed, I feel tested. I feel my faith challenged and my peace disrupted. But it is through these tests of life that I am also being molded, strengthened, and refined.

***Read James 1:12–15.***

Let me accentuate in this scripture that God does not tempt us. He doesn't place thorns in our path with the intention of seeing us stumble. He doesn't sprinkle bad soil around us to see if we can overcome and prevail. He does, however, allow us to endure trials with Him standing next to us. Sometimes the biggest test is whether we'll open our eyes to see Him in the trial with us. The tests in our lives are either going to sprout weeds and thorns we will be forced to navigate around or will breed nourishment and life into our steps as we move forward. Life gives us choices to stay stagnant and entangled with those weeds as our faith withers or to break free of them and flourish in steadfastness as we continue moving forward.

***Read James 1:3–4. When have you endured a trial or test and come out stronger walking away from it?***

Abraham certainly walked away from his test stronger in Genesis 22. The magnitude of his test is one that none can fathom I'd assume, but the intention, the struggle, and the lesson are something each of us can parallel in various ways.

My translation is the following:

God says, "Give up your only son for me, Abraham."

Abraham responds, "Okay, God. I'll do it because I love You."

Abraham loved Isaac. He just loved God more.

Sacrifice is "the act of giving up something valued for the sake of something else regarded as more important or worthy" (dictionary.com).

*When have you been asked to give something up?*

Have you given up a job you love to be in town more with

your family? Were you asked to give up your home to downsize or relocate? Did you give up your comfort to take a worthy risk? Did you give up social media to better prioritize your time? Did you give up sweets for Lent? Did you hesitate, grumble, or fight the need to give up that one thing asked of you?

Let me parallel. Were you asked to give up the only son you waited until you were one hundred years old to receive? For years, Abraham climbed spiritual mountains to step into the promise God offered through his son, Isaac, and yet Abraham didn't even hesitate to give him back to God. Abraham continued to climb and overcome the mountains and still was asked to step into another storm. It was a storm that could test his faith, tatter his peace, shatter his marriage, or symbolize genuine sacrifice and steadfast faith.

***When asked or you choose to sacrifice, do you do so willingly or begrudgingly?***

One example of sacrifice is to fast. For years, I can remember marveling at others' ability to fast from food. I have a deep appreciation for cheeseburgers and milkshakes, so I didn't think I could forego the enjoyment of them. I also had not yet been called to do so with proper motivation. When I felt the call to implement this spiritual discipline into my routine for a season, I then marveled at how adequately God equipped me for the sacrifice He desired of me. What I had denied the ability to complete and had shied away from became a monumental shift in intentionality, intimacy, and growth. Whether a small sacrifice of one meal replaced by journaling and prayer or a larger sacrifice of twenty-four hours with only water, the rewards became unexpected and powerful. It was no longer about my desire for the food and the difficulty of giving it up. It became about the someone better I was willing to give it up for.

***Are you postured to sacrifice what He asks?***

I tend to be indecisive most times, but when I believe strongly God wants me to do something, I don't tend to dawdle. I'd heard His call to fast confirmed in various forms through reading, conversations with friends and family, and mostly my own quiet time, so I did what any good planner does. I ordered a book so I could become a professional. (For the record, I do not believe simply reading one book makes you an instant pro on fasting, and it must be a genuine call from the Lord that begins after prayer and careful consideration.) Thanks to two-day shipping and some rare quiet, I consumed the book quickly and felt a mixture of motivation and nervousness but preparation.

Mind you, I do not live this open-handed on a consistent basis. As I continue to walk through our current season of heel-nipping, the weariness is too much some days. As much as I try to leave it all at His feet, I struggle to let go of too much. I hold tightly to the pieces I'm not ready to sacrifice and cling to any semblance of control I convince myself I have. When I do this, I'm communicating that I don't trust Him with it. I'm creating my own barrier from the blessings He wants to exchange for my weariness. Instead I must prepare my heart, mind, and spirit beforehand. If I am not postured to live open-handed and willing to sacrifice when and if called, am I truly living for Him or my own comfort and convenience? If I don't loosen my grasp on the people and things I value, can I truly enjoy the blessings He wants to extend?

***What person, thing, or circumstance do you grasp too tightly, preventing you from living open-handed and willing?***

As we navigated the rocky path before us, my husband became faced with a difficult decision. It was a decision I could not make for him, but I fully supported whichever path he chose. I knew he was seeking both the Lord and wise friends' counsel. I am so thankful for this because I clung too tightly throughout to the what-ifs, the worry, and the potential aftermath of either path chosen. My fists were clung too tightly to give him the fruitful wisdom he needed. My inability to open my hands and surrender not only prevented me from supporting him the way he needed, but I also almost missed God speaking through my husband.

As he confidently moved forward, I walked alongside in support, him with hands open to the Father's guidance and will and me filled with fear and tightened fists. Then just as quickly as the challenge and storm had rolled in, the clouds parted, and a ray of light showed through. My husband had prepared and postured himself to sacrifice his own comfort and well-being to heed God's call, and in response, God took the "test" away. He didn't require my husband to stand in the storm he'd been prepared for. I will never forget the words my husband spoke in reflection to being removed from the storm, "God just wanted me to be willing." He was willing to do something hard simply because God told him to. That is sacrifice and obedience.

***Are you willing to sacrifice and heed God's call no matter the cost?***

God doesn't always prevent the storm from arriving. He won't always shield us from pain, suffering, and trials. He will, however, walk through it all with us, and He does ask us to be willing to weather the storms with Him. He wants our hearts. He desires true sacrifice.

***What does true sacrifice mean to you? Read Hosea 6:6 and Romans 12:1–2.***

To know God is to faithfully love Him. To love Him is to hear and follow Him. He does call for sacrifice at times, but not at the expense of our faith. Rather it is to sharpen our faith, to strengthen our willingness, to deepen our pursuit and knowledge of His will and ways, and to fine-tune our ability to hear Him.

Truly hearing God and discerning His will is sometimes one of the biggest faith struggles. As the world offers countless distractions and shameless noise to prevent us from hearing His whispers or convince us we hear Him wrong.

In Genesis 22:1–10, Abraham is posturing his heart and preparing to obey. He arms himself with accountability and gathers the required resources (verse 3). He responds to the call. He rests in the Lord's provision (verse 8). It culminates in what I would imagine to be one of the fiercest spiritual storms of Abraham's life, the greatest form of sacrifice imaginable. My mind and heart would be spiraling. And yet, "But the angel of the Lord called to him from heaven and said, 'Abraham, Abraham!' He replied, 'Here I am'" (Genesis 22:11).

Abraham hears the Lord at exactly the moment he needs Him most. In even the darkest hour, Abraham hears God speak, "Stop." To hear this "stop," Abraham had to be postured to discern God's voice.

The only way we will discern God's voice in our darkest hour is if we have prepared, practiced, and postured to hear His voice in the calm before the storm.

***Do you tend to hear God more clearly in the calm or the storm? Why do you think many people struggle to discern God's voice? What obstacles in your life distract you from His voice? Read Matthew 19:16–22.***

Jesus audibly gave this rich young ruler direction, but the man was not postured to discern what he was being told. The man heard, "Sacrifice. Give it all up." Instead I believe what Jesus was really saying was, "Give me your heart. Give me all of you with open, willing hands." We need to discern the true sacrifice God desires of us. We need to walk in open-handed faith and obedience.

We may not be asked to give up our only child. We may not be asked to give up everything. Then again, maybe you will be asked to. At the root, it isn't about what we are or are not asked to do, but our faith may depend on our willingness to do so.

God doesn't even expect us to understand the reason He wants us to sacrifice, but He does desire our obedience, discernment, grounded faith, and willingness to sacrifice for Him.

***Read Psalm 1:2–3.***

Plant yourself in His will. Discern how He is guiding you to bear fruit. Nourish your foundation with His Word and whispers. Allow Him to point out and pull the weeds intended to entangle you. Walk in His wisdom and discernment even when it means sacrifice. Allow the trials and tests on your faith to prepare you for the battles Satan will bring before you.

Almost never will God's call involve our comfort and convenience, but our willingness and obedience will never return empty. When we let go of control, open our hands, and release our circumstances into His hands, it becomes about His will, His agenda, His purpose, and our desire to move.

In a sense, you and I are tested daily to determine if His sacrifice is worthy enough for us to obey in response.

***Read John 10:11.***

God, Jesus, our good Shepherd, sacrificed His best for us. Are you willing to do the same?

***What sacrifice are you willing to make for Him this week? Today?***

# 14

# WALKING THE ROAD TO SUCCESS

Have you ever stood on the edge of a prayer, not because your faith is strong, but because it is weak?

Our middle son lives in the city of Boston. As a mom, I love to visit, not only because I get to see my son, but also because I get to taste some amazing food! When my son and I set out on our eating adventures, we always take the subway, the T. As we approach the train and wait for its arrival, we stand behind a yellow line. That line is there for our safety. If I got too daring and crossed that line, it could end in disaster. Plus, I wouldn't be able to get my favorite pizza and cannoli. And that would be a shame!

Prayer also has a yellow line. When we stand behind the yellow line of prayer, we ask just enough to soothe our prayer conscience, yet being careful not to cross the line into the danger zone.

When I was a young girl, I was taught a phrase I added to the end of every prayer. This phrase was as rote as "In Jesus' name I pray." When I recited this phrase, all of my bases were covered from every request I had asked within this prayer. If I prayed the wrong prayer, I was covered. If I prayed the right prayer, I was covered. It kept me safely behind the yellow line, becoming so common that I became unaware that I prayed it. It became the insurance I needed to my prayers. What was the phrase? "God, if it be Your will."

This was the same prayer Jesus prayed in the garden of Gethsemane. "Father, if you are willing, take this cup from me; yet not my will, but yours be done" (Luke 22:42). So adopting this for my perfect prayer ending meant I prayed like Jesus prayed. Or did it? And then I have to ask, "Did I mean it?"

Maybe! Sometimes yes! Sometimes no!

As I continued to mature in my faith, I realized the impact of that phrase. I realized that if I really didn't mean it, then I needed to scratch it from my "sincerely," "yours truly," or "best wishes" ending. But if I left it in there, I needed to mean what I said. I needed to truly accept God's will for my prayer.

But what about that yellow line? What about going beyond standing on the edge of my prayers? When do our prayers move into the danger zone?

As we approach the end of Abraham's story, we are introduced to a man who crossed the yellow line of his prayers; he pushed past the safety zone and went boldly before the throne of God.

This man's name was Eliezer, Abraham's faithful servant. What this man did was bold, really bold. The simplicity of his prayer can change your or my life. They are five simple words wrapped within the heart of the man who wanted nothing more than to please his master.

What are these five simple words? "Lord, make me successful today."

**"Lord, Make Me Successful Today" Means Releasing the Results**

Before we can pray these five bold words, we must first release. Abraham was now toward the end of his life. He had been full and prosperous, but one final task was set before him, to find his son, Isaac, a wife.

One day while sitting in the campground, Abraham told his servant to make an oath. As his servant was making this oath, Abraham wanted him to put his hand under his thigh. This would be similar to "raise your right hand and repeat after me" kind of oath. The oath or promise Abraham asked of Eliezer was to return to the land where Abraham's relatives were and get a wife for Isaac.

Abraham wanted Eliezer to promise that Isaac would not take a wife from Canaan but from the land of Haran.

Look at Eliezer's response. "What if the woman is unwilling to come back with me to this land?" (Genesis 24:5 NIV).

"What if"... this is the question we often ask of God? What if it doesn't work? What if they are not healed? What if life doesn't get better? What if?

Eliezer questioned the results of his task so he throws out plan B. If she is unwilling "Shall I then take your son back to the country you came from?" (Genesis 24:5 NIV).

If I can't find the needle in the haystack, can I bring the haystack to the needle?

Abraham gave Eliezer a hard no. Within this no, Abraham proceeded to tell his servant that an angel of the Lord would go before him, but if by chance the woman is not willing to return to Canaan with Eliezer, "you will be released from this oath of mine" (Genesis 24:8 NIV). At the moment of this release, Eliezer was set free from the results.

Think hard with me on this one. We often pray as though the results are in our hands or our responsibility. If I pray hard enough, often enough, and loud enough, then I can control those results or at least feel a bit responsible for them. We become determined to gather as many people as possible to pray with us, as though the bigger crowd, the bigger the results. Now don't get me wrong. I am all for gathering our circle of friends for prayer, but sometimes we gather as though one more person will tip the scales for God, and He will answer with a resounding yes.

Abraham, in his kindness, allowed his servant to be released from the results. Abraham understood the importance of obedience to pursue God's desires, not the results.

Did you catch that? Abraham understood the importance of obedience to pursue God's desires, not the results!

But what if we treated prayer in the way that Abraham treated Eliezer? What if we prayed without the pressure of the results? What if we prayed in total release of what will happen? What if it is truly a prayer of surrender?

When we pray, we are often more focused on the results of that prayer than the obedience of that prayer. When the results of our prayers become our focus, we miss the incredible peace that comes from simple obedience. Focusing on the results can freeze us in our movement. Let me tell you a story.

*It was early morning, and the breakfast dishes had been placed in the sink to be washed once everyone was settled for the day. My youngest son was heading out for his final days of high school. In these days, we were in the depths of college discussions. We had done the on-site visits, the acceptance letters had come in, and the scholarship offers had arrived, so now it was decision time.*

*My son's dream since he was a young boy was to attend the University of Oklahoma and to pursue a military career. He had recently received his acceptance letter and academic scholarship information, but our funds still ran thousands and thousands of dollars short. He had also received a full ride at another school. The discussions had gotten emotional, as we knew we could not afford the University of Oklahoma. But, hey, he had gotten accepted. Wasn't that enough? So we directed him to the cheaper option.*

*Early that morning as he and I stood in the hallway heading to the garage, I was handing him his lunch, bidding him farewell for the day. Then a moment happened between my son and me that I will never forget.*

*He looked at me and very confidently told me that he was going to the University of Oklahoma. He told me that he knew that was where God wanted him to go.*

*"I'm going, Mom. I know this is where God wants me to go!"*

*We hugged goodbye, and he slipped out the door. I was left standing in that hallway with a huge pit in my stomach. How could I disappoint my son's faith? How could I tell him that what he heard from God was wrong?*

*As I walked into the kitchen to finish the breakfast dishes, God said, "Come talk with me." What could God possibly have to say to me? He knew we didn't have that kind of money.*

*I put down the dish I was cleaning and made my way to my bedroom and closed the door. God prompted me to meet Him on my knees at the side of the bed because He wanted to speak to me. This was serious!*

*As my knees lowered to the floor, the tears began to flow down my face. I felt an incredible battle within. During these moments on my knees, my faith was tested. I was afraid to let go of this because I didn't want to disappoint my son's faith. But even more than that, I didn't want to disappoint my own faith. I didn't want to claim something that I couldn't control. What if God disappointed me and I went through this surrender moment for nothing? Would I ever be able to surrender again? I battled intensely with God, telling Him that this was impossible. But there was something within me that was pushing me past the edge of my prayer. Something was telling me that I needed to cross that yellow line into the danger zone. It was time to surrender the results to God and to come boldly before His throne. Once I released the results to God, I became convinced that we needed to pause all other college pursuits and focus solely on this one university. I didn't know why or how, but that was the path we needed to pursue. Then let God figure it out for us!*

*I got up from my knees, my face red and eyes puffy … ugly cry! I walked into the room where my husband was and declared that I believed to the depths of my being that our son was supposed to fully pursue the University of Oklahoma. He looked at me as though I had a third eye, and I left the room with indescribable confidence.*

So what happened in that room that morning as I knelt broken before God? Did God reveal to me a hidden vault that He had stashed the thousands of dollars we needed? Did he show me that magic tree where money did grow? No! We were in just as much of a deficit in the funds we needed than we were when I first knelt beside my bed that morning. The only thing that changed was my faith.

In those moments on my knees, I went boldly to the throne of God. I moved from standing on the edge of prayer to crossing the yellow line into the danger zone. At that moment, I said, "Okay, God … let's do it!"

I had been released from the results. It no longer mattered what the answer was but mattered more that I had surrendered it totally to God. At that moment, I laid my request confidently at His feet.

We could easily miss the point and think all we need to do is to come boldly before God and tell him what we want, and He will do it. I mean, isn't that faith? "Ask and it will be given, knock and the door will open, seek and you will find?" But the point here is more in the surrendering of the results … truly surrendering! When we surrender the results to God, our request can be as bold as we can imagine. We need to see the God of our faith, not the God of our favor!

## THE OATH IS GIVEN, AND THE JOURNEY BEGINS

After Abraham and Eliezer finished their conversation of release, Eliezer placed his hand under the thigh of Abraham. Genesis 24:9–10 reads, "So the servant put his hand under the thigh of his master Abraham and swore an oath to him concerning this matter. Then the servant left …"

Eliezer's oath to Abraham reflected who he was as a servant, as a man. At that moment, the servant stepped past the edge of prayer and crossed the yellow line into the danger zone. It was that moment when his heart said, "Let's do it, God, and I will stand back and watch You move."

## THE STORY CONTINUES

Once this decision was made to move at the master's request, Eliezer gathered ten of his master's camels. Each camel was meticulously loaded with gifts. These weren't trinkets purchased at the local Dollar General. Instead these were gifts of gold and silver. Costly garments were placed in the satchels of each camel. And I am confident there were also costly spices from the region and various other gifts. While these camels were loaded down with wonderful things, the most precious gift rested safely in the pocket of Eliezer's coat, a gold nose ring and two gold bracelets. Reaching into his pocket to assure the safety of these items, Eliezer continued on his journey.

As he approached the town of Nahor, his destination, he paused at a well just outside the city. As he arranged the camels in a line formation, each camel knelt in order to allow rest from the long journey. But the kneeling of each camel was also a part of the servant's plan to select the bride for Isaac.

Looking toward the horizon, Eliezer was aware the day was turning to night. The timing for his journey to the well was strategic, knowing that it was in the evening when the women from the community came to the well to draw water. Looking up, he saw groups of women with large vessels balanced on their heads enjoying conversation and laughter as they talked about the events of the day.

Eliezer had strategically placed himself in a location that he knew the women of the town would frequent. So often we lay our requests before God and then walk away with no thought of how we will situate ourselves for success. As strange as this is, we also play a part in the success of our prayers. Think of it this way. When you go to buy a car, you don't go to the horse stables in hopes to find a car. You drive to the nearest car dealership, where the lot is lined with cars, therefore strategically setting yourself up for success. Eliezer was aware that in order to have better odds of finding his master's treasure, he needed to be strategically placed.

As the servant stood by the well watching the women approach for the evening draw, anticipation began to grow inside him. "He had the camels kneel down near the well outside the town; it was towards evening, the time the women go out to draw water" (Genesis 24:11 NIV).

## MAKE ME SUCCESSFUL

Then he prayed, "Lord, God of my master Abraham, make me successful today, and show kindness to my master Abraham" (Genesis 24:12 NIV).

"Lord, make me successful today … " I imagine as Eliezer was positioned at the well seeing the groups of women approaching that his dependence on God at that moment brought him hope and peace. It is amazing that when we rest our souls before our Lord, the results of our requests also rest in that hope and that peace. And yet, the prayer prayed by the servant that day seemed unbelievably bold.

How can he be so assuming of God? Maybe he added, "But, God, only if it is your will," and scripture doesn't record it. If so, his bases were covered, therefore protecting God's reputation. But Eliezer's prayer was bolder than that. He didn't need any bases covered because he blew past the yellow line, running right into the danger zone.

What would cause a simple servant to pray such a bold prayer? What would cause you to pray such a bold prayer?

On this day, the meaning of success had changed for this man. Success was not defined by results; success was defined by obedience.

Let's take a deeper look at this prayer, "Make me successful today." Taken out of context, this prayer is selfish and self-serving. But within the context of this story, we know that Eliezer has been released from the results. Once convinced of this, he stepped boldly into his mission.

When the results are no longer our concern, when we have been released of the outcome as Abraham released his servant, our prayers can be as bold as Eliezer's prayer. The danger zone of prayer will no longer feel frightening but right.

## A PLAN IS DEVISED

When we release our results of prayer to God, we tend to walk away. "God, it is now in your hands," absolving ourselves of any responsibility of the continued progress. We treat God as a toy maker. We hand over our broken toys; He returns them when they are repaired. But so often God wants us to stand and watch Him repair, handing Him the necessary tools to complete the project.

I believe that is what happened that day. Instead of walking away, he devised a plan. His heart of surrender had been made, the confidence of his success had been established, and the results were no longer his responsibility, so next was devising a plan.

> "See, I am standing beside this spring, and the daughters of the townspeople are coming out to draw water. May it be that when I say to a young woman, 'Please let down your jar that I may have a drink,' and she says, 'Drink, and I'll water your camels too' let her be the one you have chosen for your servant Isaac. By this I will know that you have shown kindness to my master." (Genesis 24:13–14 NIV)

Eliezer's plan, a simple ask, was "Please, may I have a drink of water." God's plan was a simple response, "Of course! And let me provide drink for your camels also."

The woman who responded with the reaction of God to go above and beyond the servant's request was the successful answer to his prayer. He now had a plan!

Let me tell you another story.

Two nights ago, I was caught up in the chaos of life. Anxiety had overtaken me, and I felt as though God was disappearing from my sight. The night of my surrender, I couldn't sleep. I tossed and turned for hours, grappling with my current situation. It was a situation where I felt trapped and saw no way of escape. I had battled with learning to be content and grateful for what I had, but still felt no peace and honestly was miserable. I was in the middle of writing this chapter, so that night, I felt God telling me to go back to Abraham. Go back to the story of Eliezer when he prayed for success. I was angry with God that He was throwing the same lesson I was writing into my own face, but it was exactly what I needed to hear.

As I was sitting in my chair, the hours ticked by. Eleven o'clock … midnight … one o'clock! "God, what do you want from me? I have followed, and I have obeyed!"

Then I felt as though God spoke to me. "But have your surrendered? Do you believe that the results are in My hands? Have you devised a plan?"

Needless to say, God and I had a few more hours in the night finishing that conversation. By that morning, I had surrendered the results to God and had devised a plan of movement. I had strategically written out my plan and knew exactly what I was going to do next. As I was driving to step number one, I paused at the side of the road and called my prayer warrior. After I shared my plan with her, we prayed together. Little did I know that while were praying, the plan was unfolding. As the day progressed, I saw more movement within that one day than what I had seen in weeks. I took control of the situation with God going before me with His purposed results.

You see, devising a plan of surrender to God sometimes shows itself as real before we can even say "Amen." That answer is waiting to reveal itself to us even if it isn't the answer we were looking for. But after the surrender, our hearts become moldable to whatever God desires.

## BEFORE HIS PRAYER WAS FINISHED

> Before he had finished praying, Rebekah came out with her jar on her shoulder(Genesis 24:15 NIV).

"Before he had finished praying … " He hadn't even finished his prayer. He didn't have the chance to say his closing statement. There was no "if it be Your will." There was no "Amen!"

We never know the pace at which God will move. We often complain that God is slow in answering, causing us to lose faith and become disheartened. But in the case of Eliezer, God moved so swiftly that he didn't even have the chance to open his eyes and lift his head from prayer. Before he could even finish, Rebekah came out with her jar. Because we know the end of the story, we know that Rebekah is the chosen one for Isaac. But the servant was unaware that God had moved so swiftly. So he continued in the steps of the plan that he devised.

## REBEKAH, THE FUTURE WIFE OF ISAAC

The story continues with Eliezer implementing his plan. He stayed the course, following each step.

> Before he had finished praying, Rebekah came out with her jar on her shoulder … The woman was very beautiful, a virgin; no man had ever slept with her. She went down to the spring, filled her jar and came up again. (Genesis 24:15–16 NIV)

I imagine within the servant's mind that he began to question if this were his answer. Temptation arises to preempt the plan and cause us to be enticed by the beauty of what is standing before us, but patience in the plan allows us to depend on God's guidance and not ours. So what if Eliezer had stopped working the plan because he was enamored with what stood before him? What if he had cut the plan short, assuming Rebekah was his success? What if Rebekah was just a beautiful decoy? He would have never found that out if he didn't finish the plan.

But he did finish the plan and received the answer for which he was searching. "Without saying a word, the man watched her closely to learn whether or not the Lord had made his journey successful" (Genesis 24:21 NIV).

Watching Rebekah retrieve water for him and his camels to drink, the servant was met face-to-face with his success. He reached into his pocket, taking out the gold nose ring and two gold bracelets, signifying the success of his journey for a wife for Isaac.

## SUCCESS

"… the Lord has granted success to my journey …" (Genesis 24:56 NIV). Eliezer went boldly to the throne of God and found success in his prayer.

## WRAPPING THIS UP

So what does it mean to come boldly before the throne of God? How do I move from the edge of my prayer into the danger zone of faith? What would it mean for me to pray, "Lord, make me successful today"?

First, let's start with the throne of God. Have you ever thought of what the throne of God looks like? Is it a large chair positioned on top of a long staircase? Is it a chair sitting in the meadow with birds chirping and wildflowers swaying? Is it a chair made of gold sitting amidst a castle?

Our images of the throne of God can be quite creative and vary according to each person. But I would venture to say that most of us don't feel as though it is a space that we would frequent often. It is a space to be honored and respected but not a space where we truly belong. I would never approach the throne of the Queen of England or walk into the Oval Office with confidence. Those spaces are for those who have earned the privilege to frequent them, but not for me.

With this same perspective, we often take the position we have as believers to the throne of God lightly. We look at the throne from a distance, admiring its beauty and strength. We keep clear lines drawn around it as though it is a yellow line cautioning us not to cross.

In this perspective, we are greatly mistaken. Look at this scripture, "Let's approach God's throne of grace with confidence, so that we may receive mercy and find grace to help us in our time of need" (Hebrews 4:16 NIV). I like how it states in in the New Living Translation, "So let us come BOLDLY to the throne of our gracious God."

The picture drawn for us in this scripture portrays the throne, His grace, and His mercy. It says nothing about the results of our prayers except that He will help us in our time of need. When we approach the throne of God, we find God! We find His grace and His mercy, not the granting of our request!

As God sits on His throne, He sits with grace and mercy as His backdrop. He beckons us to approach Him with boldness and confidence. As you stand on the edge of your comfortable prayer, take a step forward. As you step across the yellow line of safety, don't look down. Look up! Looking at our feet instead of His face causes us to lose perspective and direction.

Once you get to the throne, take the request you are holding in your hands and lay it at the feet of Jesus. Look boldly into His face and concentrate on the surrender.

You will never be able to lay anything at the feet of Jesus unless you approach the throne! In order to reach the feet of Jesus, you must get close to the throne.

After the servant left Abraham, he knew that his mission was to bring back a wife for Isaac; he knew that Abraham had released him from the results, but he also knew he would do whatever it took for him to succeed.

As the servant paused at the well, he prayed.

Results released.
Success asserted.
And
Obedience obtained!

Success was no longer in the results; it was in the obedience!

As my son continued his pursuit to the University of Oklahoma, every step in the journey was now bathed in faith. There was never a question from that moment on that God was going to be truly clear in His movement.

We devised a plan and pursued that plan! The first step in this plan was to make one more visit to the university. An appointment was set on the calendar to meet with the lieutenant colonel and pursue his enrollment into the ROTC program. One week before the calendar visit, the state of Oklahoma passed a new guideline stating that all ROTC students, no matter which state they came from, would receive in-state tuition. This means that his tuition portion went from $22,000 to $9,000 per year! That was a successful day!

Four years later, he was commissioned as an officer in the army at the University of Oklahoma and had also met the love of his life. Success!

What if I had not surrendered on my knees that day in my bedroom? What if I had not paused to grapple with my faith? What if I had not been obedient in my prayer? Would the results have changed? Probably not! I think God would have continued to move in the direction He desired. But if I had not surrendered that day and come boldly to the throne of God, I would have missed out! If I had stayed on the edge of my prayer and never experienced the depth of my faith, on the day of his graduation, I would have said it was a lovely day and patted my son on the back, proud of his accomplishments. But because I had that incredible moment with God on the edge of my bed, his graduation day was a glorious day of celebration of God.

Is success measured by this great story? Not at all! Our surrender measures success. It is measured by releasing the results at the feet of Jesus. Where are you standing today? Are you standing on the edge of prayer, or have you stepped into the danger zone? Can you pray, "Lord, make me successful today" and allow God to decide the results?

## TALKS WITH EMILEIGH

Boldness. Obedience. Success.

Bold as defined by my daughter is doing something that requires you to be brave, have courage, and might be hard. It could be asking a friend how you can pray for them, standing up for your faith, or crossing the yellow line of prayer for something you really desire. Perhaps the boldest prayer recorded is in Luke 22:42, "not my will, but Yours be done."

Jesus knew what lie ahead. He knew the Father's plan. He asked if it were possible to accomplish the goal another way, but He held loosely to His own will and tightly to the Father's. He prayed a bold prayer of utter surrender. He meant every word He prayed.

***Have you ever prayed for something but weren't sincere? Did you do so because you felt you should or in hopes that doing so would help you mean it?***

God, help guide my kids toward Your path for them, unless it means being a missionary overseas because I'm not sure I can handle that. God, help me choose the right church, unless people I don't agree with attend there because that's not comfortable. God, help bring healing to our family, unless it's going to involve difficult conversations that bring more tension first. God, show me if this is the new job I should take, unless it means I have to stay unhappy where I am longer. God, tell me if I should join this ministry, unless I must give up something else I love to do so. This list could continue, but I'm guessing you didn't realize how often we place stipulations on our requests. These types of prayer are not bold.

Lord, help me to live for You. Help me to be successful. Help me to align my desires with Your will.

What about the times we feel called to something but are too scared to step into the opportunity? We want our desires to align with God's will. As Christians, we are called to live for Him, and I'm not sure I know a person who doesn't want to be successful.

***When has fear or what-if held you back from something you knew you needed to do? When has the unknown or hard kept you from being bold?***

This very book has been a labor of love and healing that I almost passed by- a fear of failure, inadequacy, or time. I have had plenty of weeks and even months of silence when no words were written. I let the what-ifs stand in my way; all the noise of life distracted me from His bold calling.

***When have you believed God wanted you to do something that felt impossible?***

Abraham's servant was about to set out on a bold journey. This journey could hold obstacles and what-ifs, but Abraham's confidence in the needle in the haystack was contagious as Eliezer set out on his journey. Abraham's belief and trust that God not only could but would do the unlikely was a contagious mindset for his inner circle. Perhaps he even intentionally surrounded himself with others who held a similar level of trust in the Lord. We've read and discussed several events where Abraham's unwavering belief urged him to obedience as well as some of his weaker moments when accountability from others may have been vital. At his core, I believe Abraham rested in God's will for him and his family.

God intentionally places others in our life that can hold us accountable and challenge us to step into boldness. Melody told me, "God said you're supposed to write this book with me." I thought she was kidding. There was a laundry list of reasons I thought I couldn't or shouldn't. It was unlikely for me. I even took a half-hearted attempt at it once I relented and agreed to join this venture. She firmly but gently told me, "No. God wants more. You're capable of more." She knew God wanted me to do something bold. She knew He wanted me to take an active step of obedience and stop letting fear hold me back from not only His will but from what I would come to discover as a level of success. I needed to choose to be bold.

I needed to choose to trust His plan. We all need to surrender our will for Thy will and believe He will.

***Have you ever fallen to your knees in prayer? Does this kneeling bring you to surrender, or is there another form/posture of prayer you feel most connected/surrendered? When has coming before Him in prayer changed your faith? Was it a moment or a season?***

This temporary life is bundled with bold asks, hard no's, and everything in between. In times of bold asks, I have come to Him confidently, and in the hard no, I have been humbled to my knees. With everything along the journey, I have learned to simply bring it to Him consistently. When I take the open-handed approach of genuine surrender with all I desire and with what I hear Him saying, I am better postured to step into His will. When we lost and thought we may lose a child again, I tearfully came to God. When we encountered building concerns of our future home and familial tension, I came to Him confused. When I believed He was telling me to join the writing of this book, I was scared. These moments on my knees have been just a dose of the ways God has grown my faith. Through all of it, I have found myself unequipped to act with boldness.

***Read Hebrews 4:16 and 2 Corinthians 3:12.***

The unlikely, the unknown, and the scary-we cannot accomplish any alone. God gives us others for accountability, and He gives us all we need in Jesus. The eternal hope He offers should propel us to be bold. Even when we don't feel brave, we must still step forward and walk in obedience. For it is through the journey and often hesitant, rocky path of obedience that we step into true boldness.

***Read John 14:23–24.***

Your boldness, your faith, your trust, and your salvation isn't dependent on your obedience, but your love for Him is expressed through that obedience. It is through the love He envelops us in that we are enabled to be bold and take those steps of obedience.

Abraham's servant and even Abraham himself may not have felt bold initially, but they were obedient to the path they felt the Lord to whom loved them called them. Even as they acted in obedience, they knew the results were beyond their control, and each boldly surrendered the outcome to God's will. They surrendered their will to His will.

***Where do you need to step into obedience now? How can you prepare for this obedience and posture your heart in advance?***

With the first few chapters of this book, I would pray and ask God if this were His path, to let the words flow easily from Him through me. As chapters progressed and Melody relayed to me on more than one occasion that God told her the book would be longer than initially intended, those prayers transformed to "use me to write for You." My mind was prepared to obey, and God was posturing my heart to be bold. To obey His call, I needed to surrender my fears and inadequacies and rest in His will. I was ready to obey, but I lacked the boldness I would need to step forward.

***When has a lack of boldness delayed your ability to obey? Read Judges 6:36–40.***

The account of Gideon is rich with God's ability to take the heart of a seemingly ill-equipped young man and use him for God's greatness, for God's level of success. In this passage, God has called upon Gideon to act boldly, and yet Gideon seems to be testing God's call. He seems to doubt what He hears God directing and boldly asks for confirmation. He wants to discern His will. In Genesis 24:13–14, the servant is also coming before God for assurance and clarity. Eliezer asks for clear evidence of the answer to his prayer.

As I asked God to let words flow easily through the pages of this book, I needed to hear from God clearly. I wanted confirmation I was walking the path He intended for me.

I don't believe any of these examples are testing God but instead are cries for external confirmation of His voice and calling. We want clarity of His will before we act, and we struggle to be confident in discerning His voice. We look to others or His Word to affirm what we think is His will. His rarely audible and often subtle voice is more difficult to accept readily because we fight the need to surrender. Sometimes, even when we believe we're praying boldly or walking obediently, we can struggle to fully surrender. We can often mistake surrender as a need to step back and let God work. It's hard to believe God wants us to take part in the journey with Him, and as a result, we question His call. That's the misunderstanding of boldness, obedience, and surrender. None are one-time decisions or destinations. It's a continual journey we commit to taking with God one step at a time.

***When you feel the need to surrender, do you invite in accountability or simply quiet your heart with God? When has an undesirable answer to prayer become what you didn't know you desired?***

Surrender is a journey, and different seasons require different answers. There are moments I find myself withdrawing to quiet with God, and other times, I lean heavily on those God has led me to for accountability. I have questioned His plans. I have doubted my abilities. I have clenched my fists against His desires. It never ceases to amaze me how patient and persistent He is in pursuing me despite this.

This book was originally supposed to be six chapters. I originally wrote simple discussion questions in response to Melody's teachings. I was originally much more guarded about sharing the hard seasons and details of my life. God wanted more. I never knew His more would be exactly what I desired too. If my fists are clenched to my desires, my comfortable steps of obedience, my imposed ceiling of success, and my scope of success will never be moldable to His soaring level of Kingdom success.

If you stay comfortable under your self-imposed ceiling of success, you will never fully experience the power of His presence, the mercy of His grace, or the power of bold obedience. For His success is found in the journey of bold obedience.

***Have you ever missed an opportunity to be part of something God was doing because you resisted obedience? Because the level of success wasn't what you expected?***

My nine-year-old deems success as an A on her test at school. My seven-year-old sees winning his soccer game as successful. My best friend finds her success in living a life she loves being part of day to day. But what if failing a class leads my daughter to enroll efforts in a different subject she will need later in life (like Spanish to be a missionary)? My son may need to lose a few games so God can mold his self-control and patience. My friend will experience tough days she does not love, so she'll fall to her knees and lean on her Savior more deeply.

***Read Esther 4:14.***

In the account of Esther, another book worth a thorough reading, she acted boldly. She chose to obey. She chose to be part of God's plan for His people and her life. Did God need her? No. If she did not heed in obedience, God would have raised up another, but perhaps God had been molding, preparing, and posturing Esther's heart for His success. God's success was not dependent on Esther, and it is not reliant on you or I. He will use someone else if we resist and stand down. He does, however, desire to have us be part of both the plan and the celebration of success once He's fulfilled it.

There was evident success in saving an entire nation from massacre and rightfully celebrated. I believe the success went deeper though. Esther leaned into others in her life and invested in prayer to take steps boldly and obediently. It deepened her faith and dependence on the Lord. That's faith-altering success beyond what I presume Esther thought herself capable of that would sustain through her subsequent journey.

Abraham's servant successfully found a wife for Isaac that required him to pray boldly and trust obediently. Gideon questioned the call and asked for clarity. Esther called upon accountability in prayer and support. We all tend to take for granted the vast success God intends and invites us to be part of. We unfortunately limit His success when we impose human standards on His plans. To adjust this tendency, it just takes one step at a time toward His will and eternal success.

Surrender breathes boldness to life, and when we boldly surrender to His will, we open the door to His level of success.

***What circumstance or season are you walking through that needs a redefining of success? Where can you surrender your self-imposed results to achieve His level of success?***

"And I pray this: that your love will keep on growing in knowledge and every kind of discernment, so that you may approve the things that are superior and may be pure and blameless in the day of Christ, filled with the fruit of righteousness that comes through Jesus Christ to the glory and praise of God" (Philippians 1:9–11).

Your love for the Lord will not be deepened if you are seeking Him in obligation, but your obedience and desire to boldly grow in a relationship with Him will yield blessing, abundance, and success.

Choose boldness. Walk in obedience. Be part of His success.

# *Epilogue*

# TAKING IT TO THE TENT

Everyone likes a good love story. Tears are shed. Hearts beat fast. Palms become sweaty. We live vicariously through the lives of the untouchable people on the screen or the black-and-white letters on the pages of our books.

Why do we pursue love stories of unacquainted friends? What is in between the written words or unspoken expressions on the movie screen that make us come back for more? I often think it is because it pushes past the reality of our own lives and places us within someone else's dream. It's the "grass is greener" syndrome. If the grass in your love yard is a little brown, just hop over the fence and play in the green grass of someone else's love yard.

So let's hop in the love yard within the pages of Genesis. Abraham was reaching the end of his life, and before he left this earth, he wanted peace that his son, Isaac, was wed. But Abraham was precise in his selection and became adamant that Isaac would not marry from the women of Canaan. He wanted his servant to return to the land of Haran to find a bride for Isaac. The land of Haran had purpose and meaning for Abraham. It was where his extended family lived, which provided Abraham with familiarity with the people and their culture.

So let's finish this book with just an old-fashioned love story.

## THE STORY

Isaac had grown to be a man who loved his parents and loved God. He had been raised by a mother and father who had waited many years to hold him in their arms. The story of God had been instilled within his heart, and following God was of the utmost importance to him.

The mother he loved had recently passed, and once his mother was buried, Abraham and Isaac mourned the loss of the woman they loved. After her death, Abraham knew it was time for Isaac to marry. Since Isaac could no longer be comforted in his mother's arms, he could now find solace in the arms of a wife.

The love story that is about to unfold is one for the books. It is filled with romance and intrigue.

Suspense and surprise.

Tenderness and strength.

One where hands are joined, and love is captured

… inside a tent.

Okay, a tent is not exactly where any of us envision love captured, but roll with me on this one.

"Ticket for one please to see *Taking It to The Tent*. And where do I get the popcorn? Excuse me … pardon me … excuse me."

Popcorn topples from the overfilled bucket onto patrons sitting comfortably in their seats. Finally seated, I position my popcorn and drink, readying myself for a beautiful love story.

"Abraham was now very old, and the Lord had blessed him in every way" (Genesis 24:1 NIV).

As Abraham was now reaching the end of his life, his heart yearned to once again be with the wife he loved. He and Sarah had faced many hardships in life, and he knew he had not been the perfect husband for her, but he had loved her deeply and missed her just the same. Reckoning this within himself, he knew if the son he loved so deeply could also experience this love and devotion before he breathed his last breath, then his life would be full.

Let's take a look at the eligible bachelor. As best I can tell, the Bible does not provide a physical description for Isaac. But what we do know is that his father was wealthy, and since he was the viable heir, he too was living the life of wealth. I'm not sure about the culture in those days and the importance of physical attraction versus the attraction of riches, but I do know that in our current society, the attraction of a financially stable life could easily trump physical attraction. Would you rather have poor and pretty or privileged and plain?

So here is a highly desired bachelor living in a land of beautiful eligible women, but these women were not from his father's land of origin. So Abraham said this to his servant,

> Put your hand under my thigh, I want you to swear by the Lord, the God of heaven and the God of earth, that you will not get a wife for my son from the daughters of the Canaanites, among whom I am living, but will go to my country and my own relatives to get a wife for my son Isaac. (Genesis 24:2 NIV)

Abraham's servant proceeded to ask a few questions for clarification. Then in Genesis 24:10, it says, "Then the servant left …" The servant set out on his journey to the land of Abraham's birth. He had one goal, to find Isaac a wife!

This servant was Abraham's senior servant, but he didn't reach this position because he was cute. He was smart too. The servant strategically placed himself in a spot where he knew there would be many eligible women for Isaac. In our Christian world, it would be like attending a Bible conference for singles, like singles' bar meets Jesus.

The plan that he devised worked. He found a beautiful wife for Isaac, and her name was Rebekah. After some intense conversations with her family, specifically her father and brother, Rebekah was released to marry Isaac. "Then Rebekah and her attendants got ready and mounted the camels and went back with the man. So, the servant took Rebekah and left" (Genesis 24:61 NIV).

The movie theater goes dark. I begin to fumble to make sure popcorn and drink are readily available. My seat is in the reclining position as I wait in anticipation of what happens in this tent.

Will the lives of Isaac and Rebekah become entangled with one another? Will the union designed by man become the union blessed by God? Will their paths cross along the desert floor without their hearts connecting? Will they look beyond the other, hoping for another lover deeper on the horizon?

Gazing intently toward the movie screen, I see the perfect sunset, shades of deep orange mixed with an array of purples and pinks, the kind of sunset you can taste like cotton candy on a stick.

As I squint my eyes, I see images appearing on the screen deep within the sunset. As these images grow closer to my sight, it appears to be a caravan of camels. Is she there? Is the beautiful maiden sitting perfectly on top of the camel?

As I cram a handful of buttered popcorn into my mouth, I hope the silhouette of a woman is Rebekah. It seemed as though the servant had been successful and found a wife for Isaac. An odd jealousy rises within me, met with a growing excitement. Could I someday be that maiden that meets her prince and lives happily ever after?

As Rebekah awaits her arranged love, her heart begins to beat fast. Did she make the right decision? Should she have stayed in her homeland? What made her choose to follow a stranger into a foreign land?

Then her mind shifted to what was ahead of her. What will he look like? Will he be tall? Will his hair fall on his shoulders in long, soft curls? What will his voice sound like? Will it be one of strength? Will it be one of humility? Who is this love that awaits her touch? Questions ruminate in her mind as she sits quietly on the back of her camel.

As Rebekah's mind was attacked with the chaos of her choices, her awaited lover had quieted his spirit, enjoying the solitude of the desert within the land of Negev. The evening was still, and the night sky glowed as the sun was setting. The day had been long for Isaac as the pressures of the day and life had taken a toll on him. There was a sadness within him as he missed his mother deeply. As these pressures weighed heavily on him, he found the need to escape and find the quiet that God had created for him. As he stepped away from the well that had been named "Beer Lahai Roi," he remembered the story his parents had told him of this place. At this well, their slave, Hagar, poured out her soul to God. In the moment as she connected to the God of Abraham, she gave the well a name that captured the essence of this moment between her and God. She named the well "Beer Lahai Roi," "the well of him that lives and sees me."

Possibly this was the prayer that Isaac prayed for himself that day, "Oh, God, please see me today." As he made his way to the field, he could feel the weight of the day give way with each step. He found a place to rest and meditate. His father's servant had been away for several days, and even though he knew this was the custom, he questioned how he could love a complete stranger. What if he didn't love her? What if the servant had chosen poorly? What if the servant had not been successful in his search and he continued in life without a wife? That weight and those questions bore down on him.

As he sat in his place of contemplation, he looked toward the horizon. When he did, he saw a group of camels approaching. As the camel caravan grew closer, his eye caught a glimpse of a woman. Could this be her? Was his father's servant successful?

As the woman drew closer, Isaac couldn't help but revel in her beauty. As he was dazed in his gaze, Rebekah glanced down from her camel.

Crunch, crunch! There is silence in the theater as moviegoers watch the intensity of this moment. Crunch … crunch! The loud popcorn eater is quieted so the people seated on the edge of their seats could watch and wait as this moment unfolded.

"Rebekah also looked up and saw Isaac" (Genesis 24:64 NIV).

Still resting on her camel, Rebekah looked up. When she did, she saw this man approach her. When he got close to her, he stared deep into her eyes. Embarrassed by his intense gaze, he knew he did not want to look away, causing him to miss one moment of her beauty. Within this stare, her eyes caught his. As their eyes met, the awkwardness of the moment quickly faded. Their gaze was fixed on one another with only the desire to see more.

As she made her way down from the camel, she stood with her

feet firmly in the sand. Looking toward the servant, she asked, "Who is this man?"

The servant then smiled with satisfaction in his heart that he had been successful. He replied, "He is my master." At that moment, the servant knew the mission he had been sent out to do was complete.

Quiet sighs fill the movie theater.

As the moment closed in, Rebekah reached down to grab the edge of her veil. As she did, Isaac took one final look at her beautiful face before it was covered. The veil covering signified she had never made love to a man, therefore promising that her first touch would be his. At this moment, Isaac took a step closer.

The audience waits. Wives grab the hands of their husbands; girlfriends grab the arm of their favorite boy. Each woman is attempting to bring their man along in this moment.

Within this moment, the beauty from her eyes penetrated deep into his soul. Her eyes were as beautiful as a dark pebble lost in the white sand. As he looked deep into her eyes, he was able to see that her beauty had reached a deeper realm. It was more than just her physical beauty that captivated him. Within that one moment, he knew he could spend the rest of his life searching for ways to love her. In an instant, his love for her was celebrated.

This is getting good!

Isaac reached out his hand, brushing it gently across her arm. As his hand reached hers, he folded his strong fingers around her delicate hand. As their skin touched, he felt the softness of hers as she felt the strength of his. Her hand was soft and reserved, yet strong and capable.

Rebekah's strength ran deep. She was a mighty warrior as she chose to leave her country and come to a place filled with unknown.

As their hands touched, they both knew the God they had worshipped had brought them together. God had chosen Isaac and Rebekah to be the next union, taking His covenant to another generation.

Isaac then invited Rebekah into his tent. "So she became his wife, and he loved her" (Genesis 24:66).

## THE SERVANT

Watching Isaac and Rebekah making their way to the tent, the servant quietly smiled. The part he played in this love story was over. Leaving his gaze from the tent, the servant turned to gather Rebekah's belongings. Struggling to hold her things in his arms, he somehow managed to reach down and pick up the rope guiding the camel. He quietly left the moment, the moment God made him successful. As he walked away, a smile came to his face, and rejoicing filled his heart, knowing his mission was complete.

As he made his way back to the camp, the eyes of the people he had grown to love watched him as he made his way to his own tent. The crowd was waiting for the news of his success, but he was spent, emotionally and physically. Quietly slipping into his tent, he closed the cloth opening. As he made his was to his pallet, he began to feel the comfort of being in a familiar place, of being home. As he lay there, he began thinking about the events of the past several days. He remembered the moment he said goodbye to his master. He remembered at that moment the hope he felt as his master had given him permission to fail in his results. Obedience was all his master asked for.

The role he played would soon be forgotten, but for him, this would be a memory forever etched on his heart. This seemed like simple obedience to most, but for him, this successful journey was more than finding Isaac a wife. It was when his intangible faith became tangible, active obedience.

Rolling over to reach the flame of his candle, he blew out the light. "Tomorrow … I will tell Abraham this journey is complete!"

# *About the Authors*

**Melody Westbrook** is a common and ordinary extraordinaire. She has never authored a book prior to this one. She has spent her days as a wife and mother of three boys, treading each day to keep her head above water. She has felt the overload of laundry and captured many dust bunnies under her bed.

But in her extraordinary ordinary life, she has become the founder of The Walk Ministries and has been a pastor's wife for thirty-one years in one of the largest SBC churches in Illinois. She is a communicator around the state of Illinois, using this platform to remind woman that each and every one of them is created for a purpose. She uses her personal experience of a broken marriage and survival of childhood abuse to communicate God's redemption story. She loves teaching real stories of real life from God's word. She is tenacious and God-loving, silly and serious, people-loving, and sometimes people-pleasing. She is happy and hurting. She feels lost, and she feels found. She brings her knowledge and years of research of the Old Testament to life, allowing others to see what they may think is dead or inapplicable is actually God's story that can be written within each of us.

**Emileigh Ziebka** is new to writing as she juggles all God leads her in. She earned her MBA in college, where she met her husband of over a decade. She is active in her local church, passionately serving as a leader of young moms for over six years as well as nursery volunteer. Her time in the church nursery has provided ample training for snuggling her own four children. Since becoming a mother, she has embraced her love for encouraging and leading other young women in our desperate need for Jesus. In a world where no one seems to have time for Jesus, she fights to remind herself and others that time with Jesus is the only way to endure.

She serves with The Walk Ministries, where she enjoys facilitating conversation using the experiences of her personal life to apply biblical principles. In her free time, she loves to read, take long walks, drink margaritas with good friends, and savor fleeting moments of sanity in her beautifully chaotic life. She loves her family, friends, and Jesus fiercely. She is expectant to see how God will use the writings of these pages.

CPSIA information can be obtained
at www.ICGtesting.com
Printed in the USA
BVHW041221260423
663002BV00006B/199

9 781664 294769